PUBLICATIONS

OF THE

AMERICAN ECONOMIC ASSOCIATION

Vol. XI.   Nos. 1, 2 and 3.   Pages 1–329.

RACE TRAITS AND TENDENCIES

OF THE

AMERICAN NEGRO

BY

FREDERICK L. HOFFMAN, F.S.S.
Statistician to the Prudential Insurance Company of America

AUGUST, 1896.

With a New Introduction by
Paul Finkelman

THE LAWBOOK EXCHANGE, LTD.
Clark, New Jersey

ISBN 978-1-58477-318-4

Lawbook Exchange edition 2004, 2024

The quality of this reprint is equivalent to the quality of the original work.

THE LAWBOOK EXCHANGE, LTD.

33 Terminal Avenue
Clark, New Jersey 07066-1321

*Please see our website for a selection of our other publications
and fine facsimile reprints of classic works of legal history:*
www.lawbookexchange.com

Library of Congress Cataloging-in-Publication Data

Hoffman, Frederick L. (Frederick Ludwig), 1865-1946.
  Race traits and tendencies of the American Negro / by Frederick L. Hoffman; new
  introduction by Paul Finkelman.
      p. cm.
  Originally published: New York: Published for the American Economic Association by
  the Macmillan Co., 1896. (Publications of the American Economic Association; v. 11,
  nos. 1-3)
  Includes bibliographical references.
  ISBN 1-58477-318-9 (acid-free paper)
      1. African Americans—Social conditions—19th century. 2. African Americans—Statistics.
  3. Black race. 4. United States—Race relations. 5. Race discrimination—United
  States—History—19th century. I. Title.

E185.6.H69 2003
305.896'073'009034—dc22   2003066016

Printed in the United States of America on acid-free paper

INTRODUCTION

ON READING AND UNDERSTANDING SCIENTIFIC RACISM:
A Brief Introduction to the Work and World of Frederick L. Hoffman

Paul Finkelman
University of Tulsa College of Law

Published at the end of the nineteenth century, Frederick L. Hoffman's *Race Traits and Tendencies of the American Negro* reflects an age when racism was taken for granted, and theories of racial superiority and inferiority were widely accepted. Hoffman's book had a significant impact on American life. By employing the beguiling methodology of statistical analysis and other tools of the emerging social sciences, the work justified, among other things, massive racial discrimination in the insurance industry. Within a few years after its publication almost every white owned insurance company (the one major exception was Metropolitan Life) refused to issue life insurance policies to African-Americans. The companies based their decisions on the statistics and the conclusions found in Hoffman's book.

The reprinting of this book is timely. It appears as the nation celebrates the 50th Anniversary of *Brown v. Board of Education* (1954) and in the wake of the Supreme Court's historic reaffirmation of affirmative action in *Grutter v. Bollinger* (2003). Recalling *Brown* and coming to terms with *Grutter* reminds us of the central importance of race to the development of American society. Hoffman's book in turn, gives us insight to the world view of those who support and encouraged segregation and racial discrimination. His book helps us understand how "science," "facts," and statistical analysis could be employed to support and encourage race discrimination.

INTRODUCTION

Frederick Ludwig Hoffman was born in a small town near Bremen, Germany in 1865. His father, Augustus Franciscus Hoffman, was a lawyer, and his mother, Antoinette (von Laar) Hoffman, remained at home, running her household in the traditional role of a middle class German wife and mother. At fifteen, he left school to work as an apprentice in a mercantile firm, expecting to have a career in commerce. However, he quickly left that job and in 1884, at age nineteen, he emigrated to the United States. Hoffman held various minor jobs in his new country, living in New York, Cleveland, and then Georgia, where he worked as a shipping clerk for an oil company and met his future wife, Ella George Hay. In 1888, he moved to Boston, where he became an agent for the Metropolitan Life Insurance Company. He subsequently co-managed an independent insurance agency in Chattanooga, Tennessee and then moved to Virginia, where he served as an assistant superintendent of the Life Insurance Company of Virginia. In 1893, he became a naturalized citizen of the United States. In 1894, he joined the actuarial department of the Prudential Life Insurance Company. He would remain with that company for the rest of his career, becoming chief statistician. In 1918, he was promoted to third vice president of the company. In 1922, he gave up his executive positions at Prudential, but remained a consultant with the company until 1934. He also taught at the Babson Institute in Massachusetts and the Franklin Institute in Philadelphia, and served as president of the American Statistical Association in 1911.

As Prudential's chief actuary and statistician, Hoffman investigated the relationship between working conditions and various diseases, especially tuberculosis. His first significant article, "The Mortality from Consumption in the Dusty Trades" (U.S. Bureau of Labor, Bulletin, no. 79, 1908) led to some of the first campaigns to control work place pollution. Indeed, this work, as well as his investigations of other diseases, suggests the important tie between social science and legislation. For example, in a 1913 article, he described how air pollution in various industries led to lung and respiratory diseases.

INTRODUCTION

The article, entitled "The Menace of Cancer," led to increased focus on this disease and to his role, that year, in the creation that year of the American Society for the Control of Cancer (later the American Cancer Society). His last book, *Cancer and Diet* (1937), published when he was 72, suggests his endless search to understand how diseases might be controlled, and life-expectancy expanded.

Despite his vision of fighting tuberculosis and cancer, Hoffman was no progressive, at least in the modern sense of the word. He opposed mandatory health insurance, any form of national health care system, and even objected to public health initiatives. Hoffman believed all Americans should rely on private enterprise, like the insurance companies, or private charities, like the American Cancer Society, to solve the ills of the nation. He also accepted and, indeed, fostered the late nineteenth century arguments about race, ethnicity, and science. Hoffman believed in the superiority of the Anglo-Saxon "race," which including ethnic Germans like himself. He also believed in the fundamental inferiority of other groups, especially blacks. Hoffman's racial views were in part a product of his experiences in America. He arrived at a time when few white northerners were concerned with the fate of African-Americans, who were now a generation out of slavery. Hoffman spent only a brief time in the North, before moving South. He spent some of his first years in the United States in the South – Tennessee, Georgia, and Virginia – at a time when those states were aggressively segregating blacks and marginalizing them politically and economically. During this period lynching was more common than at any other time since Reconstruction and the social and economic status of African-Americans, especially in the South, was in rapid decline. He married into a southern white family and doubtless absorbed the racial views of his wife and in-laws. Not surprisingly, then, this young German immigrant came to see African-Americans as a "problem" which had to be dealt with, rather than as a group of oppressed people who had been denied access to jobs, education, health care, and political power.

iii

Hoffman's last book – on cancer and diet – was forward thinking and really quite modern in its approach, and was obviously written with the notion that statistical analysis would be used to help improve the status of all people. His first, and most influential book, on the other hand, went in the opposite direction. *Race Traits of the American Negro*, first published by the American Economic Association in 1896 and reprinted here, had a profoundly negative affect on African-Americans. The book would be used to justify racial discrimination in a variety of ways. For example, Hoffman demonstrated that at all ages blacks had a lower life expectancy than whites. He found that black mortality rates for most age groups were nearly twice those of whites. Most of the major players in the insurance industry used Hoffman's findings to justify refusing to sell life insurance policies to blacks. There is some evidence that some southern white politicians used Hoffman's work to argue for black disfranchisement.

Hoffman's conclusions about race and disease stand in stark contrast to his later work on tuberculosis, cancer, and other diseases. He correctly tied these diseases to social, economic, and environmental conditions. But, when it came to African-Americans, Hoffman was certain that black mortality and black health were a function of the innate racial traits of blacks. Ignoring the recent history of slavery, and seemingly oblivious to the social and human costs of segregation, Hoffman assumed that disease and poverty were a result of racial inferiority, rather than social discrimination or a heritage of bondage.

Hoffman believed that the numbers don't lie and concluded that the grim statistics he compiled on black life in American proved that blacks were racially – genetically – inferior to whites. In his preface he claimed that as a person of German birth he was "free from a personal bias which might have made an impartial treatment of the subject difficult." He argued that by "making use of the statistical method" (p. v) it would be possible for readers to reach the same conclusions he reached. He collected voluminous statistics on American life, usually comparing data on blacks with white and recent immigrants. There is data on yellow fever deaths, the rate of alcoholism, insanity, poverty, overall death rates, and the like. There is also social data on diseases, birth rates, out-of-wedlock birth rates, and crime rates. The statistics he gathered remain a tremendously useful source for legal scholars, historians, and social scientists. Even as we reject his theories and explanations, modern scholars can make use of his tables, charts, and calculations.

Hoffman's book appeared in the same year that the Supreme Court decided *Plessy v. Ferguson* (1896), upholding racial segregation at the state level. By this time segregation was in place in much of the South and dramatically growing throughout the region. Already some southern states had taken steps to disfranchise black voters. Others would soon follow. This was also at a time when the social and economic status of African-Americans had reached its lowest point since the end of slavery. They were poorer, less educated, and more isolated than any other social group. Ninety per cent of blacks lived in the South, the nation's poorest region. Thus, they were the poorest of the poor, the least educated in a region that led the nation in illiteracy. The data Hoffman found proved this, and showed how it led to greater mortality, and, as its proponents argued, it justified discrimination. Thus, Hoffman's book would help create the intellectual and statistical arguments in favor of both disfranchisement and segregation.

It is not surprising that the conditions would lead to the higher mortality rates Hoffman found for blacks. Poverty, after all, has always been associated with high mortality rates. Other groups in American society also had high mortality rates. Eastern European Jewish immigrants, crammed into the lower east side of New York City suffered from unconscionably high tuberculosis rates. As Hoffman, himself, would demonstrate some years later, workers in textile factories and coal mines died from respiratory diseases at very high rate. It would have been logical for Hoffman to conclude that blacks suffered high rates of mortality because of their social conditions. But, as the title of his book indicates, Hoffman did not reach this conclusion. Instead, he argued that the "Race Traits" of blacks led to their condition. Reflecting the social darwinism of his age, he attributed the alarming statistics concerning African-Americans to what he called their "low state of morality." He also rejected the notion that public policy or private charity could change the social condition of blacks. On the contrary, he believed that "modern educational and philanthropic efforts" had made blacks even more "dependent on the white man" than they were as slaves. Thus, he concluded that "Unless a change takes place, a change that will strike at the fundamental errors that underlie the conduct of the higher races towards the lower, gradual extinction is only a question of time." (p. 329)

Race Traits helps us better understand how segregation could be so easily perpetuated, and how racism and racial thought could permeate society. One need not have been a racist at heart to be persuaded by Hoffman's data and his interpretation. Indeed, given the context of the times, only those inclined to believe in human equality and racial fairness, would take the time to carefully examine Hoffman's data and carefully analyze his conclusions. Such a careful examination would of course reveal that throughout his book Hoffman confused results with causes. Because blacks were largely uneducated, Hoffman concluded they were inherently less intelligent than whites; because they suffered more from disease than whites, Hoffman concluded they were inherently unhealthy; because they lacked resources, Hoffman concluded they must not have the same work ethic as whites. Most importantly, because they had a high mortality rate – due to their poverty and their lack of access to education and health care – Hoffman concluded they were a dying race. With these conclusions, he encouraged the insurance industry to reject black applicants, and more significantly, he provided a "scientific" justification for wholesale discrimination in the United States.

Reading Hoffman is painful and yet critically important. It enables us to see a world where science and racial thought worked hand-in-hand to create a Jim Crow society. It also reminds us that science and statistics are tools and not oracles. They can be used, or misused, for good or evil. Hoffman's contemporaries used his data to justify discrimination, disfranchisement, and segregation. But, the same data in the hands of modern scholars and policy makers might lead to a redoubling of efforts to create better schools, better opportunities for health care, and better nutrition for the least fortunate and least affluent in our society. Thus, the value of returning to Hoffman's book is not merely historical. The book also serves as a reminder of how citizens, scholars, and policy makers of the twenty-first century can learn from the failure of vision and values of leaders of the late nineteenth century.

PUBLICATIONS

OF THE

AMERICAN ECONOMIC ASSOCIATION

Vol. XI.   Nos. 1, 2 and 3.   Pages 1–329.

RACE TRAITS AND TENDENCIES

OF THE

AMERICAN NEGRO

BY

FREDERICK L. HOFFMAN, F.S.S.

Statistician to the Prudential Insurance Company of America

AUGUST, 1896.

PUBLISHED FOR THE
AMERICAN ECONOMIC ASSOCIATION
BY THE MACMILLAN COMPANY
NEW YORK
LONDON : SWAN SONNENSCHEIN & CO.

PRESS OF
ANDRUS & CHURCH,
ITHACA, N, Y.

PREFACE.

About ten years ago I began, for my own information, the collection of vital and social statistics of the colored population of this country. The first results of these investigations were published in the *Arena* in April, 1892; a second contribution was published in the *Medical News* in September, 1894, and a third, dealing with the Negro in the West Indies, appeared in the *Publications of the American Statistical Association*, in 1895. The large body of facts accumulated has made a more elaborate treatment seem feasible and the final result is the present work.

At the commencement of my investigation, especially in regard to longevity and physiological peculiarities among the colored population, I was confronted with the absence of any extensive collection of data free from the taint of prejudice or sentimentality. Being of foreign birth, a German, I was fortunately free from a personal bias which might have made an impartial treatment of the subject difficult. By making exclusive use of the statistical method and giving in every instance a concise tabular statement of the facts, I believe that I have made it entirely possible for my readers to arrive at their own conclusions, irrespective of the deductions that I have made.

During the course of my inquiry it became more and more apparent that there lie at the root of all social difficulties or problems, racial traits and tendencies which make for good or ill in the fate of nations as well as of individuals. It became more apparent as the work progressed, that, in the great attempts at world bettering, at the amelioration of the condition of the lower races by those of a higher degree of culture and economic well being, racial traits and tendencies have been almost entirely ignored. Hence a vast sum of evil consequences is met as the natural result of misapplied energy and misdirected human effort.

The need therefore, of a presentation of the facts as they pertain to racial differences between the white and colored populations of this country, and the consequent differences in the tendencies of the two races, seemed sufficiently clear to demand that publicity should be given to such facts as I had been able to collect; and while I have ventured at times to add my own deductions, or interpretation of their meaning, such deductions or interpretations are subject to the reader's own verification in view of the facts themselves.

The close relation of social and moral phenomena to economics, is, I believe, fully demonstrated by the results of this work. The absolute need of a more searching investigation of the underlying principles of human progress or retrogression, becomes more than ever apparent. In the words of Mr. Bryce: "But for one difficulty the South might well be thought to be the most promising part of the Union, that part whose advance is likely to be swiftest, and whose prosperity will not be least secure. This difficulty, however, is a serious one. It lies in the presence of seven million Negroes."

If this be true, it behooves the general government as well as the governments of the several states, to institute annually such inquiries in regard to the material and social condition of the colored race as will demonstrate beyond a doubt the existence of vital factors affecting its progress or retrogression. Such inquiries would be free from the sectional prejudice or sentimental regard of those who are now arrayed on either side of the " race question."

If such an investigation were undertaken by the Department of Labor, it would lead to very beneficial results by furnishing a basis for definite conclusions as to the results of philanthropic and charitable efforts in behalf of the colored race. In the absence of this much needed government investigation, the present inquiry may serve a useful purpose in stimulating others to special inquiry along the many lines indicated.

In the preparation of this work, extending over so many years, I have been materially aided by so many public and private individuals in all parts of this country and the West Indies, that it would be impossible to make a proper acknowledgement of my obligations in each individual case. To all those who have so kindly aided me with advice or documentary evidence, I extend my most sincere thanks, and trust that the results of the investigation will prove a compensation for the personal inconvenience I may have caused them.

I am, however, especially indebted for advice and information to Mr. Carroll D. Wright, the Commissioner of Labor, Dr. John S. Billings, U. S. A., Dr. S. W· Abbott, secretary of the Massachusetts state board of health, Dr. Arthur Newsholme, Brighton, England, M. Charles Letourneau, secretary of the Anthropological Society of Paris, Mr. S. P. Smeeton, the registrar-general of Jamaica, Mr. Archibald Allison, the colonial secretary of Bermuda, Dr. D. T. Rogers of Mobile, Ala., Dr. H. B. Horlbeck of Charleston, S. C., Dr. Gordon De Sassure, of the same city, Dr. Jerome Cochrane, of Montgomery, Ala., and Emmons Clark, Esq., secretary of the New York board of health.

I am indebted to Professor W. F. Willcox for most valuable assistance in the prosecution of the investigation and final publication of the results; also to the publication committee of the American Economic Association, but especially to Mr. F. S. Kinder of Cornell University, for considerable and valuable assistance in the reading of the manuscript and proofs for final publication. To the librarian of the Public Library of Newark I am under obligations for exceptional privileges afforded in the use of a valuable collection of transactions of scientific societies, as well as of other valuable publications not easily obtainable. Most of all am I indebted to my wife for her kindly and sympathetic assistance and many personal sacrifices during the early years of my labors. Without her encouragement and never failing sympathy, the completion of this work would not have been possible in a business life where only spare hours could be devoted to an investigation of this nature.

In an investigation extending over so many years, and involving so large a number of calculations and statistical quotations, errors are almost unavoidable. But having taken every precaution to insure absolute accuracy, I feel confident that no error sufficient to affect the conclusions has occurred. If the work accomplishes its purpose and leads to a more searching investigation into the underlying causes of race progress or retrogression ; if it leads to more scientific attention to the relations between the superior and inferior races, as contrasted with the present dangerous method of guess work, it will not have been written in vain. For after all it is a question of *living beings* and not of theories; and no philanthropy or charity that in all its missionary efforts has not been able to save the *living man*, has any claim to be called successful. Race deterioration once in progress is very difficult to check, and races once on the downward grade, thus far at least in human history, have invariably become useless if not dangerous factors in the social as well as political economy of nations.

FREDERICK L. HOFFMAN.

761 Broad Street, Newark, N. J.,

July 28, 1896.

TABLE OF CONTENTS.

THE RACE TRAITS AND TENDENCIES OF THE AMERICAN NEGRO.

CHAPTER I.

POPULATION.

The progress of the colored population in the United States, and more particularly in the southern states, has for more than fifty years past been a matter of the most serious concern to those who have observed the results of the presence of a large and growing negro population. The natural bond of sympathy existing between people of the same country, no matter how widely separated by language and nationality, cannot be proved to exist between the white and colored races of the United States. To-day, after thirty years of freedom for the negro in this country, and sixty years in the West Indies, the two races are farther apart than ever in their political and social relations. To-day, more than ever, the colored race of this country forms a distinct element and presents more than at any time in the past the most complicated and seemingly hopeless problem among those confronting the American people.

It is therefore a matter of the utmost importance that the true condition of this population should be fully understood in all its intricate details, to eliminate every possible doubt as to the seriousness and importance of the problem to the people of the southern states as well as the larger cities of the North and West. In the endless

discussions that have been carried on for years past as
to the condition and future of the colored people, the
fact that there is a northern side to the question has never
been fully taken into account.   Only by means of a thorough analysis of all the data that make up the history of
the colored race in this country can the true nature of the
so-called 'negro problem' be understood and the results
of past experience be applied safely to the solution of
the difficulties that now confront this country in dealing
with the colored element.

The most threatening danger, numerical supremacy,
may be considered as having passed away, if indeed it
ever existed in fact. Leaving aside the results of the
eleventh census, which clearly proved a smaller increase
in the colored population than in the native white, the material is abundant and will be fully presented in this monograph, to prove that, independent of the census returns,
the gradual decrease in the decennial growth of the
colored population can be fully explained.

During the past decade, however, according to the
census returns, the increase in the colored population of
the southern states has been so much less than that of
the white race, and so much less than the believers in
Professor Gilliam's prediction had cause to expect, that
the accuracy of the census has been disputed by many,
even though they had no means whatever at their command of proving the truth of their charges. Since
many of the tables and calculations in this paper are
necessarily based on the eleventh census it may not be
out of place for me to state that after the most careful
analysis of the results in this and many other investigations I am convinced that the eleventh census was as
carefully taken as any one of the ten preceding enumerations. This conviction is based principally on a study

of the age distribution of the population, which is probably the most delicate test applicable to census work.

During the ten years, 1880–1890, the colored population of the southern states increased only 13.24 per cent., in contrast with an increase of 23.91 per cent. for the white population of the same section. The total white population of the country at large increased 26.68 per cent., and the total colored population 13.51 per cent. during the same period. This result, therefore, disproves Professor Gilliam's prediction that the increase of the colored population would be 35 per cent. per decade, and makes impossible the realization of the further prediction, which has been so widely copied, that in seventy or eighty years the blacks will largely predominate in every southern state. Professor Gilliam, as so many other writers on this subject have done, relied in his calculations on only one element of the natural increment of a population, namely, the birth rate; he ignored the far more important influence of the death rate. To what absurdities such calculations may be carried is perhaps best illustrated by the following table

COMPARATIVE ESTIMATES OF THE PROBABLE COLORED POPULATION OF THE UNITED STATES.

	United States Census.	Estimate of Darby.[1]	Estimate of De Bow.[2]	Estimate of Kennedy.[3]	Estimate of Prof. Gilliam.[4]
1830	2,328,642	2,893,731	. . . . .	. . . . .	. . . . . .
1840	2,873,648	4,114,709	. . . . .	. . . . .	. . . . . .
1850	3,638,808	5,756,079	. . . . .	. . . . .	. . . . . .
1860	4,441,830	7,860,118	4,319,452	. . . . .	. . . . . .
1870	4,880,009	10,669,236	5,296,235	5,407,130	. . . . . .
1880	6,580,793	14,329,701	6,494,334	6,591,292	. . . . . .
1890	7,470,040	19,208,740	7,962,004	7,909,550	. . . . . .
1900	8,458,952[5]	25,825,878	9,766,884	9,491,459	12,000,000

[1] "View of the United States." (Philadelphia, 1828). Pages 438–40.

[2] "South and West," Vol. II, page 305.

[3] Preliminary report on the eighth census, page 7.

[4] "*Popular Science Monthly,*" Vol. XXII, page 437. (For the Southern States only).

[5] Estimated by the writer.

of comparative estimates, by a number of writers, of the colored population in the United States at different periods of time.

Of the various estimates here brought together, those of De Bow and Kennedy come nearest being approximately correct, while those of Darby and Gilliam are far out of the way. Darby made no allowance for a possible increase in the death rate, nor could he foresee the emancipation of the slaves in 1863. Both De Bow and Kennedy were thoroughly familiar with the vital statistics of the negro, and so made allowance for a probable gain of the death rate on the birth rate, as well as for a probable decrease in the latter. Professor Gilliam, who had at his command the mortality statistics of southern cities—especially of Savannah, Charleston, Mobile, New Orleans and Richmond—could easily have ascertained the element of error that vitiated his elaborate calculations. His assumption that the colored population would for years to come increase at the rate of 3.5 per cent. per annum was justified neither by past experience nor by the returns of the census of 1880. The census of 1870 was admittedly defective and this consideration should have prevented him from using the rate of increase in this decade as a formula for calculating the colored population for the next century. As has been stated, the rate of increase during the decade 1880–90 was considerably less for the colored population than for the whites; whereas Professor Gilliam estimated the probable annual gain of the southern white population at only two per cent., in contrast with an assumed gain of 3.5 per cent. per annum for the colored population. Thus he estimated a probable colored population for 1900 of twelve millions: in all probability it will not reach seven and a half millions. According to Professor

Gilliam's method of calculating, the population in 1890 should have been slightly in excess of nine millions, while the census showed only 6,741,941 in those states.

ESTIMATE OF THE COLORED POPULATION OF SOUTHERN STATES, 1880–1900.

	Prof. Gillian's Estimate.	Result of the Census.
1880	6,000,000	5,953,903
1890	9,039,470[1]	6,741,941
1900	12,000,000	7,634,450[2]

[1] Calculated by the writer in accordance with Prof. Gilliam's method.
[2] Calculated by the writer in accordance with the method of Dr. Farr.

These examples illustrate the uselessness of attempts to arrive at accurate results on the basis of enumerations which do not show the underlying elements of the population or afford the means of stating the probable tendency of a population for a long period of years. Reasoning from gross results in this as in other branches of statistical inquiry must be useless and misleading.

I have gone into considerable detail in my account of the elements of the colored population in order that those who have neither time nor opportunity to consult the original reports may know the sources of the information and the basis of the tables which are introduced in other parts of this work. Only after a comprehensive study of the intricate details of these elements can the nature of the problem as to the future of the negro and his relation to the white race in this country be understood.

The table which follows shows, for periods of thirty years each, the progress of the colored and white populations in the country at large during the present century. I have selected this method because there is no apparent need of giving the results of all of the eleven enumerations of the population, and also because the use of the defective census of 1870 is thereby avoided.

POPULATION OF THE UNITED STATES, 1800 to 1890.

	White Population.	Colored Population.[1]	Per ct. of White.	Per ct. of Colored.
1800	4,306,446	1,002,037	81.12	18.88
1830	10,537,378	2,328,642	81.90	18.10
1860	26,922,537	4,441,830	85.62	14.13
1890	54,983,890	7,470,040	87.80	11.93

[1] Previous to 1860, Chinese and Indians were counted as colored; for 1860 and 1890 these are excluded.

It will be observed that the proportion of whites in the total population has gradually increased from 81.12 per cent. in 1800, to 87.80 per cent. in 1890. This increase in the proportion of whites is to a considerable extent due to the large immigration in the past fifty years. The southern states, however, have been affected but very slightly by foreign immigration. The table which follows shows that the proportion of the colored to the white population has increased in some states and decreased in others during the past sixty years. During the period 1860–1890 the proportion of whites increased in seven out of the thirteen southern states. During the last census period the proportion of colored to whites increased in only two of these thirteen states—Mississippi and Arkansas; all the other states show a considerable decrease.

PERCENTAGE OF NEGROES[1] IN TOTAL POPULATION—1830-1890.

PRINCIPAL SOUTHERN STATES.

	1890	*1860*	*1830*
Maryland,	20.69	24.91	34.88
District of Columbia,	32.80	19.07	30.81
Virginia,	38.37	34.39	42.69
North Carolina,	34.67	36.42	35.93
South Carolina,	59.85	58.59	55.63
Georgia,	46.74	44.05	42.57
Florida,	42.46	44.63	47.06
Kentucky,	14.42	20.44	24.73
Tennessee,	24.37	25.50	21.43
Alabama,	44.84	45.40	38.48
Mississippi,	57.58	55.28	48.44
Louisiana,	49.99	49.49	58.54
Texas,	21.84	30.27	. . .
Arkansas,	27.40	25.55	15.52

[1] Persons of African descent only.

That this condition is not due to any decided tendency on the part of the colored population to migrate to northern states is clearly borne out by a careful study of the census returns. The most satisfactory method of arriving at a definite result is probably a comparison of the native resident populations—that is of the numbers of those living in the states in which they were born. In this comparison only the native whites are taken into account and compared with the native colored. I have abstracted from the census volume the returns for five representative southern states, and calculated from the actual returns the proportionate increase in the native white and native colored elements. For purposes of comparison the percentages which the population so defined makes of the total white and the total colored population, respectively, are also given.

POPULATION BORN AND LIVING IN STATE.[1]

	1890 Native Whites.	1880 Native Whites.	Increase 1880–90.	Per ct. of increase 1880–90.	Percentage of total White Population. 1890.	1880.
South Carolina, .	435,594	363,576	72,018	19.81	95.55	94.77
Georgia, ...	873,234	717,276	155,958	21.74	90.35	88.93
Alabama, ...	660,848	506,917	153,931	30.37	80.68	77.67
Mississippi, . .	440,670	353,247	87,423	24.75	82.04	75.09
Louisiana, ...	444,230	341,974	102,256	29.90	87.18	85.03

COLORED.

	Native Colored 1890.	Native Colored. 1880.	Increase 1880–90.	Per ct. of increase 1880–90.	Percentage of total Colored Population. 1890.	1880.
South Carolina, .	677,175	588,819	88,356	15.01	98.28	97.45
Georgia, ...	798,747	677,938	120,809	17.82	93.01	93.50
Alabama, ...	607,058	507,716	99,342	19.57	89.39	84.60
Mississippi, . . .	622,996	509,938	113,058	22.17	83.68	78.21
Louisiana, . . .	478,655	386,348	92,307	23.89	85.58	79.89

[1] Census of 1890, Vol. I, Population, pp. CVI.

PERCENTAGE OF DECENNIAL INCREASE IN THE RESIDENT NATIVE
POPULATION OF FIVE SOUTHERN STATES.

	Native White.	Native Colored.	White over Colored.
South Carolina, . . .	19.81	15.01	4.80
Georgia, ...	21.74	17.82	3.92
Alabama, ...	30.37	19.57	10.80
Mississippi, ...	24.75	22.17	2.58
Louisiana, ...	29.90	23.89	6.01

These tables prove conclusively the steady gain of the
native white on the native colored population, and the
larger natural increase—excess of births over deaths—
in the white population. This is most marked in Alabama, and least so in Mississippi. But it is remarkable
that the latter state should show even the slight excess
in favor of the white race that it does, since the increase in
the total colored population has been greater than the
increase of the white race, owing to a considerable
migration of colored people from other states to the low-
lands of the Mississippi. The small increase in the
colored population of Alabama is to a great extent due
to the drifting of the Negroes into the large cities which
have grown up in that state during the past decade, in
which the mortality among the colored is higher than
that recorded for any other American cities at the present time.

The tendency of the colored population to leave the
country and congregate in the large cities either of the
South or North, is one of the most distinct phenomena
of the past thirty years. Immediately previous to the
outbreak of the war the colored population of the larger
southern cities formed but a small proportion of the
aggregate population of these cities. If, for purposes of
illustration, we take the fourteen largest cities of ten
southern states we shall find that in 1860 only 18.85 per
cent. of the population of these cities was colored, as

compared with 36 per cent. of the colored in the total population at large of the ten states. In 1890 the states under consideration contained sixteen large cities with 29.08 per cent. of colored population, while in the total population of these states the proportion of colored was nearly the same as in 1860, or 35.96 per cent. The next three tables give, first, the aggregate and the colored population of ten southern states at the censuses of 1860 and 1890, together with the proportion of the colored in the total population; second, the same information for fourteen cities in 1860, and for sixteen in 1890; third, the increase in the white and the colored population during the thirty years 1860–90 for the states, the cities named, and the states excluding the cities. The last may be considered for the present purpose as rural, although many cities of considerable population are included.

PROPORTION OF THE COLORED IN THE TOTAL POPULATION OF TEN SOUTHERN STATES.—1860 AND 1890.

	Total Population, 1890.	Colored Population.	Per ct. Color'd	Total Population, 1860.	Colored Population.	Per ct. Color'd
Delaware	168,493	28,386	. . .	112,216	21,627	. . .
Maryland.	1,042,390	215,657	. . .	687,049	171,131	. . .
Dist. of Col.	230,392	75,572	. . .	75,080	14,316	. . .
Virginia .	1,655,980	635,438	. . .	1,596,318	548,907	. . .
S. Carolina	1,151,149	688,934	. . .	703,708	412,320	. . .
Georgia . .	1,837,353	858,815	. . .	1,057,286	465,698	. . .
Kentucky.	1,858,635	268,071	. . .	1,155,684	236,167	. . .
Tennessee.	1,767,518	430,678	. . .	1,109,801	283,019	. . .
Alabama .	1,513,017	678,489	. . .	964,201	437,770	. . .
Louisiana.	1,118,587	559,193	. . .	708,002	350,373	. . .
10 S. States	12,343,514	4,439,233	35.96	8,169,345	2,941,328	36.00

PROPORTION OF THE COLORED IN THE TOTAL POPULATION OF SIX-
TEEN SOUTHERN CITIES, 1860 AND 1890.

	Total Population 1890	Colored Populat'n 1890.	Per ct. Color'd	Total Populat'n 1860.	Colored Populat'n 1860.	Per ct. Col'd.
Wilmington, Del. . .	61,431	7,644	. . .	21,258	2,214	. .
Baltimore, Md. . .	434,439	67,104	. . .	212,418	27,898	. .
Washington, D. C.	230,392	75,572	. . .	75,080	14,316	. .
Norfolk, Va. . . .	34,871	16,244	. . .	14,620	4,330	. .
Richmond, Va. . .	81,388	32,330	. . .	37,910	14,275	. .
Charleston, S. C. .	54,955	30,970	. . .	40,522	17,146	. .
Atlanta, Ga. . . .	65,533	28,098	. . .	9,554	1,939	. .
Augusta, Ga. . . .	33,300	15,875	. . .	12,493	4,049	. .
Savannah, Ga. . .	43,189	22,963	. . .	22,292	8,417	. .
Louisville, Ky. . .	161,129	28,651	. . .	68,033	6,820	. .
Chattanooga, Tenn.	29,100	12,563	. . .	. . .	. .	. .
Memphis, "	64,495	28,706	. . .	22,623	3,882	. .
Nashville, "	76,168	29,382	. . .	16,988	3,945	. .
Birmingham, Ala .	26,178	11,254	. . .	. . .	. .	. .
Mobile, Ala. . . .	31,076	13,630	. . .	29,258	8,404	. .
New Orleans, La. .	242,039	64,491	. . .	168,675	24,074	. .
16 Southern Cities.	1,669,683	485,477	29.08	751,724	141,709	18.85

INCREASE—WHITE AND COLORED POPULATION OF TEN SOUTHERN
STATES, 1860-1890.

	Population of Ten Southern States.		Population in Large Cities.		Population in States Excluding Cities.	
	White.	Colored.	White.	Colored.	White.	Colored.
1860	5,228,017	2,941,328	610,015	141,709	4,618,002	2,799,619
1890 . . .	7,904,281	4,439,233	1,184,206	485,477	6,720,075	3,953,756
Increase.	2,676,264	1,497,905	574,141	343,768	2,102,123	1,154,137
Increase per ct.	51.19	50.93	94.11	242.60	45.52	41.23

The summary of the first two tables is given in the
third, in which also the white population is given.
As shown by this table the white population of
the ten southern states increased 51.19 per cent. during the thirty years 1860–90, while the colored population increased at almost the same rate, or 50.93 per
cent. Considering the population of the cities it is
shown that the white population increased 94.11 per

cent., as compared with an increase of 242.60 per cent. for the colored during the same period. This phenomenal increase in the colored population of southern cities during the past thirty years is perhaps the most convincing evidence of the changed conditions at the South, as affecting the future of the colored population. After all that has been said on the modern tendency of civilized peoples to leave the country for the cities, there are probably no other instances of such wholesale migration to the city as is here shown. In marked contrast with this enormous increase in urban population stands the small increase in the colored population of the rural sections of the states under consideration, a rate of increase considerably below the rate shown to prevail for the white race. Since 89.07 per cent. of the colored population of these ten states still live in the rural sections of the country, the fact that the rate of increase there should be less for the colored than for the white race is highly significant. If we compare the urban with the total population in 1860, 11.67 per cent. of the white population lived in the large cities, increasing during thirty years to only 14.89 per cent.; in contrast with an increase from 4.82 per cent. of colored urban population in 1860 to 10.93 per cent. in 1890.

PERCENTAGE OF WHITE AND COLORED POPULATION LIVING IN THE LARGE CITIES OF TEN SOUTHERN STATES IN 1860 AND 1890.

	WHITE.		COLORED.	
	1860.	1890.	1860.	1890.
Population of Ten States	5,228,017	7,904,281	2,941,328	4,439,233
" of 16 Large Cities	610,015	1,184,206	141,709	485,477
Percentage in Large Cities	11.67	14.89	4.82	10.93

During the last decade this migratory tendency of the colored population has been more pronounced than ever, affecting not only the large cities but also those of proportionally small colored population. I have grouped the cities into two classes, those with a colored population in 1890 of 10,000 to 20,000, and those with more than 20,000. The per cent. of increase is larger for the small than for the large cities, but the numerical increase in the large cities was more than twice that in the other group. The white population of these cities increased at a lesser rate than the colored, which agrees with the results of the comparison made in preceding tables for the period 1860–90.

POPULATION OF THE LARGE CITIES.—1880–1890.

	White Population.		Colored Population.	
	1890.	1880.	1890.	1880.
Washington, D. C	154,695	107,714	75,572	52,135
Baltimore, Md	367,143	278,584	67,104	53,716
New Orleans, La	177,376	158,367	64,491	57,617
Philadelphia, Pa	1,006,590	815,362	39,371	31,699
Richmond, Va	49,034	35,765	32,330	27,832
Charleston, S. C	23,919	22,699	30,970	27,276
Nashville, Tenn	46,773	27,005	29,382	16,337
Memphis, Tenn	35,766	18,677	28,706	14,896
Louisville, Ky	132,457	102,847	28,651	20,905
Atlanta, Ga	37,416	21,079	28,098	16,330
St. Louis, Mo	424,704	328,191	26,865	22,256
New York, N. Y	1,489,627	1,185,843	23,601	19,663
Savannah, Ga.	20,211	15,041	22,963	15,654
Total Population	3,965,711	3,117,174	498,104	376,316
{ Increase, 1890 over 1880 .	. . . .	848,537	. . .	121,788
{ Increase, Per Cent. . . .	. . . .	27.22	. . .	32.36

TEN CITIES WITH FROM 10,000 to 20,000 COLORED POPULATION IN 1890.

	White Population.		Colored Population.	
	1890.	1880.	1890.	1880.
Chicago, Ill	1,084,998	496,495	14,271	6,480
Brooklyn, N. Y	795,397	558,427	10,287	8,095
Cincinnati, O	285,224	246,912	11,655	8,179
Kansas City, Mo	118,821	47,613	13,700	8,143
Norfolk, Va	18,617	11,898	16,244	10,068
Augusta, Ga	17,395	11,771	15,875	10,109
Mobile, Ala	17,429	16,885	13,630	12,240
Chattanooga, Tenn	16,525	7,807	12,563	5,082
Houston, Tex	17,178	. 10,026	10,370	6,479
Birmingham, Ala	14,909	. . . .	11,254	. . . .
Total Population	2,386,493	1,407,834	129,849	74,875
{ Increase, 1890 over 1880 .	. . . .	978,659	. . . .	54,974
{ Increase, Per Cent	. . . .	69.51	. . . .	73.42

These two tables forcibly illustrate the importance of the negro problem to all sections of the country, since the tendency here shown to exist must, if not checked in a few decades, materially increase the colored population of all the large cities of the country. It will surprise many to be told that Philadelphia has a colored population of almost forty thousand; this number being exceeded in only three other cities, Washington, Baltimore and New Orleans. And while the colored element forms a far more important factor in the large cities of the South than in those of the East and West, still it presents in the latter no less serious problems, but of a different nature and more complex in form. For in the large cities of the South the colored population is fairly well distributed over the whole city, with the exception of Richmond, where the larger portion of it is contained in a single ward. In the cities of the North and West the negroes are crowded into a very few wards. In Richmond the negro district is designated "Africa," and it may be truthfully said that in each of the large cities of the North and West in which the colored people have settled in sufficient numbers, one may find an "Africa" of the Richmond type. The two tables below show for six cities of the North and West and six of the South the distribution of the colored population by wards according to the census of 1890. These tables are the first, I believe, to present with a considerable degree of accuracy the massing of the colored population

DISTRIBUTION, BY WARDS, OF THE COLORED POPULATION OF SIX LARGE NORTHERN CITIES. (CENSUS 1890).

Wards.	Chicago.	Boston. 25 Wards.	New York. 24 Wards.	Brooklyn. 26 Wards.	Phil'a. 34 Wards.	Cincinnati. 30 Wards.
1 . . .	3,381	56	124	272	794	171
2 . . .	2,744	24	19	70	522	1,759·
3 . . .	2,997	50	17	193	861	59
4 . . .	722	143	40	494	2,573	487
5 . . .	401	40	61	502	2,335	482
6 . . .	33	55	108	84	125	1,286
7 . . .	3	50	9	611	8,861	21
8 . . .	4	388	687	44	3,011	238
9 . . .	16	2,547	1,126	417	497	480
10 . . .	73	· 226	76	709	798	257
11 . . .	222	1,099	10	1,910	11	12
12 . . .	335	123	3,951	. . . .	338	21
13 . . .	695	47	9	94	539	2
14 . . .	41	46	130	1	1,379	194
15 . . .	49	23	2,201	60	1,751	242
16 . . .	14	784	2,188	397	104	633
17 . . .	51	622	105	13	124	782
18 . . .	610	389	434	52	11	1,589
19 . . .	98	777	1,933	589	275	589
20 . . .	. . . . .	127	4,782	799	1,333	590
21· . . .	38	45	546	228	93	162
22 . . .	88	32	4,275	164	1,798	134
23 . . .	149	200	495	214	1,026	185
24 . . .	306	47	275	958	930	199
25 . . .	18	185	. . . .	1,190	260	378
26 . . .	41	. . . .	. . . .	222	1,375	202
27 . . .	88	. . . .	. . . .	. . . .	2,077	103
28 . . .	53	. . . .	. . . .	. . . .	644	130
29 . . .	36	. . . .	. . . .	. . . .	1,476	137
30 . . .	479	. . . .	. . . .	. . . .	1,789	131
31 . . .	42	. . . .	. . . .	. . . .	16	. . . .
32 . . .	218	. . . .	. . . .	. . . .	382	. . . .
33 . . .	19	. . . .	. . . .	. . . .	190	. . . .
34 . . .	207	. . . .	. . . .	. . . .	1,073	. . . .
Total .	14,271	8,125	23,601	10,287	39,371	11,655

DISTRIBUTION BY WARDS OF THE COLORED POPULATION OF SIX
LARGE SOUTHERN CITIES.—(CENSUS 1890.)

WARDS	Charleston, S. C. 8 Wards.	Norfolk, Va. 6 Wards.	Mobile, Ala. 8 Wards.	Atlanta, Ga. 6 Wards.	Louisville, Ky. 12 Wards.	New Orleans, La. 17 Wards.
1	1,518	2,272	1,891	6,749	1,087	2,753
2	2,763	1,526	207	3,233	748	3,270
3	3,008	3,122	61	3,899	1,777	9,475
4	4,914	8,617	257	6,390	2,982	3,555
5	4,187	157	1,124	3,172	3,664	6,676
6	5,447	550	2,735	4,655	1,699	3,740
7	3,332	. .	5,138	. .	876	7,729
8	5,801	. .	2,217	. .	2,663	1,330
9	. .	. .	. .	. .	3,356	2,664
10	. .	. .	. .	. .	4,883	4,311
11	. .	. .	. .	. .	3,789	5,260
12	. .	. .	. .	. .	1,127	2,572
13	. .	. .	. .	. .	. .	2,174
14	. .	. .	. .	. .	. .	1,274
15	. .	. .	. .	. .	. .	4,492
16	. .	. .	. .	. .	. .	1,982
17	. .	. .	. .	. .	. .	1,234
Total,	30,970	16,244	13,630	28,098	28,651	64,491

of northern and western cities into a few wards—which
as a rule are the most undesirable sections of the cities.
With the data given it will be easily possible for the
resident of any one of the cities to verify the writer's
statements. It needs to be observed that this tendency
is much more manifest in the North than in the South.
It may be that the distribution of the colored population
in the southern cities appears more even from the fact
that the subdivisions are larger than in the northern and
western cities.

The tendency towards concentration is more distinctly
presented by taking the total of the colored population
of a few wards and comparing this number with the
white population of the same wards. If we take, for
instance, Chicago, we shall find that out of the 14,271
colored persons living in that city, 9,122 or 63.90 per
cent. were living in three wards, which contained at the
same time only 6.3 per cent. of the total white popula-

tion.   In other words, these three wards contained almost two-thirds of the total colored, and less than one-
fourteenth of the white, population.   This condition is
met with more or less in every city of any importance
in the North and West.   In the case of the six cities,
selected for the purpose of illustration, the facts are
brought out clearly in the table below :

PERCENTAGE OF THE WHITE AND COLORED POPULATION LIVING IN
THREE WARDS WITH LARGEST COLORED
POPULATION. (CENSUS 1890).

	White Population. 1890.	White Populat'n in Three Wards.	Per- centage of Tot'l White.	Colored Populat'n 1890.	Colored Populat'n in Three Wards.	Per- centage of Tot'l Color'd
Chicago	1,084,998	68,408	6.30	14,271	9,122	63.90
Boston	439,887	47,862	10.88	8,125	4,430	54.52
New York	1,489,627	469,751	31.53	23,601	13,008	55.11
Brooklyn	795,397	79,958	10.05	10,287	4,058	39.44
Philadelphia . .	1,006,590	52,909	5.26	39,371	14,445	36.69
Cincinnati	285,224	23,606	8.28	11,655	4,634	39.75
Six Cities . . .	5,101,723	742,494	14.55	107,310	49,897	46.49

The concentration according to this table would seem
to be greatest in Chicago and least in Philadelphia, while
the percentage of whites living in the three wards with
largest colored population is least in Philadelphia and
greatest in New York.   The conclusion would seem to
be warranted that the most unfavorable conditions for the
colored population as indicated by the disproportionate
number of whites in the same localities are to be found
in Chicago and Philadelphia.

How far this is true for the former city is demonstrated by the maps attached to the volume of " Hull
House Maps and Papers," modeled after Mr. Booth's
great work on the " Life and Labour of the People of
London."   The work, which seems to have been done with
exceptional care, was under the direction of Mrs. Florence
Kelley, chief factory inspector of Illinois, who had

charge of the investigation made by the United States Bureau of Labor of the slums of large cities. The two maps attached to this volume show the concentration of the colored population of the area investigated, which includes parts of the three wards referred to in the table above. One map shows the nationality and color of the inhabitants of the section, the other the houses designated as 'brothels.' The first reveals that the colored population is concentrated in a very limited area, which at the same time contains but a small number of whites, while the rest of the section, inhabited by various nationalities, does not appear to contain a single house inhabited by a colored person as a home. The second map shows that the section inhabited almost exclusively by colored persons is also the section which contains all the houses of ill-fame in this part of the city.

So far as my personal investigations have gone, the condition shown to exist in Chicago is found more or less in all of the other large cities of the North and and West. In Philadelphia, Chicago, Boston and Cincinnati, the large majority of the colored population is found to be living in the worst section of the city, a section in which vice and crime are the only formative influences. The Negro in the North and West therefore presents an even more serious problem than the Negro in the South, if mere numbers are disregarded.

In most of the states of the North and West the rural counties are showing a constant decrease in the colored population, the cities a constant increase. In Missouri, for instance, out of a total of 115 counties, 74 show a falling off in colored population during the ten years 1880–1890, while the five largest cities show a considerable increase. In Indiana, which state at one time was threatened with an invasion of Negroes from the southern states, the colored population has decreased in 48 counties. In Ohio 47 counties show a falling off in colored population, while seven cities of the state show an increase of a little more than nine thousand during the last census period. For the two states, Ohio and Missouri, I have worked out a table in which the growth of the urban at the expense of the rural population is brought out with singular force.

COLORED POPULATION OF THE RURAL AND URBAN SECTIONS OF
OHIO AND MISSOURI, 1880 AND 1890.

	OHIO.		Increase.
	1890.	1880.	1880–90.
Total Colored population	87,113	79,900	7,213
City of Cincinnati	11,655	8,179	
Cleveland	2,989	2,038	
Columbus	5,525	3,010	
Dayton	2,158	991	
Springfield	3,549	2,360	
Toledo	1,077	928	
Xenia	1,868	1,943	
Total Colored population of 7 cities . .	28,821	19,449	9,372
Remainder of State	58,292	60,451	[1]2,159

	MISSOURI.		Increase.
	1890.	1880.	1880–90.
Total Colored population	150,184	145,350	4,834
City of St. Louis	26,865	22,256	
Hannibal	2,073	1,838	
Kansas City	13,700	8,143	
St. Joseph	3,686	3,227	
Springfield	2,258	1,494	
Total Colored population of five cities .	48,582	36,958	11,624
Remainder of State	101,602	108,392	[1]6,790

[1] Decrease.

We see that in two of the richest agricultural states of the Union the colored population is leaving the farms for the cities. In both states the rural sections show an actual decrease in the population while the cities alone show an increase. This increase is therefore not a natural one, that is, an excess of births over deaths, but is largely due to migration. There is no corresponding tendency of the colored population to migrate from one city to another. Most of the new comers are from the country, but the city Negro rarely returns to the country. The tendency must in the end cause a general decrease of the colored population of the northern states, since the very heavy death rates of the Negro population of the large cities is not overbalanced by a greater birth rate.

In the southern states this tendency prevails, but to a less extent, on account of the very large rural population in which losses by migration to the towns would easily be balanced by a more favorable birth rate. In many sections of the South, however, the Negro seems more and more to drift into those counties and tiers of counties where his people are largely in the majority. Such counties form what is known as the 'Black Belt,' of which the most important sections are the Mississippi river belt which stretches from the Gulf to Memphis, and the belt of the South Central States, which passes through central Mississippi, Alabama, Georgia and the southern part of South Carolina.

An aggregation of the colored population is to be found in every southern state such as I have shown to exist in the northern cities.

In all these aggregations the colored people are in the vast majority, but this does not seem to prevent the whites from maintaining control of public affairs. Even in counties where the Negroes outnumber the whites fifty to one the principal offices of the county are in the hands of the latter.

I have deemed this point of sufficient importance to abstract from the census returns a table for the principal southern states showing the concentration of the colored population in certain counties, which at the same time contain but a very small proportion of whites. In some instances, it will be observed, the whites are but a very small fraction of the total population. This tendency, if persisted in will probably in the end prove disastrous to the advancement of the colored race, since there is but the slightest prospect that the race will be lifted to a higher plane of civilization except by constant contact with the white race.

PROPORTION OF COLORED TO WHITES IN SELECTED COUNTIES OF SEVEN SOUTHERN STATES, 1890.

Counties.	Whites.	Colored.	Col'd to 1,000 Whites.
ALABAMA.			
Bullock	6,055	21,005	3,469
Dallas	8,016	41,329	5,156
Greene	3,235	18,771	5,802
Hale	5,180	22,321	4,309
Lowndes	4,563	26,985	5,914
Marengo	7,946	25,149	3,165
Montgomery	14,682	41,485	2,826
Perry	6,812	22,516	3,305
Russell	5,814	18,729	3,221
Sumter	5,943	23,631	3,976
Wilcox	6,794	24,022	3,445
ARKANSAS.			
Chicot	1,392	10,023	7,200
Crittenden	2,050	11,890	5,800
Jefferson	10,951	29,908	2,731
Lee	4,691	14,187	3,024
Phillips	5,695	19,640	3,449
FLORIDA.			
Jackson	6,332	11,211	1,771
Jefferson	3,558	12,199	3,429
Leon	3,121	14,631	4,688
GEORGIA.			
Burke	5,817	22,680	3,899
Dougherty	1,975	10,231	5,180
Green	5,332	11,719	2,198
Hancock	4,739	12,410	2,619
Harris	5,999	10,797	1,800
Houston	5,272	16,341	3,100
Monroe	6,621	12,516	1,890

Counties.	Whites.	Colored.	Col'd to 1,000 Whites.
Oglethorpe	5,686	11,264	1,981
Steward	4,198	11,484	2,736
Sumter	7,008	15,098	2,154
Wilkes	5,616	12,464	2,219
LOUISIANA.			
Caddo	8,003	23,541	2,942
Concordia	1,757	13,112	7,463
De Soto	6,638	13,220	1,992
East Carroll.	997	11,360	11,394
East Feliciana	5,196	12,707	2,446
Iberville	6,696	15,142	2,261
Madison	931	13,204	14,183
Tensas	1,153	15,492	13,436
West Feliciana	2,276	12,785	5,617
MISSISSIPPI.			
Adams	6,128	19,895	3,247
Claiborne	3,533	10,980	3,108
Grenada	3,896	11,076	2,841
Holmes	7,084	23,883	3,371
Jefferson	3,589	15,356	4,279
Leflore	2,597	14,267	5,494
Lowndes	6,009	21,036	3,501
Madison	6,031	21,290	3,530
Marshall	9,731	16,306	1,676
Noxubee	4,709	22,629	4,805
Sunflower	2,530	6,850	2,708
Tunica	1,259	10,895	8,654
Washington	4,838	35,530	7,344
Wilkins	3,962	13,626	3,439
Yazoo	8,690	27,701	3,188
SOUTH CAROLINA.			
Abeville	15,142	31,705	2,094
Beufort	2,695	31,421	11,659
Berkely	7,687	47,739	6,210
Chester	8,482	18,178	2,143
Clarendon	6,987	16,246	2,325
Colleton	14,032	26,245	1,870
Edgefield	17,340	31,916	1,841
Fairfield	7,139	21,460	3,006
Georgetown	4,053	16,840	4,155
Hampton	6,827	13,717	2,009
Newbery	8,966	17,468	1,948
Orangeburg	15,654	33,738	2,155
Richland	11,933	24,885	2,085
Sumter	11,813	31,792	2,691
Williamsburg	9,355	18,420	1,969

Desirable as it would be to go into the details of this
tendency of the Negroes to congregate in certain rural
sections of the South, as has been done for the large
cities, it is not possible to do so here. The many
changes that have been made in the area of such
counties as it would be most desirable to investigate,
make a thorough study of this phase of the problem
exceedingly difficult. In the state of Alabama, for
example, nearly all of the counties have undergone
some changes in area during the past thirty years, with
the exception of Dallas and Sumter counties, for which
the statistics are very interesting and instructive.

PROGRESS OF THE POPULATION OF TWO COUNTIES OF ALABAMA.
1850-1890.

	DALLAS Co.		SUMTER Co.	
	White.	Colored.	White.	Colored.
1850	7,461	22,566	7,369	14,881
1860	7,785	25,840	5,919	18,116
1870	8,552	32,152	5,202	18,907
1880	8,425	40,007	6,451	22,277
1890	8,016	41,329	5,943	23,631

The colored population in both counties has increased
largely during the past forty years, while the white population has remained almost stationary or has actually
decreased. Part of the larger increase of the colored population is no doubt the result of migration from other
sections of the state; a migration which, however, must
have taken place previous to 1880, since, during the decade 1880-90 the increase in the colored population of
both counties has been below the average.

The preceding table may be compared with the following which shows for four counties with a large white
population the white and colored population for the last
three census years.

PROGRESS OF THE POPULATION OF FOUR COUNTIES OF ALABAMA.
1870-1890.

	BLOUNT CO.		CLEBURN CO.	
	White.	Colored.	White.	Colored.
1870	9,263	682	7,441	576
1880	14,210	1,159	10,308	668
1890	20,155	1,770	12,427	791

	JACKSON CO.		WALKER CO.	
	White.	Colored.	White.	Colored.
1870	16,350	3,060	6,235	308
1880	21,074	4,033	8,978	501
1890	24,179	3,840	14,422	1,656

The table shows that there is a similar tendency toward concentration on the part of the white population. Though this tendency does not seem general, the whites in these counties have made gains in population considerably in excess of the average rate of increase. If the general tendency is due to emigration of the whites from the counties now gaining in colored and decreasing in white population, the fate of the Negro West India Islands will overtake the Negro Gulf states of the South.

The tendency to migrate to large cities and to certain rural portions of the southern states, is not in the nature of an exodus. In only a very few instances have wholesale migrations taken place, and these as a rule have met with disaster and have proved a disappointment to those who looked forward to colonization as a means of solving the so-called " race problem." Probably the most notable instance was the so-called " Negro exodus from the southern states" during the year 1879. The movement assumed such proportions that a special committee of the United States Senate was appointed to investigate the causes which led to the emigration of colored people from North Carolina, Louisiana, and other states, largely to Kansas and Indiana. The com-

mittee held elaborate hearings, the results of which have
been published in a work of three volumes, forming a
valuable body of facts for study.[1]

The main causes of this exodus would seem to have
been politicians, railways and land agents. There had
been some discontent on account of the restriction and
deprivation of the right to vote, but on the whole the
colored people seemed previous to this time to have been
contented. The exodus was largely the result of external causes and, as was expected at the time, proved a
failure. A few instances must suffice to make this point
clear, since I cannot go into the details of the movement.
But I wish to show that it was not so much the dissatis-
faction of the colored people with the prevailing conditions in the southern states as it was the result of a
concerted arrangement of outsiders to induce them to
leave the plantations for the farms and cities of the
West.

One Benjamin Singleton appeared before the committee as a witness and testified that he was the "father of
the exodus," and that he had brought to Kansas, mostly
from Tennessee, 7,432 colored people during the period
1869–79. The people, according to this "father of the
exodus," settled in Lyons and Cherokee counties, Kansas.
He asserted also that the emigrants he had taken to
Kansas "were happy and doing well" and that he was
"the whole cause of the emigration to Kansas."[2] The
census returns of the past three decades fail to support
this assertion; for according to the ninth, tenth and
eleventh censuses there never were, and are not to-day,

[1] Report and Testimony of the Select Committee of the United States
Senate to investigate the causes of the removal of the negroes from
the southern states to the northern states. 46th Cong., second session,
Washington, D. C., 1880. (Three Volumes.)

[2] Senate Report, Vol. I, p. XIII.

one-third of this number of colored persons in the two counties named. In fact during the past decade the very small number of Negroes in these two counties has decreased, in contrast with a large increase in the white population.

PROGRESS OF THE POPULATION OF CHEROKEE AND LYON COUNTIES, KANSAS, 1870–1890.

	CHEROKEE Co.		LYON Co.	
	Colored.	White.	Colored.	White.
1870	134	10,899	126	7,888
1880	1,861	20,031	1,027	16,298
1890	1,342	26,421	1,031	22,163

The statement made, that 7432 colored people settled in those two counties of Kansas cannot, therefore, have been true. The aggregate population of these counties has steadily increased, as is evidenced by the last state census (1895) which gives to Lyon county a population of 23,795 and to Cherokee 30,651. In view of this progressive increase in the aggregate population it is remarkable that the colored population should show a decline. According to the reports of the Kansas Bureau of Agriculture the general economic condition of these counties is excellent, the aggregate value of agricultural produce is considerable, the assessed valuation being about seven million dollars for the former and four millions for the latter. There is a large variety of industries in agriculture and mining, and the section would seem to be one where almost any class of people would 'increase and multiply.'

Among the many statements made before the committee as to the probability of the colored people meeting with success in the northern states, is one by Senator Blair who was a member of the committee. In reply to a statement by the chairman, Mr. Vance of North Carolina, that he would not advise negroes to go to New Hampshire, Senator Blair replied : " Well, I would, and

I will tell you another thing, that twenty thousand Negroes would do well in New Hampshire.   I have known
a *good many*[1] Negroes up in New Hampshire and I
never saw one that had any trouble in getting along
on account of the climate.   I extend a cordial invita-
tion to them to come to New Hampshire; twenty
thousand of them could get along there and have a
chance of making a living. ''[2]   New Hampshire had a
colored population of 651 in 1790, 520 in 1850, and 614
in 1890.   It would therefore seem that the cordial invi-
tation of the Senator of that state had not been heeded.
That the climate does play an important part in the
mortality of the Negro will be shown in another part of
this monograph, in which the mortality of the race
will be dealt with.

Another interesting phase of the problem was brought
out in the testimony of a colored witness from Bolivar
county, Miss.   In reply to the question of the chairman
of the committee as to the causes of the exodus from
his county the witness replied: '' So far as the exodus
from our county is concerned I don't believe there ever
would have been any man to leave there if it had not
been for a colored man that lives in Helena, by the name
of Dr. C——.   He came down here in '78 and he got it
into the minds of the people there that they could go to
Liberia; that there was one tree there that bore the
bread and another that bore the lard and they had nothing at all to do but to go to one tree and dry the fruit
that gave the bread and to the other tree and cut it and
set a bucket under it and catch the lard.   It was the
most outrageous thing ever perpetrated on an ignorant
race in the world.''[3]

[1] The italics are the writer's.

[2] Report and Testimony of Select Committee, etc., Vol. III., p. 34.

[3] *Ibid.*, Vol. III, page 520.

In reply to the question of the chairman, " Is there another place within your knowledge where the colored people are so well off as they are in Bolivar county?" witness replies, " No sir, there is nowhere that they could be better off if they would do only what they ought to do and be industrious and work as they ought to work to make their own way."[1] It may be of interest to compare the progress of the colored with that of the white population of this county for the past fifty years for the purpose of showing how far the statements of this witness are supported by the facts. In addition to the data for Bolivar county, I give in the table below the same facts for Washington county which adjoins Bolivar.

PROGRESS OF THE POPULATION OF BOLIVAR AND WASHINGTON COUNTIES, MISSISSIPPI, 1840–1890.

	BOLIVAR CO.		WASHINGTON CO.	
	White.	Colored.	White.	Colored.
1840	384	972	654	6,633
1850	395	2,182	546	7,843
1860	1,393	9,078	1,212	14,467
1870	1,900	7,816	2,164	12,405
1880	2,694	15,958	3,478	21,861
1890	3,222	26,737	4,838	35,530

The Negroes according to the above table are largely in the majority and increasing at a rate out of proportion to the normal increase in the population at large. The large increase is partly due to migration since a natural increase in ten years of 10,779 in a population of 15,958 would be impossible.

The most emphatic prediction was probably that of a colored witness from Natchitoches parish, La., who expressed himself as follows in reply to the question of Mr. Windom as to the probable effect on this exodus of the election of a Democratic President: " The effect would

[1] Report and Testimony of Select Committee, etc., Vol. III, page 523.

be to create a great deal of consternation among them ;
I think it would cause them to leave the southern states,
not in a systematic way at all, but as they started away
this last year to go to Kansas, pell-mell—a regular
stampede—I am satisfied it would."[1] Such was the
gloomy prediction. Twice since then a Democratic
President has been elected and the predicted exodus has
—not taken place. Much to the contrary the colored
population of Nachitoches parish has increased from
12,020 in 1880 to 15,551 in 1890, and the white population of the same parish has made a corresponding
progress. So far as my information goes, no consternation
was created by the news of the election of Mr. Cleveland
in 1884 and 1892, and there was no stampede of any
kind.

The instances here quoted prove how far mere opinion
may mislead even the most sincere well wisher of the
colored race, and show the absolute necessity of a body
of carefully collected and thoroughly digested facts
from which to make deductions as to the present and possible future condition of the negro of the South. The
wholesale migration of the colored population of the
southern states to other sections of the United States, or
even to other countries, as Mexico and Liberia, may be
considered as the most remote possibility ; and it may
be safely asserted that all of the attempts in this direction have practically proven failures.

It would go beyond the purpose of this monograph were
I to attempt even an outline of the history of negro colonization, but I will quote the results of the most recent attempt, that of colonizing American negroes in the state of
Durango in Mexico. Some seven to eight hundred
families entered into an agreement with a syndicate, by

[1] Report and Testimony of Select Committee, etc., Vol. II, page 443.

which they were to have 60 acres of land or more, according to size of family, forty acres to be planted in cotton and fifteen in corn, and properly tilled under supervision; the right being reserved, in case of default, to employ labor at the expense of the colonist. Five acres were given rent free for the sustenance of each family. In addition, water for irrigation was to be furnished free, as well as farming implements, mules and teams for farming purposes, and food for the same. The colonists were to perform all labor and receive one-half of the crops. Houses, fuel and water were provided free, and rations, medicines, etc., were furnished at cost to be repaid out of the crops. Land was set apart for one church and one school house to each one hundred families. The colonists were to receive one-half of the cotton seed as well as one-half of all the other products raised by them, and they obligated themselves to sell to the promoters all their corn, cotton and cotton-seed at the market prices. The cost of transportation was to be advanced, and to be repaid out of their share of the crops.

The agreement was to last for five years. It did not last one year. The whole plan proved a dismal failure and a considerable pecuniary loss to those who directed it, as well as a loss of time, money, and even life, to the colonists. The Negroes proved unreasonable and of far less service than had been expected. They were controlled largely by bad leaders of their own race who stirred up strife, and they were induced to leave 'by a little rascal who had been but recently released from the Georgia penitentiary.' The colony came to an inglorious end.

As to the fitness of the Negroes for the work they had agreed to perform, and which, as has been pointed out in the above summary of the agreement, was almost identical with southern farm labor, I cannot do better than quote portions of a special report to the *Evening Post*, dated July 8, 1895. " In the course of these conferences with the Negroes it became evident that they are, as a class, incapable of assimilating readily with new surroundings or of applying to them the first dictates of common sense. They are superstitious, suspicious and easily swayed by the intriguers among them. The impression left on the mind of an unprejudiced observer was, in short, that seventy-five per cent. of the Negroes had left home from a love of novelty and adventure, had exhausted these delights and were bent on repudiating their agreements and forcing their partners in the contract to restore them to their homes without regard to right or reason. The conclusion drawn from a close study of this colony was, I regret to say, that it was foredoomed to failure. While the region in which it was laid was no paradise, it was free from the objections incident to most of the similar previous efforts of this sort. Whether wisely or mistakenly guided, every endeavor was made to meet the reasonable requirements of the colonists. To those who interest themselves in the future of the Negro this experiment presents little cause for congratulation. It indicates, that the same limitations which hinder his advancement at home, are equally apparent when he changes his habitation and that until he is capable of self control and intelligent application among the surroundings with which he is familiar there is but small hope that he will succeed amid strange environments. . . If this experiment is entitled to rank as an example it would seem that the ordinary Negro ' hand' of the southern states, whatever are his trials and tribulations at home, is more likely to be satisfied there than when transported to other, even if more favorable scenes."[1]

I have quoted from the report of Mr. Mackie at considerable length because a correct view of the colonization question is of the utmost importance. Colonization is still advocated with persistency by many who see in it the only solution of the so-called race question of the South. If the Negro cannot be colonized under such favorable conditions as the experiment in Mexico presented (and no charge has ever been made that it was not honestly managed on the part of the promoters of the scheme) the sooner this is realized the better.

It has been shown that the Negro has failed to gain a foothold in any of the northern states as an agricultural laborer; it has been shown that he has remained in the South, contrary to the many predictions of wholesale migration; and lastly it has been shown that he has failed in the most recent experiment of colonization. The conclusion to be drawn from the statistical tables previously presented would be that he is in the South as a permanent factor, with neither the ability nor inclination to leave this section in large numbers, for the North or for foreign countries. The observed tendency to drift into the cities, there to concentrate in the most undesirable and unsanitary sections, is therefore of considerable importance, since it is most likely to be persisted in with increasing force in the future. The loss thus sustained by the rural districts of the South is not very large numerically nor proportionally, and the evil effect will be more felt by the cities which are thus augmented in population of an undesirable character. The further tendency to concentrate into certain sections of the South, especially those which already possess a pre-

[1] Charles Paul Mackie in the New York *Evening Post.*

ponderating colored population, presents the most serious aspect of the problem. We have here to deal with large numbers; which must have a corresponding effect on the welfare of the individual state thus affected, as well as on the nation at large.

CHAPTER II.

VITAL STATISTICS.

" Mortality statistics surpass all other vital statistics in importance, whether they are considered from a social, an actuarial or a sanitary standpoint."—*Newsholme.*

This part will be devoted almost exclusively to a discussion of the mortality statistics of the colored population, together with such information pertaining to the white population as will bring out the most important differences in the vitality of the two races. Desirable as it would be to have as a basis a comparative statement of the birth rates of both races, it must be admit ted that information on this point is almost entirely wanting, and that no trustworthy conclusion as to the comparative fecundity can be arrived at. In the forthcoming eleventh census reports on mortality, by Dr. Billings, we may expect to find the best that can be done in this direction at the present time; and a comprehensive discussion of the comparative mortality may enable us to make up for the want of reliable information as to the comparative fecundity.

That the birth rate of the Negroes is in excess of that of the white population is probably true even at the the present time, at least as compared with the native whites. That it is not as high as has often been stated, however, is proved by the fairly accurate statistics of the West Indies. In Alabama we have had for a series of years a commendable attempt to collect information in this line, but with a varying degree of success. For some of the northern states, especially Rhode Island,

3

Connecticut and Massachusetts, valuable information has been collected but in view of the differences in the age distribution of the colored population of those states as compared with the whites, it is difficult to arrive at a correct estimate. It would appear, however, that in the northern states the Negro mortality is in excess of the natality; while the reports for Alabama show a birth rate equal to twice the death rate. Among the whites of Alabama the reports show three births to one death. The admitted defects of the Alabama reports may be assumed to affect the rates for both races in the same degree, and the excess of natural increase in the white population as compared with the colored is probably correctly represented by the table below:

VITAL STATISTICS OF THE WHITE AND COLORED POPULATIONS OF
ALABAMA, 1888-1893.

	White Population.			Colored Population.		
	Births.	Deaths.	Ratio of Births to Deaths.	Births.	Deaths.	Ratio of Births to Deaths.
1888 . .	10,841	3,673	. . .	8,263	4,046	. . .
1889 . .	14,649	5,066	. . .	9,765	4,994	. . .
1890 . .	13,631	4,716	. . .	9,955	5,005	. . .
1891 . .	11,484	3,827	. . .	9,138	4,283	. . .
1892 . .	10,819	3,720	. . .	8,237	4,100	. . .
1893 . .	12,453	3,945	. . .	9,961	4,406	. . .
1888-93	73,877	24,947	2.96 to 1	55,319	26,834	2.06 to 1

In Rhode Island, Connecticut and Massachusetts the vital statistics for the colored population have been collected for many years, but it is only for the first named state that I am able to give the returns for a period of some length. For Massachusetts the information has been collected but not published, excepting for the year 1888. The data so far as they have come to my notice, are contained in the following three tables, all of which show a mortality in excess of the registered births.

VITAL STATISTICS OF THE COLORED POPULATION OF RHODE ISLAND.

Period.	Births.	Deaths.			
1861–70	1,131	1,153	Excess of Deaths		22
1871–80	1,615	1,573	"	Births	42
1881–90 . . .	1,954	1,860	"	Births	94
1891–93	558	690	"	Deaths	132
1861–93	5,258	5,276	"	Deaths	18

VITAL STATISTICS OF THE COLORED POPULATION OF CONNECTICUT.

Period.	Births.	Deaths.			
1881–85	1,340	1,391	Excess of Deaths		51
1886–90	1,374	1,554	"	"	170
1891–93	939	990	"	"	51
1881–93	3,653	3,925	"	"	272

VITAL STATISTICS OF THE COLORED POPULATION OF
MASSACHUSETTS, 1888.

Births 511
Deaths. 579
Excess of Deaths 68

The three tables support each other and leave no doubt as to the excessive mortality and low birth rate of the colored population in the northern states. Possibly the omission of births would be balanced by omissions of deaths and proportionally the result would be the same even under the most perfect registration system.

The low vitality of the colored race in the North did not escape the notice of the officials in charge of the registration records, and some of the editorial comments may not be out of place here. Dr. Fisher, for many years the registrar of vital statistics of Rhode Island, refers to the subject in the second annual report of the state board of health, as follows: " The circumstances favorable to the promotion of the physical health of the colored population are believed to be at least quite as favorable and ample in Rhode Island as in any other northern or eastern state. When we find that in a period of eighteen years the excess of births over deaths is only 42, and having full knowledge of the fact that the state is annually having accessions to the number of colored people by immigration and these accessions largely in the periods of life between twenty and forty years, we must conclude, however reluctantly, that the race is not self-sustaining in this latitude."[1]

Dr. Snow, the eminent registrar of Providence arrived at practically the same conclusion nearly twenty years before the above was written, and makes use of the following language, which seems justified by the facts quoted : " During the past four years, 1855–58 inclusive, 176 colored children have been born in this city, of which 88 were males and 88 were females. During the same period there have been 206 deaths of colored persons, or 29 more deaths than births. The colored population is evidently not self-sustaining in this city." [2]

Mr. Appolino, one time registrar of Boston, in his report for 1862 concludes that, " in each of the aspects in which the subject may be viewed the colored race seems, so far as this city is concerned, to be doomed to extinction." [3] During the period of seven years preceding 1862 there had been reported 304 births of colored children in Boston and 500 deaths ; which facts fully justify the conclusion of Mr. Appolino, than whom Boston never had a more able and conscientious registrar.

These conclusions, based, not on chance observation or opinion, but on registration data, are in contrast with the view of those who have held that the Negro could live in the northern as well as in the southern states of the

---

[1] Second Annual Report of the Rhode Island Board of Health, (1880), p. 107.

[2] Annual report for 1858, p. 3.

[3] Annual report for 1862, p. 7.

Union. One instance of the latter claim has been given,[1] and I select out of many others the statement of the author of the " History of the Maroons." In relating the transfer of the Maroons to Nova Scotia, he speaks of the effect of the climate as follows: " It is proved, by experience, that the Negro race can endure the severity of a cold climate as well as white people, if equally clothed,"[2] The writer did not state on what experience this observation was founded but goes on to say that the Maroons were later on removed to the Coast of West Africa, much to their own satisfaction.

The vitality of the Negro may well be considered the most important phase of the so-called race problem; for it is a fact which can and will be demonstrated by indisputable evidence, that of all races for which statistics are obtainable, and which enter at all into the consideration of economic problems as factors, the Negro shows the least power of resistance in the struggle for life.

Most writers who have dealt with the subject from this standpoint have referred to the excessive mortality of the colored race. Most of the officials of the health offices of southern cities have from time to time discussed the waste of life among these people. Some have essayed to treat of the causes, and others of the means of prevention; but thus far no effectual remedy has been suggested which would even slightly improve the present condition, a condition which, unchecked, must lead eventually to extermination, at a rate far more rapid than the recent census returns would indicate.

In the second annual report of the Atlanta board of health, occurs the following reference to the excessive colored mortality: " The disparity in the relative death

[1] Page 25.
[2] R. C. Dallas, " History of the Maroons," (London, 1803), Vol. II, p. 199.

rates of the whites and Negroes is striking and invariable. The record in this city does not differ from that of other cities. The fact is significant and full of melancholoy interest, and unless the figures in the cities are reversed by the statistics from the rural districts, the fate of the race will not be difficult to read."

The second annual report of the National Board of Health, edited by the foremost medical authorities of the time, gives expression to the following opinion: " These figures (vital statistics of Cuba), demonstrate conclusively, as the statistics of all southern countries have invariably done, that the old idea that the Negro surpassed the white in enduring tropical or southern climates was false; and that in truth the colored death rate is habitually greater," [1]

This concensus of opinion of northern and southern authorities is fully supported by all the available data. It is true that most of the collected statistics have reference only to the large cities; but in view of the tendency of the colored population to migrate from the country to the cities in ever increasing numbers, and at the age period most favorable for a low general death rate, the proof of an excessive mortality rate is of the greatest economic and social significance. The following table will show the comparative death rates of the white and colored populations of ten southern cities for the period 1890–94. The rates are calculated on the basis of the census of 1890 in accordance with the method of Dr. Farr. The mortality figures have been obtained from the annual reports of the health officers of the respective cities. The rates will differ from those calculated by the city authorities, who make use of no uniform method in calculating the increase in the population.

[1] Annual report, National Board of Health, 1880, p. 224.

COMPARATIVE DEATH RATES OF THE WHITE AND COLORED POPU-
LATIONS OF TEN SOUTHERN CITIES, 1890–1894

	Washington, D. C.		Baltimore, Md.		Richmond, Va.		Memphis. Tenn.		Louisville, Ky.	
	White.	Col'd.	White.	Col'd.	White.	Col'd.	White.	Col'd.	White.	Col'd.
1890 . .	18.97	34.74	21.96	32.28	22.31	37.86	17.84	24.58	27.64	28.79
1891 . .	19.37	33.27	20.87	32.47	20.75	34.17	17.73	25.33	16.84	37.02
1892 . .	20.70	32.57	21.55	31.55	18.26	33.14	15.56	31.86	17.84	29.42
1893 . .	21.33	32.79	18.58	30 33	18.16	32.05	12.35	29.96	16.96	26.85
1894 . .	18.62	30.85	17.81	30.47	15.20	25.46	11.84	29.84	15.99	25.47
1890–94	19.80	32.78	20.01	31.39	19.03	32.45	14.84	22.12	17.04	27.41

	Atlanta, Ga.		Savann'h, Ga.		Charleston, S. C.		Mobile, Ala.		New Orleans, La.	
1890 . .	18.92	32.26	24.70	37.86	21.36	42.20	21.57	34.51	25.96	40.73
1891 . .	18.64	31.36	22.29	31.25	23.00	43.61	21.50	29.56	24.65	37.18
1892 . .	16.44	29.35	21.83	33.62	24.25	41.36	23.93	32.96	26.16	41.59
1893 . .	15 21	28.92	21.51	30.79	22.02	39.81	20.91	32.62	24.53	39.65
1894 . .	12.58	22.27	18.16	28.61	19.62	39.80	19.59	28.65	23.04	37.97
1890–94	16.17	28.59	21.43	32.26	22.05	41.34	21.44	31.60	24.85	39.42

COMBINED MORTALITY RATE OF TEN CITIES, 1890–1894.

Death rate, White, ... 20.12
Death rate, Colored, ... 32.61

It will be observed that the mortality among the
colored exceeds that of the whites in each of the ten
cities embraced in the above table, which includes most of
the principal cities of the South. The difference in the
comparative mortality of the two races is greatest for
Charleston and least for Memphis, but the percentage of
excess is greatest for Charleston and least for Mobile.
In the former city the Negro death rate is 87.5 per cent.
above that of the whites, and in the latter 47.4 per cent.
For the ten cities combined the mortality of the Negroes
exceeds that of the whites by 12.49 per 1,000 of population or by 62.1 per cent.

The results of this comparison therefore support the
opinions of the authorities previously quoted, even in

the case of those sections of the south which have been
considered least favorable for the white population.
The comparative rates are based on an aggregate white
population of 5,371,355 with 108,045 deaths, and an aggregate colored population of 2,085,679 with 68,012
deaths. The period of observation covered five years in
which the health of each race was normal and not dis-
turbed by epidemics.

The facts brought out in the above table relate to
about 416,000 of the total colored population. Even if
the Negro mortality in the country districts were less
than that of the whites, which it is not, the fact that
so large a portion of the colored population is affected
by the high death rate named must prove an important
factor, economic as well as social and moral, in the
progress of the race. Whatever the causes may be to
which we must attribute this difference in the statistics
of the two races, they deserve to be fully investigated.

The foregoing table, giving only the gross death rates
of the two races, is fairly reliable for southern cities,
since the age distribution of the two races is nearly the
same in each of them. But to fully comprehend the
significance of the higher mortality of the colored population it will be necessary to consider the mortality rate
for the different periods of life. In the large cities of
the North and West the age distribution of the colored
population is so radically different from that of the
white that a gross death rate is of no value and is even
misleading.

The age distribution of the two races in two southern
and two northern cities is given in the table below, which
has been calculated from the census.

COMPARATIVE AGE DISTRIBUTION OF THE WHITE AND COLORED
POPULATIONS OF FOUR CITIES.—(1890.)

AGES.	New York.		Brooklyn.		Charleston.		New Orleans.	
	Percentage.		Percentage.		Percentage.		Percentage.	
	White.	Col'd.	White.	Col'd.	White.	Col'd.	White.	Col'd.
Under 15 . .	28.9	19.2	30.8	24.4	30 46	32.95	32.52	32.06
15–20 . .	9.9	7.6	9.8	8.7	10 85	9 82	10.79	9.86
20–25 . .	11.7	13.0	10.9	12.6	10.47	11.19	10.70	10.49
25–35 . .	20.2	27.3	18.9	22.2	15.74	16.84	16.33	15.06
35–45 . .	13.3	18.8	12.6	16.4	12.17	13.58	11.42	12.97
45–55 . .	8.8	9 0	9.0	8.9	9.42	8.17	8.83	9.99
55–65 . .	4.6	3.1	5.0	4.2	6.33	3.85	5.60	5.25
Over 65 . .	2.6	2.0	3 0	2.6	4.56	3.60	3.81	4.32

According to this table the proportion of Negroes in the
northern cities is largest for the age periods in which the
mortality is least, that is from fifteen to forty-five years.
This excess of adults at middle age is due solely to the
constant influx of young people from the southern states.
The result is that the gross death rate for the colored
population is not so high as it would be if the age distribution were the same as that of the whites. In the
southern cities the differences, it will be observed, are
very slight and the gross death rates of those cities are
therefore more reliable than those of the large cities of
the North and West, which understate the facts. This
element of error is eliminated in the following tables
which show for six cities the comparative death rates of
the two races at various periods of life. For the four
northern cities the death rates are given for eight periods
and for Baltimore and the District of Columbia for four.
It is very unfortunate that in the reports of Dr. Billings,
from which the tables have been compiled, a different
method should have been employed for the two groups
of cities, thus making an exact comparison impossible.

DEATH RATES OF FOUR CITIES FOR 1890, CALCULATED FOR EIGHT AGE GROUPS.[1]

AGES.	New York.		Brooklyn.		Boston.		Philadelphia.	
	White.	Col'd.	White.	Col'd.	White.	Col'd.	White.	Col'd.
All Ages, ...	28.47	37.47	25.41	34.99	24.62	33.29	22.28	32.42
Under 15 . .	47.06	87.42	40.69	69.45	40.20	78.40	34.89	69.24
15–20 . .	5.65	14.32	5.42	12.54	7.27	9.69	6.17	13.61
20–25 . .	9.84	16.12	8.60	15.95	9.76	17.64	8.81	14.50
25–35 . .	14.15	19.24	12.65	11.53	12.43	14.72	10.85	15.21
35–45 . .	20 91	25.29	15.93	21.79	16.37	18.98	13.60	17.16
45–55 . .	29.30	35 56	23.03	34.02	21.71	36.07	18.98	29.41
55–65 . .	48.45	79.05	40.60	47.93	36.45	51.55	31.56	40.09
65 and ov.	105.16	94.86	96.09	144.37	94.01	113.51	88.88	116.49

[1] Still-births included.

DEATH RATES OF BALTIMORE AND WASHINGTON, D. C., FOR 1890, CALCULATED FOR FOUR AGE GROUPS.[2]

Ages.	Baltimore, Md.		Washington, D. C.	
	White.	Colored.	White.	Colored.
Under 5 years . . .	80.27	171.78	65.04	159.93
Under 15 years . . .	30.71	64.24	23.90	57.00
15–45 years . . .	8.99	14.88	9.29	17.09
45 years and over. .	37.49	42.31	33.88	47.60

[2] Still-births excluded.

It will be observed that the gross death rates for the colored population exceed those of the white and this too, in view of the fact just stated, that the age distribution of the colored is far more favorable for a low general death rate than that of the white population. Considering the mortality rates for various age groups it will be noticed that for the earliest period the difference is enormous. In New York for instance the white population for the age group 0—15 shows a death rate of 47.06 per thousand while that of the colored population for the same age period is 87.42 per thousand. The same disparity is to be observed in all of the other cities to a greater or less degree, and it is not until we reach the higher age periods that we find the mortality rates of the two races nearing each other. Even at the highest ages the white mortality rate rarely approaches the colored. Only in one instance does it rise above. Before considering the comparative differences in the mortality of the two races for the different age periods, in the cities of the North, I would direct the attention of the reader to the following tables for three cities of the South, all of which may be considered representative of the respective sections in which they are located. The tables have been calculated by the writer on advance statistics of the age distribution of the population, kindly furnished him for this purpose by Mr. Carroll D. Wright, the acting superintendent of the census. The mortality returns have been obtained from the board of health reports of the respective cities for the year 1890. The age groups differ from those of the preceding table, giving the mortality for ten year periods after the age of ten. But for the want of uniformity in the mortality returns of southern cities it would have been possible to give similar tables for other cities. However, the cities furnishing reports for the above tables may be assumed to represent fairly the prevailing conditions in other cities of the south.

NEW ORLEANS.—1890.

	WHITE.			COLORED.		
Ages.	Population.	Deaths.	Rate per 1000.	Population.	Deaths.	Rate per 1000.
0–1 . . .	3,842	1,035	269.4	1,290	555	430.2
0–5 . . .	19,134	1,428	74.6	6,787	805	118.6
5–9 . . .	19,466	98	5.0	7,145	70	9.8
10–19 . . .	38,216	165	4.3	13,179	154	11.7
20–29 . . .	34,467	377	10.9	12,091	277	22.9
30–39 . . .	24,502	509	20.8	9,169	270	29.4
39–49 . . .	17,551	475	27.1	7,337	256	34.9
49–59 . . .	12,661	534	42.2	4,642	244	52.6
59–69 . . .	7,634	501	65.6	2,476	221	89.3
69–79 . . .	2,879	354	123.0	1,065	176	165.3

CHARLESTON.—1890.

	WHITE.			COLORED.		
Ages.	Population.	Deaths.	Rate per 1000.	Population.	Deaths.	Rate per 1000.
0–1 . . .	494	99	200.4	758	350	461.7
0–5 . . .	2,285	148	64.8	3,455	517	149 6
5–9 . . .	2,365	8	3.4	3,391	37	10 9
10–19 . . .	5,231	17	3.3	6,428	104	16.2
20–29 . . .	4,420	42	9.5	6,503	170	26.1
30–39 . . .	3,406	47	13.8	4,635	112	24.2
40–49 . . .	2,526	57	22.6	3,208	98	30.6
50–59 . .	1,859	47	25.3	1,674	72	43.0
60–69 . . .	1,184	69	58.3	1,031	79	76.6
70–79 . . .	440	47	106.8	407	66	162.2

RICHMOND.—1890.

	WHITE.			COLORED.		
,0–1 . . .	1,102	206	186.9	625	331	529.6
0–5 . . .	4,942	332	67.2	2,772	496	178.9
5–9 . . .	4,871	40	8.2	3,063	57	18.6
10–19 . . .	10,420	58	5.6	7,134	78	10 9
20–29 . . .	9,859	113	11.5	7,387	134	18.1
30–39 . . .	7,053	98	13.9	4,634	99	21.4
40–49 . . .	5,030	92	18.3	3,488	92	26.4
50–59 . . .	3,539	100	28.3	1,853	92	49.7
60–69 . . .	2,119	101	47.7	1,021	75	73.5
70–79 . . .	834	104	124.7	380	46	121.1

COMPARATIVE DEATH RATES FOR THREE SOUTHERN CITIES.
DEATHS PER 1000 LIVING AT SAME AGE. (1890.)

	New Orleans.		Charleston.		Richmond.	
Ages.	White.	Colored.	White.	Colored.	White.	Colored
0–1 . . .	269.4	430.2	200.4	461.7	186.9	529.8
0–5 . . .	74.6	118.6	64.8	149.6	67.2	178 9
5–9 . . .	5.0	9.8	3.4	10.9	8.2	18.6
10–19 . . .	4.3	11.7	3.3	16.2	5.6	10.9
20–29 . . .	10.9	22.9	9.5	26.1	11.5	18.1
30–39 . . .	20.8	29.4	13.8	24 2	13.9	21.4
40–49 . . .	27.1	34.9	22.6	30.6	18.3	26.4
50–59 . . .	42.2	52.6	25.3	43.0	28.3	49.7
60–69 . . .	65.6	89.3	58.3	76 6	47.7	73.5
70–79 . . .	123.0	165.3	106.8	162.2	124 7	121.1

I have given all the data from which the rates were calculated, in order to enable the reader to form his own opinion as to the value of the results. The three tables fully support the previous conclusions for northern cities and show that the greatest excess of mortality amongst the colored falls on the early age groups. The excess at the very early ages, *i. e.*, from birth to the end of the first year and to the end of the fifth year is, however, not as great proportionately as the excess at the age periods immediately following; but the actual excess, the greatest waste of life, falls on the earliest age group. The economic importance of this fact cannot be overestimated. An excessive infant mortality, such as we meet with among the white population in all parts of the country, has at all times been the concern of the philanthropist and economist, but nowhere else do we meet with such a frightful infant mortality as we find prevailing among the colored population of the large cities, both North and South. In one city, Richmond, over half of the Negro children die under one year, a mortality so great that no greater fecundity could balance the loss. The increase of the population which we observe in all cities of the South and North, must therefore be largely due to migration from the country. In the cities of the South there is less difference in the death rates of the two races as the higher age groups are reached, but in only one case is there a difference in favor of the colored race. These differences are brought out in the tables which follow, in which the percentage of excess of the Negro mortality over the white is shown for three age periods, first for Washington and Baltimore, second for the three southern cities, to which is added a comparative table for four northern cities.

COMPARATIVE MORTALITY OF WHITES AND NEGROES[1] IN BALTIMORE AND WASHINGTON, 1890.

Ages.	BALTIMORE.			WASHINGTON.		
	White.	Col'd.	Col'd over White. Per cent.	White.	Col'd.	Col'd over White. Per cent.
0 to 15 . . .	30.71	64.24	109.2	23.90	57.00	138.5
15 to 45 . . .	8.99	14.88	65.5	9.29	17.09	84.0
45 and over. .	37.49	42.43	13.2	33.88	47.60	40.5

[1] Vital Statistics of Washington and Baltimore, 1890, p. 6.

4

COMPARATIVE MORTALITY OF NEGROES AND WHITES.

	Four North'n Cities.[1]	Four South'n Cities.[2]		Excess of Negro Mortality.
		White.	Colored.	
0–1	230.92	240.57	467.67	94.4 per cent.
0–5	72.74	72.17	144.38	100.1 "
5–10	7.50	5.51	12.58	128.3 "
10–20	5.45	4.58	12.11	164.4 "
20–30	9.37	10.95	21.58	97.8 ',
30–40	13.60	18.76	25.11	33.9 "
40–50	19.49	24.88	32.32	29.9 "
50–60	26.57	37.71	47.64	26.3 "
60–70	56.88	61.70	78.18	26.7 "

[1] Boston, St. Louis, New Haven and Cincinnati.
[2] Savanah, New Orleans, Charleston and Richmond.

The percentage of excess in Negro mortality is here shown to be highest for the period of life under fifteen, next highest from fifteen to forty-five and lowest for the age periods over forty-five. There are slight deviations from this rule but none which materially affect the conclusion that the young generation of the colored population shows the highest, and the oldest generation the lowest, percentage of mortality above that of the white race.

It may be of value to show briefly the influence of sex on this excessive mortality. I have abstracted, in part, from the reports of Dr. Billings, the comparative mortality of the two sexes for three cities for eight age groups. I have selected the three northern cities where females largely predominate and the increase in the population is largely due to migration from the country. The tables are deserving of consideration as showing the effects of city life on the colored population of middle age.

COMPARATIVE MORTALITY OF WHITE AND COLORED ACCORDING
TO AGE AND SEX.—1890.

NEW YORK.

	Males.		Females.	
	White.	Colored.	White.	Colored.
All ages	31.15	42.06	25.87	33.01
Under 15 . . .	51.15	96.76	42.97	78.23
15–20 . . .	6.25	18.82	5.13	10.86
20–25 . . .	11.47	21.17	8.52	11.47
25–35 . . .	15.54	21.40	12.71	17.02
35–45 . . .	23.30	29.69	18.32	20.45
45–55 . . .	31.86	40.68	26.60	30.20
55–65 . . .	53.88	98.16	43.41	65.82
65 and over,	107.99	87.72	102.84	98.51

BOSTON.

	Males.		Females.	
All Ages. . . .	25.96	31.56	23.37	35.32
Under 15 . . .	43.18	75.22	37.18	81.40
15–20 . . .	7.22	9.58	7.31	9.80
20–25 . . .	10.88	15.76	8.79	19.76
25–35 . . .	12.85	15.51	12.03	13.60
35–45 . . .	17.54	23.97	15.15	12.59
45–55 . . .	23.39	31.39	19.94	41.90
55–65 . . .	38.02	52.98	35.12	50.00
65 and over,	97.19	129.03	91.72	105.69

PHILADELPHIA.

	Males.		Females.	
All ages	23.85	36.02	20.79	29.23
Under 15 . . .	37.22	75.81	32.51	63.12
15–20 . . .	6.49	15.01	5.89	12.66
20–25 . . .	10.12	19.75	7.64	10.46
25–35 . . .	11.28	14.12	10.43	16.24
35–45 . . .	15.30	20.52	11.91	13.55
45–55 . .	20.85	33.67	17.20	25.48
55–65 . . .	36.44	47.70	27.42	34.57
65 and over,	93.51	155.26	85.35	96.47

PERCENTAGE OF COLORED MORTALITY OVER WHITE, ACCORDING
TO AGE AND SEX.

	MALES.			FEMALES.		
Ages.	New York. Per. Ct.	Boston, Per Ct.	Philadelphia. Per Ct.	New York. Per Ct.	Boston. Per Ct.	Philadelphia. Per Ct.
All ages	35.0	21.6	51.0	27.6	51.1	40.6
Under 15 . . .	89.2	81.6	103.7	58.8	116.2	94.2
15–20 . . .	201.0	32.7	131.3	111.7	20.4	114.9
20–25 . . .	84.6	44.9	95.2	34.6	124.8	36.9
25–35 . . .	38.4	20.7	25.2	33.9	13.1	55.7
35–45 . . .	27.4	36.7	34.1	11.6	*	13.8
45–55 . . .	27.7	63.4	61.5	13.5	109.6	48.1
55–65 . . .	82.2	20.5	30.1	51.6	42.4	18.8
65 and over,	*	32.8	66.0	*	4.2	13.0

*White mortality in excess of colored.

The excess in the Negro mortality rate varies considerably for some age groups, which is due, in part, to the small numbers on which the ratios are based. However, for the age periods under 25, the excess of mortality is greater for males than for females and almost without exception the numerical mortality for colored males is in excess of that of the females at all periods of life. The most important exception is to be observed in Boston where the mortality of females under 25 is in excess of the male mortality. In New York and Philadelphia the females with slight and unimportant exceptions have a lower mortality rate than the males, irrespective of race and age. In Boston white females at all ages, excepting fifteen to twenty have a more favorable mortality rate than males, while colored females have a lower mortality only after the age twenty-five. This favorable rate for females is due in part to the greater liability of the male to accidental death, more frequent exposure to the inclemency of the weather, and last, not least, to his more pronounced criminal tendencies. Females also are usually employed as domestic servants and in consequence are better cared for in every respect than the colored male, who only too often leads the life of a vagrant and roust-about in search of something to do, honest or otherwise.

The effect of conjugal condition on the mortality rate is fairly well brought out in a table for Washington and Baltimore abstracted from the report of Dr. Billings. The respective death rates are given for two age periods and afford an interesting comparison. It must be taken into consideration, however, that the conjugal condition of the colored population is not so clearly defined as it is for the white race. This is easily understood when I mention the fact that over 25 per cent. of the colored children born in Washington are reported as illegitimate, as compared with less than 3 per cent. for the whites. It is probable, however, that all those who had borne children were enumerated as married, or at least those who were living under the conditions of married life.

DEATH RATES OF THE WHITE AND COLORED POPULATIONS
ACCORDING TO CONJUGAL CONDITION.

	MALES—AGES 15-45.				FEMALES—AGES 15-45.			
	Washington.		Baltimore.		Washington.		Baltimore.	
	White.	Col'd.	White.	Col'd.	White.	Col'd.	White,	Col'd.
Single . . .	10.47	18.58	9.19	13.75	6.44	14.50	6.53	13.20
Married . .	9.06	16.67	8.98	13.49	9.56	16.72	9.76	16.31
Widowed. .	40.17	50.51	26.95	30.93	13.65	15.12	12.02	14.36
	MALES—45 AND OVER.				FEMALES—45 AND OVER.			
Single . . .	48.23	69.33	35.70	60.81	26.04	37.61	37.79	46.05
Married . .	29.94	40.75	31.22	39.60	18 05	28.50	24.13	24.77
Widowed . .	80 12	99.42	74.59	83.48	42.00	56.37	54.85	46.01

It remains for me to add to the present series of tables two which have some bearing on the condition of life of the colored population in our large cities, namely those showing altitude and density of population. It is a favorite argument with some authors who have written upon the causes of the excessive mortality of the colored race, that the low social and economic conditions of these people, as well as the general unsanitary condition of their dwellings, are largely responsible for their higher mortality. In a word, they attribute to the environment most of the ills that at present affect so seriously the duration of life for the colored race. These writers argue that, given the same social, economic and sanitary conditions of life, the colored race would enjoy the same health and favorable death rate as the white population. The powerful influences of a bad heredity are almost wholly ignored and the greatest stress is laid upon the effect of the environment. I therefore call attention to the tables below, which, so far as I am aware, present certain facts not hitherto published.   It is true that the Surgeon-General of the Army,[1] as well as Dr. Cunningham of the Alabama Penitentiary,[2] have called attention to the fact that even under the same conditions, subject to the same regulations, fed and clothed in the same manner as the white man, doing the same class of work, the Negro is still subject to a higher death rate; but the statements of these two high authorities have never been duly considered by those who believe so firmly in the all powerful effect of the ' milieux.'

DEATH RATES OF THE WHITE AND COLORED POPULATION AT ALL AGES AND UNDER 5 YEARS FOR TWO CITIES, ACCORDING TO ALTITUDE.—1886-1890.

Average Altitude	Washingon. All Ages.		Baltimore. All Ages.		Washingon. Under 5 yrs.[1]		Baltimore. Under 5 yrs.[1]	
(In feet.)	White.	Col'd.	White.	Col'd.	White.	Col'd.	White.	Col'd.
Under 25	21.26	37.48	23.63	44.65	78.85	167.69	86.92	203.30
25- 50	19.83	37.06	21.84	36.51	71.41	155.21	76.96	194.03
50- 75	17.24	31.87	21.64	34.34	57.59	159.57	78.78	155.68
75-100	15.67	32.55	18.31	28.03	52.30	157.89	66.16	148.39
Over 100	17.24	31.23	17.16	28.21	57.87	136.11	58.70	145.53

[1] Exclusive of still births.

DEATH RATES OF THE WHITE AND COLORED POPULATION OF TWO CITIES, ACCORDING TO DENSITY OF POPULATION.—1886-1890.

WASHINGTON.	All Ages.		Under 5 years.[1]	
Persons to the Acre.	White.	Colored.	White.	Colored.
Under 25	18.51	35.46	60.94	161.77
25-50	18.54	31.19	66.31	148.49
50 and over	17.78	34.72	64.34	163.98
BALTIMORE.				
Under 50	22.73	39.13	80.11	196.40
50-100	18.34	27.74	66.91	149.34
Over 100	21.58	36.98	77.87	171.65

[1] Exclusive of still births.

[1] John Moore, Annual report, Surgeon-General of the Army, 1889, p. 18.
    [2] *Medical News*, Feb. 3, 1894.

The above two tables are of great value as evidence that environment has less effect on the duration of life than have the factors of race and heredity. It will be observed that even under the most favorable conditions as indicated by a high altitude and low density of population, the excessive Negro mortality rate remains comparatively the same. The per cent. of excess in the rate for the population living under the most unfavorable conditions as indicated by the degree of altitude, is 76.29 for Washington and 88.95 for Baltimore, while for the population under the most favorable conditions the excess is 81.15 per cent. for the former and 64.39 per cent. for the latter city. The evil effect of a low altitude is too well known to need more than a reference to it, and the importance of these remarkable facts will be fully understood by those familiar with the influence of soil moisture on mortality. I give similar information for the age group under five, and also with respect to the effect of density of population, to assist those who wish to trace more fully the effect of environment on the mortality of the colored race. It may be of interest here to give the comparative distribution of the white and colored populations of Washington and Baltimore according to altitude. It will be seen that in the two cities the Negroes live in larger proportion in the most favored localities so far as indicated by a higher altitude. Hence the gross death rate of the colored race is only slightly if at all affected by either altitude or density, both of which are factors of the highest importance in the duration of life in the white race. The conditions of life therefore, so far as these two factors are concerned, would seem to be of less importance than race and heredity.

DISTRIBUTION OF THE WHITE AND COLORED POPULATIONS OF TWO
CITIES ACCORDING TO ALTITUDE.—(Percentage of total population.)

Average Altitude in feet.	Baltimore, Md. 1890.		Washington, D. C. 1890.	
	White. Per Cent.	Colored. Per Cent.	White. Per Cent.	Colored. Per Cent.
Under 25	18.01	12.53	14.53	19.62
25–50 . . .	25.58	19.01	25 62	15.14
50–75 . . .	14.59	12.77	38.55	40.86
75–100. . .	20.25	18.72	14.94	17.79
100 and over	21.57	36.97	6.36	6.59

The natural question in view of this proof of an excessive mortality of the colored race, an excess met with
under all the varying conditions, locality, age, sex, conjugal condition, altitude and density of population, is,
whether the unusual mortality has always existed or is
of recent origin, *i. e.*, whether the excessive mortality is
a result of new conditions of life or is a fundamental
race trait. It will always be difficult to answer this
question satisfactorily, since the mortality statistics
for the early part of the present century are wanting in
details, without which it is difficult to arrive at a satisfactory conclusion. The higher rate of increase of the
colored population during the period preceding the war
would indicate that during slavery the mortality was
not so high, at least not in the United States, as it has
been since emancipation, while the gradual lowering of
the decennial rate of increase would indicate that a process of deterioration has been going on ever since 1810,
but less intense before emancipation than during the
past thirty years.

So far as I have been able to ascertain, the only fairly
complete record of white and Negro mortality for a considerable length of time has been kept in the city of
Charleston, for which city we are fortunate enough to
have an almost unbroken record from the year 1822.
Through the kindness of Dr. H. B. Horlbeck, the health

officer of Charleston, I have been able to obtain a statement of the comparative mortality of the two races from
1822 to 1894, excepting the war period, when no data of
value were collected. To Dr. Gordon de Sassure of the
same city I am indebted for a copy of the census of
Charleston for 1848, which is a document of great statistical and historical value. I am therefore able to in-
clude in the table which follows, some statistics which
have seldom been used, and which I trust will be of
value to those who are interested in the course of the
mortality of the two races. I have also obtained from
Dr. T. S. Scales, former health officer of Mobile, a partial
statement of the white and colored mortality of that city
for the period 1843–55, with some years missing. For
Savannah I have compiled the mortality returns for the
period preceding the war, from the very valuable essay of
Dr. Eugene Corson on the "Vital Equation of the Colored Race." For all recent years I have made use of the
official board of health reports for the various cities. The
death rates are based on the population estimated in accordance with Dr. Farr's method for intercensal years,
thus insuring uniformity and freedom from the individual guess work. It is of course unfortunate that the
periods under observation are not always the same, but
this is unavoidable in view of the dearth of data.

COMPARATIVE MORTALITY OF SOUTHERN CITIES FOR VARIOUS
PERIODS OF TIME.

MOBILE, ALA.			CHARLESTON, S. C.		
Periods.	White.	Colored.	Periods.	White.	Colored.
1843–46	45.83	23.10	1822–30	32.73	28.16
1847–50	42.53	31.19	1831–40	25.24	25.02
1852–55	54.39	34.70	1841–50	16.17	19.77
1876–80	24.64	39.74	1851–60	29.79	34.12
1881–85	26.14	36.26	1866–75	25.56	41.98
1886–90	23.92	35.11	1876–85	24.32	43.83
1891–94	21.40	30.91	1886–94	22.26	44.06

COMPARATIVE MORTALITY OF SOUTHERN CITIES FOR VARIOUS
PERIODS OF TIME.

SAVANNAH, GA.			NEW ORLEANS, LA.		
Periods.	White.	Colored.	Periods.	White.	Colored.
1856–60	37.19	34.07	1849–60	59 6	52.1
1861–65	50.19	49.65	1871–73	28.63	44.61
1866–70	33.16	57.26	1875–79	31.25	40.22
1871–75	32.70	44.82	1880–84	25.01	52.33
1876–80	38.60	51.66	1885–89	23 81	35.22
1881–85	27.02	41.67	1890–94	24.85	39.42
1886–90	22.52	37.26			
1891–94	21.43	32 26			

The table before us presents with a fair degree of accuracy the course of the death rates for both races for
long periods of time. While the point to be brought
out by this table is not as clear as would be desirable, it
is shown that for the white population there has been a
considerable and fairly constant fall in the death rate;
while for the colored population the mortality at the
present time would seem to be higher as a rule than it
was forty or fifty years ago. For Charleston the records
are the most complete and therefore the most satisfactory
from a statistical standpoint, and they show clearly the
unfavorable change in the mortality rate of the colored
race.

If we combine the periods under observation so that
one period is formed by the years before the war and the
other for the period of freedom, we have a more compact
body of data in which the possibility of accidental variation is eliminated. By this method the death rate of the
white population of Charleston is shown to have been
25.60 before the war and 24.04 for the period 1866–94,
giving a *decrease in the white mortality* of 1.56 per
1,000. The mortality rate of the colored population
during the same period *increased* from 26.45 during
1822–60 to 43.33 during 1866–94, or 16.88 per 1,000.

In Mobile the mortality rate of the whites *decreased* from 48.26 during the period 1843–55 to 24.13 for the period 1876–94 while in the same interim the Negro mortality rate *increased* from 30.31 to 35.60 per 1,000.

For these two cities therefore the conclusion is warranted that the Negro mortality has largely increased since emancipation, and that too in the localities considered most favorable for the race. What is here shown to be true for two cities, each of which represents different conditions of life, economic as well as climatic and sanitary, we may assume to hold fairly true for other sections of the south. The proverbial longevity of the Negro has probably never existed as a matter of fact, but we have an abundance of testimony, unfortunately little of it statistical, that previous to emancipation the Negro enjoyed health equal if not superior to that of the white race. Consequently the proved tendency towards a higher death rate must be considered an evidence of race deterioration, which in part will explain the gradual lowering of the rate of increase of the colored population, brought out more distinctly than ever by the census of 1890.

The above facts, however, are insufficient for a determination of the importance that should be attached to the increasing mortality rate of the colored race. This is brought out by comparing the death rates at various ages and periods of life.

The first table has been compiled in part from the valuable report of De Saussure on the census of Charleston in 1848,[1] and in part from a table of Charleston death rates previously given. At the same time the per cent. of excess in the Negro mortality rate over the white, or

[1] Census of the city of Charleston for the year 1848, by J. L. Dawson, M.D. and H. W. De Saussure, M.D. Charleston, S. C., 1849.

vice versa, is shown in a separate column. The rates have been calculated in conformity with others of the same kind, namely, on the living population for the same ages.

COMPARATIVE MORTALITY FOR CHARLESTON, S. C., 1848 AND 1890.
(Deaths per 1,000 living at same ages.)

| | 1848. | | 1890. | | Excess of Col'd motality over White. | |
| | White. | Col'd. | White. | Col'd. | 1848. | 1890. |
					Per ct.	Per ct.
Under 5	31.1	75.0	64.8	149.6	141.1	130.9
5–10	5.8	3.9	3.4	10.9	——[1]	220.6
10–20	3.0	11.1	3.2	16.2	261.3	406.3
20–30	11.2	12.3	9.5	26.1	9.8	174.7
30–40	16.1	15.3	13.8	24.2	——[1]	75.4
40–50	21.8	21.9	22.6	30.5	0.5	35.0
50–60	28.4	28.3	25.3	43.0	– ——[1]	70.0
60–70	47.5	58.8	58.3	76 6	23.8	31.4
70–80	97.3	106.3	106.8	162.2	9.2	51.9

[1] White mortality in excess of colored.

This table is most interesting and valuable from an economic or other scientific standpoint. We can here trace the rate of the mortality through the various stages of life and compare the two races at two radically different periods, the one under slavery, the other under freedom. During the former, according to this table, the mortality of the colored exceeded that of the white population for the age period 0–5 by 141 per cent., and in 1890 by 131 per cent. For the second age group the Negro mortality rate for 1890 was 221 per cent. higher than that of the whites, in contrast with a former excess in the mortality of the whites for this age group. For the two next higher age groups the rate is almost double at the present time what it was before emancipation, and for the next three groups a former mortality rate favorable to the colored race has been changed into one largely unfavorable. At the most advanced ages the numbers are rather small and the excess of Negro mortality at these periods is difficult to define.

As general inferences to be drawn from the table before us it may be safely concluded that the Negro mortality rate has increased for all periods of life ; that the excess of Negro mortality over that of the whites previous to emancipation existed to a considerable degree for only two age periods below the age sixty, but that at the present time it is to be observed at all ages. At the present time the excess is greatest for the first generation, and least for the third—if we divide the whole of life into three periods as has been done heretofore. It would seem therefore, that the young generation is the one least fit for race survival, and the consequent loss of social effectiveness, as Mr. Kidd calls it, is enormous. The great difference in the expectation of life for the two races is brought out with scientific accuracy in the following life table, abstracted from the census of 1880. No official life tables have been compiled since that year.

COMPARATIVE EXPECTATION OF LIFE FOR WHITE AND COLORED PERSONS IN FOUR SOUTHERN CITIES IN 1880.[1]

AGES.	Washingt'n, D.C. 1880.		Baltimore, Md. 1880.		Charleston, S. C. 1880.		New Orleans, La. 1880.	
	Whites. Years.	Col'd. Years.	Whites. Years.	Col'd. Years.	Whites. Years.	Col'd. Years.	Whites. Years.	Col'd. Years.
0 . . .	42.36	25.25	38.18	23.26	38.34	21.82	38.10	25.56
5 . . .	51.85	44.48	51.72	44.32	48.10	40.68	47.88	40.76
10 . . .	48.71	42.13	49.66	42.40	44.24	37.96	44.16	37.50
20 . . .	40.42	35.34	41.50	36.62	36.24	31.60	35.80	30.63
30 . . .	33.64	30.22	34.74	30.64	30.08	27.14	29.35	26.98
40 . . .	27.36	24.63	28.05	24.68	24.60	21.51	23.78	22.49
50 . . .	21.06	18.90	21.27	18.92	18.80	15.72	18.62	17.78
60 . . .	15.01	13.70	15.01	13.42	13.14	11.04	13.58	13.22
70 . . .	9.98	9.19	10.24	8.87	8.81	7.90	9.43	8 98
80 . . .	6.70	6.37	7.14	6.38	6.59	5.94	6.73	6.46

[1] Census of 1880, Vol XII, pages 773-783.

This table shows the expectation of life at ten selected ages for both races, in representative southern cities, bringing out in a forcible way the difference in the vitality of the two races. In the District of Columbia a white person at the age of thirty for instance would have a chance of living about three and a half years longer than a colored person of the same age; in Baltimore about four years, and in New Orleans two and a half years. But this is an age at which the general mortality is very low for both races. At all the earlier ages the differences are of course much greater. The excessive mortality at the very early ages of course affects the mortality at the older ages by reducing the differences between the two races. For the periods of old age the expectation of life is almost the same for both races. A clear idea as to the effect of an excessive mortality is brought out by means of a life table showing the number surviving at various ages out of a million born. Such a table has been abstracted from Dr. Billings' report on the vital statistics of the tenth census, those for the eleventh census not having as yet been made public.

COMPARATIVE APPROXIMATE LIFE TABLES FOR FOUR SOUTHERN CITIES, SHOWING THE NUMBER OF SURVIVORS AT SELECTED AGES.

(Abstracted from the Report of the 10th Census, Vol. XII, pp. 773-783.)

Ages.	Washington, D. C. 1880.		Baltimore, Md. 1880.	
	Whites.	Colored.	Whites.	Colored.
0	1,000,000	1,000,000	1,000,000	1,000,000
5	739,661	499,169	664,869	458,964
25	662,723	401,081	579,191	361,966
45	516,330	291,601	468,126	268,706
65	326,461	158,444	301,471	150,481
85	49,104	17,807	48,985	15,676
	Charleston, S. C.		New Orleans, La.	
0	1,000,000	1,000,000	1,000,000	1,000,000
5	715,404	465,753	712,193	548,488
25	635,585	357,608	634,301	426,354
45	455,493	249,404	448,348	271,075
65	258,954	105,958	238,176	134,717
85	24,609	6,405	34,754	14,990

This table reads that in the city of Washington out of a million whites born during the year 1880, 739,661 will survive to their fifth year, while only 499,169 of the colored population will survive, a difference of 240,492 lives. This represents an enormous economic loss. For if we take into consideration the number of years of life lost through such an excessive mortality, we have a fair means of estimating the resulting economic loss. It would be impossible to consider this point at length, but I subjoin a brief abstract of the life table of Charleston for 1880, which shows for both races, with distinction of sex, the number of years of life remaining at various ages.

NUMBER OF YEARS OF LIFE REMAINING TO SURVIVORS AT SELECTED AGES, ACCORDING TO COLOR AND SEX.

| | Charleston, S. C.—1880. | | | |
| | White. | | Colored. | |
Ages.	Males.	Females.	Males.	Females.
10 . .	13,874,245	17,070,833	8,273,445	8,400,897
25 . .	9,077,720	11,803,905	5,213,560	5,397,550
45 . .	4,025,910	5,973,925	2,199,075	2,396,175
65 . .	955,885	1,804,695	431,860	530,400

The economic loss involved in such a great waste of life is difficult to estimate, but it seems clear that a race which has only about one half of the effective economic force of another race must needs prove more of an economic hindrance than a help. Even if the race were gifted with an abnormally high birth rate, which it is not, it could not overcome the effect of the high death rate. This abnormal condition will in part explain the large amount of poor relief and the large number of pauper funerals of colored persons in the large cities of the South. It does not come within the province of this paper to discuss the purely economic aspects of the race tendencies of the colored population, but I have touched upon this point as one which is deserving of a more careful consideration by the student of social and economic problems than has thus far been devoted to it.

I have thus far discussed only the purely statistical aspects of the excessive mortality of the colored race as contrasted with that of the white population. I have shown by indisputable evidence, collected from all sections of the country in which the colored element is present in sufficient numbers, and from which information has been obtainable, first, that the colored race is subject to an excessive mortality in the cities of the North and West as well as in the South ; second, that the mortality rate of the race is on the increase ; third, that the excess of mortality of the negroes over whites is greatest for the youngest generation, and least for the generation which grew up largely under slavery influences ; fourth, that the increase in the mortality rate affects principally the earlier ages, and that in consequence the number surviving to the productive and reproductive ages is far less, proportionately, for the colored population than for the white ; fifth, that to this abnormal condition the constant lowering of the decennial rate of increase for the colored population must be attributed, which tendency if persisted in must lead to a decrease in the population at an ever increasing rate ; and finally, that the economic loss involved in so high a mortality must prove a serious hindrance to the economic development of the sections of the country or of the large cities in which the colored population is found in large numbers.

Causes of the Mortality.

Having shown the general movement of the population, and the comparative mortality, I may now consider the causes of the high mortality, with the two-fold purpose of tracing the physiological history and consequent race traits, and showing the race tendencies brought out by a study of the causes of disease and mortality, its prevalence at various periods of time, and in different sections of the country. To do the subject complete justice is impossible here, and only the most important and interesting phases can be discussed. There is a large body of facts, although less than I expected to find, which is available for the study of the comparative susceptibility to disease and death, for the two races.

It was a frequent argument with southern physicians, before the war, that no northern or European physician could successfully treat a colored person in view of the radical differences existing between the two races and the consequent difference in results from medical treatment, the Negro yielding less readily to such treatment than the white man. It was argued, and with considerable force, that physicians who were to practice among the colored population should be especially educated for their work.

Since the war the medical journals often urge the need of colored physicians. The *Medical News* (October 6, 1894) declared that "although some forty million dollars had been spent in the literary education of the colored race since the war, it was doubtful whether forty cents had been spent for medical education for colored men." The *News* referred to the fact that probably not one-half of the colored population receive medical attention, and maintained that a liberal proportion of colored physcians would materially alter the present condition and its consequent waste of life.

As to the amount of money spent in the education of colored young men for medical work, I may state that according to the official reports of the Bureau of Edu-

5

cation for the year 1891–92, there were in this country five institutions for the education of colored persons in the professions of medicine, dentistry and pharmacy, with a total attendance of 457 pupils. The amount expended on these institutions is not stated, but it must be considerable, at least a good deal more than forty cents.

As to the second point, I cannot do better than to quote from the reports of the health officer of Savannah for recent years, in which the subject of non-medical attendance of colored people is fully discussed. Referring to the excessive mortality of colored children the report says : " The neglect of children by Negro parents is so often apparent to your health officer that he must call your attention again to the matter. In many instances they will not call in a physician when the city provides them free medical attendance."[1]   In his report for the following year Dr. Brunner refers again to the same subject as follows :

" Fifty per cent. of the children who die never receive medical attention.   In many instances the parents will not call in a physician, claiming the children died before they could go for a physician, although a cross examination will always show that the children had been sick from two to ten days before they died."[2]   Again in his report for 1893 : " For years the city of Savannah has furnished gratuitous medical advice and medicine, and the Negroes persistently refuse to accept them, at least for their children. Can the city do more? Is there any other move to make save that of appeal to the law to force parents to care for their offspring ?"[3]

And finally in the report for 1894 : " We must have

---

[1] Annual report, City of Savannah, 1890, p. 125.
[2] *Ibid.*, 1891, p. 157.   [3] *Ibid.*, 1893, p. 160.

stringent laws covering the criminal neglect of negro parents who allow their children to sicken and die without making an effort to obtain the services of those physicians who are paid by the city to give such people gratuitous medical attention. The appointment of a negro physician may do some good; it will be an experiment, but one worth trying."[1]

In other cities of the South the conditions are more or less the same. The claim that colored physicians are more appreciated than whites is not supported by the facts. Colored physicians charge less and give more credit, and largely for this reason gain practice among the members of their own race; but whenever accessible a white physician will be preferred. Such at least has been my observation.

The indifference as to medical attendance in cases of illness of their children is due to ignorance rather than to criminal neglect. The negro has a habit of dosing himself and his children on every possible occasion, and the drugging of infants with paregoric and even with laudanum is very frequent, the use of castor oil being also extremely liberal; hence the neglect to call a physician, even when the city provides one free of charge. In Richmond, Va., the percentage of cases of non-medical attendance is considerably less than in Savannah, and the difference may be almost solely attributed to a higher degree of education, which exhibits itself in the management of every day affairs. The number of

[1] The annual report of the health officer for 1895 contains the following reference to the result of this experiment: "One of these physicians (for the care of the indigent sick) is a colored physician who was appointed with a view of getting at the class of unfortunate negroes who, even when well are unable to take care of themselves. The appointment is a satisfactory one. Proof of which is in evidence from his weekly reports rendered to this office." (Annual reports, City of Savannah, 1895, pp. 213-14.)

colored physicians in Virginia is very large, and a few years ago the Petersburg *Daily Herald*, a race organ, suggested that they form a state association. The high death rate of the colored population of southern cities cannot, therefore, fairly be attributed to the want of doctors either white or colored.

In some of the West India islands practically the whole of the population are without medical attendance in case of illness or death. In Jamaica for instance, 75 per cent. of the deaths during 1894 were registered without a medical certificate. In some of the parishes of the island the per cent. of non-medical cases is even greater. The registrar, Mr. S. P. Smeeton, in his report for 1895 observes, however, that in the city of Kingston the percentage of such cases is much less, and concludes that "the lack of professional testimony is not altogether attributable to unwillingness on the part of the people to resort to the doctor's aid, but to some considerable extent may be owing to the difficulty of obtaining such assistance at a cost within their means and at a distance within their reach."[1]

This conclusion would seem to be fairly warranted in view of the fact that the number of physicians in the island is very small. In 1849, according to the report of the Registrar General for 1889, the number of registered physicians was 126, as against 85 in 1889, of whom 9 were absent from the colony. Thus in spite of a considerable increase in the population the number of physicians has actually decreased. The evil therefore is one which cannot be eradicated without a considerable improvement in the moral and economic condition of the population, together with an increase in the knowledge of the plain everyday duties of life, such as

[1] Report of the Registrar-General for 1895, p. 3.

regulates the life of the white population with which they come in daily contact.

In previous tables the excessive mortality of infants and children has been fully brought out; and the repeated reference to the subject by the health officer of Savannah and other southern cities, makes it advisable that the causes of child *mortality* should be discussed before any other. The subject divides itself naturally into two parts: first, premature and still births, and second, deaths after birth. As regards the former our information is necessarily incomplete. All statistics dealing with still-births of the colored race must for many years be wanting in completeness. Even for the white population the information is wanting in accuracy. But the mortality rate for the two races is perhaps sufficiently brought out in the two following tables for Washington and Baltimore to show the comparative mortality from premature and still births for the white and colored populations.

DEATHS FROM PREMATURE BIRTH AMONG THE WHITE AND COLORED POPULATIONS OF WASHINGTON, D. C., AND BALTIMORE, MD., 1890.
(Per 100,000 of Population at all Ages.)

	White.	Colored.
Washington, D. C.	32.97	67.37
Baltimore, Md.	45.76	69.84

DEATHS FROM STILL-BIRTH.
(Per 100,000 of Population under one year.)

	White.	Colored.
Washington, D. C.	6.528	20.152
Baltimore, Md.	7.024	16.988

The two tables show practically the same result as regards the excessive pre-natal mortality among the colored people in these two cities, and the significant fact is brought out that the inordinate mortality of the race at all ages affects pre-natal existence in the same manner. As to the causes of infant and child mortality we have some valuable information in two tables abstracted from the report of Dr. Billings on the vital statistics of Baltimore and Washington, from which report the preceding tables also have been compiled. The causes taken into consideration are those which most seriously affect the duration of life during infancy and early childhood.

DEATHS FROM DEBILITY, INANITION AND ATROPHY.[1]

(Per 100,000 of population under 1 year.)

	White.	Colored.
Washington	4.181	10.045
Baltimore	4.800	11.884

DEATHS FROM DIARRHŒAL DISEASE.

(Per 100,000 of population under 1 and under 5 years.)

	0—1		0—5	
	White.	Colored.	White.	Colored.
Washington. . . .	6.220	11.952	1.737	3.299
Baltimore	7.732	14.565	2.157	3.895

[1] Vital Statistics of Washington and Baltimore, 1890, pp. 28 and 29.

The mortality from diarrhœal diseases is largely subject to sanitary conditions, which no doubt have some influence in producing a Negro mortality rate nearly a hundred per cent. higher than that of the whites. Deaths from inanition, debility and atrophy are largely the result of inferior organisms and constitutional weakness, which as we shall see later on is one of the most pronounced race characteristics of the American Negro. The terms, however, cover unrecognized consumption, scrofula and other tubercular diseases. As it has well been said by a close observer of Negro mortality in the West Indies, Dr. McHattie, the registrar-general of Antigua, "These are not diseases at all but merely names, all of which have nearly the same meaning and indicate that 91 infants died in Antigua in 1889 from diseases inherited from their parents, who in the majority of these cases are broken down by disease consequent on vice, immorality and debauchery, and who impart such enfeebled constitutions to their offspring that they cannot live a few months even under the most favorable circumstances."

The registrar-general of Trinidad in quoting the above remarks agrees that they are as applicable to the island of Trinidad, and on the general subject of infant mortality quotes further from the report of Dr. McHattie : " Since 1884 there has been an increase of nine per cent. in the mortality from the causes under consideration (inanition, debility, and atrophy) and nothing will materially lessen the number of deaths of infancy but a change in the moral condition of our people, and this change under existing conditions is hopeless, impossible. An improvement in the dwellings of our laboring population must precede any hope of 'moral improvement, for where marriage is ignored, and where men, women and children are crowded together in one small room for all domestic purposes, day and night, the possibility of any moral sentiment existing among those who live in this manner is precluded, and children growing up in the midst of such surroundings cannot possibly have any sense of shame or decency ; so that the evils of the system are perpetuated. The chance therefore of materially lessening the death rate from the causes just mentioned seem very remote."

Mr. H. J. Clark, the learned registrar-general and superintendent of the census of Trinidad for 1891, does not fully agree with Dr. McHattie as to the applicability of the above remarks to conditions affecting child life in Trinidad, but he attributes it to the same cause as Dr. Brunner of Savannah, *i. e.*, that the principal cause of the difference between the coolie and creole populations (which is here to be observed as well as everywhere else) is due to neglect and inattention on the part of the creole parents, partly, he regrets to say, to wilful or thoughtless neglect, and partly unavoidable, owing to the long absence of many of the parents in the pursuit of their daily occupations.[1]

It cannot be argued that the coolie population is better off in either the material good things of life, as Professor Ely puts it, or from a sanitary or any other standpoint. In fact, I understand, and have seen some figures in proof, that the creole of Trinidad is paid a slightly higher wage for the same labor than is paid the coolie immigrant. It may be of interest here to show the comparative mortality of the creole and coolie population in this island.

COMPARATIVE INFANT MORTALITY AMONG THE GENERAL (NATIVE)
AND THE EAST INDIAN (COOLIE) POPULATIONS, 1889–1890.[1]
(Rates per 1,000 living births.)

	1889	1890.
Creole population	199.75	185.83
East Indian (Coolie population) . .	134.28	134.92

[1] Report of the Registrar-General of Trinidad for 1890, p. 17.

The difference in mortality of the two races is not so pronounced as between the white and colored populations of American cities, but is sufficiently large to establish substantially the same race tendency to premature death among the colored population of the West Indies that we meet with among the colored population of this country. In some of the British colonies, Guiana for instance, the infant mortality is much higher, being reported at 237 deaths under one year per 1,000 births.

[1] Report of the Acting Registrar-General of Trinidad for 1890, p. 18.

In British Guiana we are informed conditions exist similar to those we have met with in Antigua, Trinidad and our Southern cities, namely, extreme neglect on the part of the parents of colored children.

According to a report of a former United States Consul at Georgetown, British Guiana, the children of the colored population of that colony "suffer greatly from hunger, rarely getting more than one meal a day."[1] In St. Lucia the infant mortality is reported as 221 per 1,000 births. In both of the latter colonies the pre-natal mortality, (*i. e.*, still-births), is very great.

The facts here brought together for southern cities as well as for the islands of the West Indies so fully support each other as to warrant the conclusion that the excessive infant mortality among the colored population is largely the result of individual neglect, as well as in part due to inherited organic weakness, and only to a limited extent to the conditions of life.

Considering now in particular the principal diseases to which the Negro is liable, and which will more clearly than any other series of facts bring out his race traits and tendencies, we shall first have to consider *consumption* as the most important of all. A volume could easily be written on this one disease and its influence on the destiny of the colored race. Few writers on Negro mortality have failed to discourse upon the excessive mortality due to this cause, and but few have failed to recognize the fact that this most dreaded of all diseases is constantly on the increase among the colored population of this country. The opinion of southern physicians who practiced among Negroes before the war was almost unanimous that consumption was less frequent among the colored population than among the whites. I am

---

[1] Consular report for September, 1892, page 90.

able to furnish statistical support for this opinion by a table of comparative death rates from this disease for Charleston, for the periods 1822–48 and 1865–94. The rates have been calculated in the same way as the general death rates; but in their proportions to the hundred thousand of mean population, to make the respective rates more intelligible.

CONSUMPTION IN CHARLESTON, S. C., 1822-1894.
(Death rates per 100,000 of Population.)

Period.	White.	Colored.
1822–30	457	447
1831–40	331	320
1841–48	268	266
1865–74	198	411
1875–84	255	668
1885–94	189	627
1822–1848	347	342
1865–1894	213	576

According to this table the mortality from consumption has almost steadily decreased for the white population. It decreased for the colored population from 1822 to 1848 at almost the same rate as for the white population; but since emancipation the rate has largely increased and is now more than three times as great as for the white population. Comparing the former period with the latter we find that while the white mortality has decreased 134 per 100,000 the colored mortality has increased 234 per 100,000. This change in the susceptibility of the colored race to consumption, if supported by other facts, may be considered, next to the excess in infant mortality, a distinct race characteristic, and one which must needs have the most pronounced effect upon the numerical as well as the social and moral progress of the race.

Gould in his classical work on the " Statistics of the

Sanitary Commission," observed "the inordinate mortality and singular susceptibility to fatal diseases exhibited by the colored troops."[1] Unfortunately Mr. Gould was not permitted to make use of the available material for a study of the disease prevalence among the colored troops. We have, however, in the "Medical and Surgical History of the War" a mine of valuable information which will afford the diligent student of the influence of race on mortality the most exceptional opportunities. Another work of the greatest possible value is the report of Dr. Baxter on the "Anthropological Statistics of the United States Army," which presents the results of measurements of over a million of recruits during the war. The two works combined furnish data for a concise description of the colored male at the time of the war, and, what is of most importance, during the war. To this we can add the medical reports of Dr. Robert Reyburn while in charge of the Hospitals of the Freedmen's Bureau, in operation for the period 1865–72. We can therefore trace the pathological history of the colored race during the period of transition from slavery to freedom, with a degree of accuracy unequaled in the history of any other race.

The table below shows the number of rejections per thousand recruits examined for enlistment into the army during the war period 1861–65. The rates are based on examinations of 315,620 white and 25,828 colored recruits.

[1] "Statistics of the Sanitary Commission," page 602.

NUMBER OF REJECTED RECRUITS PER 1,000 EXAMINED FOR
SPECIFIED DISEASES.[1]

	White Recruits.	Colored Recruits.	Excess of	
All specified diseases	264.1	170.2	White over Col'd	
Rheumatism	4.8	3.7	"	"
Consumption	11.4	4.2	"	"
Disease of Nervous system	11.5	7.8	"	"
" Circulatory "	25.5	12.2	"	"
" Respiratory "	10.1	4.2	"	"
" Digestive "	84.3	50.1	"	"
" Urinary "	2.5	.7	"	"
" Generative "	6.4	4.4	"	"
" Organs of Locomotion .	30.4	18.7	"	"
" Cellular-tissue	.9	.4	"	"
Hernia	39.8	38.3	"	"
Syphilis	3.8	10.7	Col'd over White	
Scrofula	2.8	3.8	"	"

The table includes rejections for various causes and
groups of causes and will be referred to in connection
with the discussion of other diseases which is to follow. It
is shown that out of a thousand white applicants for enlistment 264 were rejected for diseases in general, while
11.4 were rejected for consumption.   Among the colored
applicants only 170 were rejected for diseases in general
and 4.2 for consumption.   This would prove that before
the war the colored males of military age were far less liable to consumption than the whites and the result would

[1] Medical statistics of the Provost-Marshal General's Bureau, Vol. II, page 431,
etc.

There is evidently an error in the tables of the first volume of the
Provost-Marshal General's report, in which, on chart IV, the rate of
rejections of native whites for consumption is given as 18.4 per 1,000
examined, and for colored, 7.04. On page 431, Vol. II, of the same
work, where the original figures are given, the rate for native whites
is given as 11.4, and for colored 4.8. The latter are evidently correct,
since the following are the facts from which the rates were calculated :
Number of whites examined, 315,620; rejected for consumption,
3,605 ; rate per 1,000, 11.4. Number of colored examined, 25,828 ;
rejected for consumption, 108 ; rate per 1,000 examined, 4.18. I have
therefore substituted the rates given on page 431, Vol. II, in place of
those first given as found on chart IV, Volume I.

support the Charleston figures showing consumption to be about equally prevalent among the whites and colored. Since the men examined were drawn from the population at large and in many, perhaps the majority of instances, from the country districts, the excess of consumption among the whites would seem plausible. Dr. Buckner, who examined over 1,600 Negroes, reports that " except for being over age or under, very few were rejected, not perhaps more than ten per cent. Tuberculosis is very rare among them; and contrary to the generally received opinions in the slave states, they are not, as far as my experience goes, more subject to scrofulosis than other people."[1]

Other opinions as to the comparative infrequency of consumption among the colored population before the war could be quoted, but would only prove repetitions of the opinion of Dr. Buckner, who, as examining surgeon of the district of Kentucky had most excellent opportunities for observation.

If we now consider the mortuary experience of the colored troops during the war we shall find that the subsequent experience did not justify the sanguine anticipations of those who had previously pronounced the Negro in every way the equal if not the superior of the white for military service.

[1] Report of Provost-Marshal General, vol. I, p. 379.

AVERAGE ANNUAL RATES OF DISEASE AND DEATH IN THE U. S.
ARMY DURING THE WAR.[1] (Per 1,000 of mean strength.)

	White Troops. (1861–65)		Colored Troops. (1863–65)	
	Cases.	Deaths.	Cases.	Deaths.
Average annual rates for all diseases,	2434 64	53.48	3298 96	143.40
Continued fevers	40.29	11.60	22.99	12.45
Typho-malarial fevers.	22.38	1.68	41.05	6.78
Malarial fevers	522.34	3.36	829.58	10.03
Diarrhœa and dysentery	711.46	15.62	839.38	35.27
Eruptive fevers	46.61	4.50	92.29	18.36
Syphylis, Gonnorhœa and Orchitis,	82.04	.06	77.74	.17
Rheumatism, acute and chronic . .	144.33	.20	178.54	1.23
Consumption	6.06	2.18	7.26	6.31
Disease of the nervous system . . .	76.31	1.84	130.51	4.25
" " Circulatory system,	11.27	.69	8 50	2.44
" " Respiratory "	261.80	7.40	354.74	32.35
" " Digestive " .	252.79	1.71	295.92	5.06
Urino-genital disease	13.41	.18	16.45	.68

This table shows disease prevalence and consequent
mortality from various causes for white and colored
troops per 1,000 of mean strength. The mean strength
of white soldiers per annum was 431,237 while the mean
strength of colored soldiers was 60,854. The numbers
for the colored troops are therefore sufficiently large to
compare the morbidity and mortality of white and colored troops. According to this table the average mortality of white troops from all causes was 53.48 per
1,000 of mean strength, while for the colored troops the
rate was 143.40, or almost three times as great. The
number of cases of disease was 2,435 per 1,000 of mean
strength per annum for the white troops, and 3,299 per
1,000 for the colored troops.

For the disease under consideration the death rate was

[1] Medical and Surgical History of the War of the Rebellion. Medical volume,
part Third, page 13.

In army medical statistics the number of cases of attacks or such
as lead to hospital attendance is recorded and calculated on the mean
strength. Hence if the rate of diseases is 2,000 per 1,000 of mean
strength, this means that on an average every man was twice under
medical observation as a patient.

2.18 per 1,000 for the white troops and 6.31 for the colored, almost three times as great. The disease prevalence due to this cause was almost the same, that is, 6.06 for the white and 7.26 for the colored troops. The latter figures are of most value since they are not subject to an uncertain element affecting the mortality rates, namely, the fact that on account of the homeless and poverty-stricken conditions of the colored patients, they would remain longer in the hospitals than the whites, many of the latter going back to their homes as soon as this could be done without risk. The figures, however, show clearly that consumption was slightly more prevalent as a disease among the colored troops than among the whites during the war. In view of the fact that it was shown to have been less prevalent previous to the war we must believe either that the increased prevalence was caused by the consequences of active military service or that it was present in its incipient stages in the recruit who succumbed as soon as he was exposed to the hardships of military service. Certain aspects of this important point have been fully discussed in the able and comprehensive report of Dr. Sanford B. Hunt on the " Negro as a Soldier, " which was prepared for the use of the Sanitary Commission, and was reprinted in the *Anthropological Review* for 1869, pp. 40-54.

Dr. Hunt in discussing the physical and pathological peculiarities of race characteristics of the Negro refers to the prevalence of consumption and its remote causes as follows : " In *pulmonary diseases* we find the *only* excessive cause of mortality in the Negro which seems to be inherent to his constitution. . . . While it must be admitted that temporary causes [conditions of life] had much to do with the frequency of lung diseases among Negroes, it will still be found that they are vastly more liable to this source of mortality than the whites. . . It was found that when fairly enlisted, clothed and fed, and subjected to the same methods of life as the white soldier, he still exhibited a far greater ratio of deaths from pulmonary disease."

"We are compelled, then, to believe that, independent of external causes, [conditions of life] the Negro is far more susceptible to pulmonary disease than the white. The physiological cause of this cannot, perhaps, be demonstrated; but great weight is due to the hypothesis that he has a tropical or smaller lung. . . . A careful series of weights of normal lungs, to contrast with weights for an equal number of whites, is a great desideratum. It should be re-enforced by measurements and the volume and the expansibility of the living thorax. At present we are only able to suggest that, if the Arctic lung requires a capacity equal to the absorption of oxygen enough to convert into carbonic acid gas forty-five to fifty ounces of carbon daily, in order to maintain the animal heat in these cold regions, it would be in accordance with the economy of nature to suppose that the oxygen capacity of a tropical lung would be smaller than the Arctic, in the same ratio as the amount of carbon required to maintain animal heat in the sultry climate of the Equator." But this, Dr. Hunt adds, "is not yet proven."[1]

We have therefore a perfect agreement of the highest authorities, and on the basis of undisputed facts, that during the war consumption was relatively more prevalent among the colored troops than among the white. We have also fairly satisfactory evidence that consumption was comparatively less frequent among the general colored population before emancipation; and, in con-

[1] Journal of Anthropology, (London, 1869,) Volume VII, pp. 47-48

nection with the statistics of Charleston showing a considerable increase in the mortality from this cause among the colored population, we are forced to conclude that the inordinate susceptibility of the colored race to this most fatal disease is of comparatively recent growth. This conclusion is further supported by some very valuable statistics of the comparative mortality of the white and black troops in the West Indies and on the West coast of Africa.

The information I have been able to obtain covers two periods, one for the years 1817–1835, and the other for the years 1886–92. The statistics for the first period were collected for the well known report of Major Tulloch, while the more recent figures have been compiled from the reports of the medical department of the British Army.

AVERAGE RATE OF MORTALITY FROM DISEASES OF THE LUNGS, PER 1,000 OF MEAN STRENGTH, FOR THE PERIOD 1817-36.[1]

Locality	White troops	Colored troops.
West Indies.	10.4	16.5
Sierra Leone	4.9	6.3
Cape of Good Hope . . .	2.4	3.9

[1] London Quarterly Review, July, 1840, pp. 73 and 80 ; also Journal of the Royal Statistical Society, Vol. I, p. 129, *et seq.*

The West Indies show the largest proportionate Negro mortality from respiratory diseases, while in the native country of the Negro, his mortality, though slightly in excess of that of the white troops, is less than one-fourth the rate prevailing in the West Indies. Now we have considerable testimony to the effect that consumption among the natives of Africa is an infrequent disease. Indeed, the statistics of the colonial hospital of Sierra Leone[1] for the period of 1853–54 show that out of 113 deaths from all causes among the liberated slaves cared

[1] Journal, Royal Statistical Society, Vol. XIX., pp. 60–81.

6

for at the hospital, only four were from consumption, and ten from diseases of the respiratory organs. The ages of the patients are not given, but they were probably largely adults.

The very small number of deaths from diseases of the lungs here shown for the native African, would support the view of M. Quarterfrages, that consumption among Negroes in Africa is not a common disease.[1] If we now compare the mortality from this disease among the white and colored troops in the West Indies at the present time, we shall find that the susceptibility of the colored race to this malady has largely increased. The statistics are for the period 1886–92 and are the latest which have come to my notice.

COMPARATIVE MORTALITY AND ADMISSIONS TO THE HOSPITALS FOR TUBERCULAR DISEASES AMONG THE WHITE AND COLORED TROOPS IN THE WEST INDIES.[2]

(Rates per 1,000 of mean strength, 1886–1892.)

	Admissions.	Deaths.
White troops.	1.3	0.26
Colored troops.	7.6	2.69

The above table shows only the mortality from tubercular diseases and is, therefore, not strictly comparable with the last table, but it is plainly seen that the excess of Negro mortality from lung diseases has largely increased during recent times in the West Indies, as well as in the United States. In Africa the rate is even higher, but there are no data from which a comparison could be made between the white and colored populations in the same locality. In West Africa, among the colored troops, the mortality from tubercular diseases was 4.23 per 1,000 and the admission rate 8.5. The disease, therefore, was only slightly more prevalent than in the

[1] "Pygmies", p. 85.
[2] Army Medical Report, 1893, (London, 1895,) pp. 188–191.

West Indies, but more fatal. Since many of the colored troops in West Africa had served in the West Indies, the disease may have been more confined to them than to the natives of Africa. The reports do not give exact information on this point.

Among the general population of the West Indies, consumption at the present time is a very common disease. In Trinidad, the rate for consumption is 292 per 100,000 of population, and 229 per 100,000 for respiratory diseases. In Jamaica, the average mortality from consumption was 175 per 100,000, while for Kingston Parish the rate was 435. The enormous difference between the two rates is more apparent than real, in view of the want of proper medical attendance in the country districts. The general death rate of Kingston is only about two per thousand above the rate for the whole island. The true rate for consumption will probably lie between the two.

In Hayti, we are officially informed that "pulmonary diseases are almost unknown, excepting among the natives with whom it is always hereditary."[1] This official statement is in contrast with the statement of Mr. Steward who maintains that "consumption does not prevail at Port au Prince, where enlightened negro physicians control sanitation.[2]" We have it on the authority of Mr. Froude and Sir Spenser St. John that the sanitary condition of Port au Prince makes the place utterly unfit for residence, and this view is confirmed by a friend of the writer who visited Hayti about a year ago. That the disease must be rather frequent among the natives is perhaps proved by a singular custom prevailing in the island. According to Dr. R. Percy Crandall,

[1] Government Handbook of Hayti, p. 71.
[2] *Social Economist*, Oct., 1895, p. 207.

U. S. N., " when a consumptive dies the entire contents
of the room in which he dies are either destroyed or are
thrown into some place set aside by the government for
that purpose. * * * Cases have occurred where
small houses have been burned to the ground to prevent
the spread of the disease. " This advanced view of the
contagious nature of consumption may, however, have
materially prevented the spread of the disease.

We may now consider the prevalence of the disease
immediately after the war. We have the record for the
city of Charleston for the years 1865–94, according to
which the colored population had a death rate from consumption of 363 per 100,000 above that of the whites.[1]
We have also the record of the hospital service of the
Freedmen's Bureau, from which the following abstract
has been compiled, showing at the same time the prevalence of other important diseases, and the resulting
mortality.

CAUSES OF THE MORTALITY AMONG THE WHITE AND COLORED
PATIENTS OF THE FREEDMEN'S BUREAU UNDER TREAT-
MENT FROM 1865 TO JUNE 30, 1872.[1]

	White patients.	Rate per 1,000	Colored patients.	Rate per 1,000
Number of patients.	22,053		430,466	
Deaths from all causes	735	33.3	18,027	41.9
" " Miasmatic diseases	288	13.1	8,364	19.4
" " Enthetic "	9	.4	160	.4
" " Dietic diseases.	7	.3	49	.1
" " Constitutional diseases . .	65	2.9	2,371	5.5
" " Nervous " . . .	46	2.1	765	1.8
" " Circulatory " . . .	10	.5	357	.8
" " Respiratory " . . .	48	2.2	1,814	4.2
" " Digestive " . . .	59	2.7	1,302	3.0
" " Urinary " . . .	13	.6	228	.5
" " Diseases of women	8	.4	184	.4
" " all other causes	182	8.3	2,433	5.7

[1] " Type of Disease among the Freed people of the United States," by Robert Reyburn, M. D., Washington, D. C., 1891, page 16, *et seq.*

[1] See page 70.

The total number of white patients under treatment was 22,053, and of colored patients 430,466. The ages of the patients are not given, but it is evident from the report of Dr. Reyburn that persons of all ages and both sexes came under the charge of the relieving officers. The total of deaths from all causes for the white population was 735, and for the colored population 18,027. The rate of mortality was, therefore, 33.3 per 1000 patients for the whites, and 41.9 per 1,000 for the colored, an excess of about 25 per cent. For constitutional diseases the mortality rate was 3.0 for the whites, and 5.5 for the colored, an excess of 80.3 per cent. For consumption and respiratory diseases the whole number of deaths and the death rates per 1,000 patients were as follows :

MORTALITY FROM CONSUMPTION AND RESPIRATORY DISEASES.[1]

	Consumption.		Respiratory Diseases.	
	Number of Deaths.	Per 1,000 Patients.[2]	Number of Deaths.	Per 1,000 Patients.[2]
Colored Patients	1,787	4.2	1,814	4.2
White Patients	47	2.1	48	2.2

[1] "Type of disease," page 16, *et seq.*
[2] In all 430,466 colored and 22,053 white.

For both diseases the Negro mortality was about 100 per cent. above that of the whites, which is in marked contrast with the former infrequency of the disease among the general colored population. In this case, too, we have two populations practically alike, subject to the same conditions of life, the same medical treatment and under the same relieving officers of the government. It would even be natural to suppose that the white patients were of a class which had suffered and endured much before they became practically government paupers, yet we have the proof before us that they were less liable to death from consumption and disease of the respiratory organs than the colored population.

This assertion contradicts the opinion of Dr. Reyburn, who on the strength of the foregoing statistics concludes that " they are quite sufficient to disprove the statements so commonly made concerning the extreme liability of the colored race to scrofula and pulmonary tuberculosis. So far from these two diseases being almost universally prevalent amongst the colored people in the southern states, these people seem to be no more subject to them than the whites who live under like conditions in our large cities. Scrofula and pulmonary tuberculosis are, in part, caused by a neglect of the laws of hygiene and sanitary science. These diseases do not seem to be any more destructive to the colored race than to the white."[1]

It is difficult to understand how Dr. Reyburn could arrive at this conclusion, which is neither supported by his own facts nor by the medical experience of the army. According to a previous table,[2] the mortality from consumption was 6.31 for colored and 2.18 for the white troops during the war. According to Dr. Reyburn's report the mortality from this cause was 4.2 per 1,000 of colored patients, and only 2.1 per 1,000 of white patients. And we shall see later on that this disparity between the mortality rates, as shown for consumption, prevails to an even greater extent in the mortality from scrofula and other diseases. But if Dr. Reyburn had been entirely correct as to the equal prevalence of consumption and scrofula at the time the colored patients came under his observation, it can be proven that at the present time the colored race is subject to an inordinate mortality from consumption and respiratory diseases, which will menace the very existence of the race in the not far distant future.

[1] *Medical News*, Dec. 2, 1893.
[2] Page 74.

The table which follows gives the comparative mortality per 100,000 living population for fourteen representative American cities with large colored populations. The rates are for the year 1890 and are based on the population returns of the census. The mortality has been compiled from the health reports of the respective cities.

MORTALITY FROM CONSUMPTION—FOURTEEN AMERICAN CITIES.
Rates per 100,000 of Population.—1890.

	White.	Colored.
Charleston, S. C.	355.4	686.3
New Orleans, La.	250.3	587.7
Savannah, Ga.	371.1	544.0
Mobile, Ala.	304.1	608.2
Atlanta, Ga.	213.8	483.7
Richmond, Va.	230.5	411.1
Baltimore, Md.[1]	250.6	524.6
Washington, D. C.[1]	245.0	591.8
Brooklyn, N. Y.[1]	284.9	539.0
New York, N. Y.[1]	379.6	845.2
Boston, Mass.[1]	365.8	884.8
Philadelphia, Pa.[1]	269.4	532.5
St. Louis, Mo.	159.9	605.9
Cincinnati, Ohio	239.1	633.3

[1] Reports of Dr. Billings, Census of 1890.

Without exception the mortality rates of the colored race are largely in excess of the rates for the white population. The rates are highest in New York and Boston, but this is due to a certain extent to the larger proportion of colored persons in those cities between the ages of 15 and 45, for which period the mortality from consumption is greatest.[1] The actual difference in mortality for the white and colored from this disease is more clearly brought out in the table below, which shows the comparative mortality from this cause for two cities at two age periods. These cities fairly represent the mortality of the colored population in the other large cities.

[1] See page 41.

MORTALITY FROM CONSUMPTION IN TWO CITIES BY AGE GROUPS.
1890.[1]

	White.	Colored.	Per ct. of Col'd above White.
Ages 15-45.			
Baltimore, Md.	313.07	592.37	89.21
Washington, D. C.	293.69	658.14	124.09
Ages 45 and over.			
Baltimore, Md.	449.99	569.26	28.73
Washington, D. C.	369.54	727.27	96.80

[1] Report of Dr. Billings, Vital Statistics of Washington and Baltimore, Census of 1890, p. 32.

It will be observed at a glance that the mortality is most excessive at the period of middle life, that is, among those who largely represent the present generation, born or raised during the period of freedom. The age group above 45 represents largely those who were under the influence of the conditions of servitude; but it is among this class that we find a greater power of resistance to disease and death than among the generation following emancipation and the participation of the Negro in the active struggle for life. It will be of interest to trace the effect of age on mortality even to the youngest generation; and this is done for deaths from pneumonia, since the mortality from this cause more accurately measures the power of vital resistance at the early ages. The statistics are for the same two cities and for four age periods. The rates are per 100,000 living at the same age.

MORTALITY FROM PNEUMONIA IN TWO CITIES.[1]
(Death rate per 100,000 living at same age.)

	White.	Colored.	Col'd over White. Per ct.
Ages 0 to 5.			
Baltimore, Md.	645.01	2,158.95	234.72
Washington, D. C.	466.17	1,642.15	252.26
Ages 5-15.			
Baltimore, Md.	37.52	105.01	179.87
Washington, D. C.	28.08	119.72	326.35

[1] Report of Dr. Billings, Census of 1890, p, 32.

| | Ages 15-45. | | Col'd over White. |
	White.	Colored.	Per ct.
Baltimore, Md.	74.20	123.74	66.76
Washington, D. C.	69 32	194.00	179.86
	Ages 45 and over.		
Baltimore, Md.	323.93	360.53	14.39
Washington, D. C.	274.18	446.28	62.77

This table presents the life history of the race as affected by the mortality from a single cause. For Baltimore the mortality among the colored for the age group 0–5 exceeds that of the white population by 234.7 per cent; for the age group 5–15, 179.9 per cent.; for the group 15–45, 66.8 per cent., and for the last group 14.4 per cent. For Washington the excess of Negro mortality over the white is 252.3 per cent. for the age group 0–5; 326.4 per cent. for group 5–15; 179.86 per cent. for group 15–45 and 62.8 per cent. for group 45 and over. We are led to ask, can the "conditions of life" have anything to do with this gradual decrease in the proportionate colored mortality as we reach the age groups which represent the "old stock"? Is it not self evident that it is the working of the law of physiological heredity rather than the effects of environment that we have here to deal with?

Pneumonia as well as consumption is excessively prevalent among the colored population in all parts of the country. I have dealt to such a considerable extent with the mortality from consumption that I shall confine myself in the consideration of pneumonia to the following statistics of comparative mortality from this cause for six representative cities. The table has been compiled from the reports of Dr. Billings.

MORTALITY FROM PNEUMONIA IN SIX CITIES—1890.[1]
(Rate per 100,000 of Population.)

	White.	Colored.
Baltimore, Md.	174.86	350.69
Washington, D. C.	140.28	352.72
New York, N. Y.	336.46	389.50
Brooklyn, N. Y.	277.47	493.33
Boston, Mass.	249.84	325.96
Philadelphia, Pa.	180.31	356.67

[1] Reports of Dr. Billings, Census of 1890.

The table shows that consumption is not the only disease excessively prevalent among the colored population. We shall see later on that there are other diseases of no small degree of importance which prevail to a larger extent among the colored than among the whites. Consumption and pneumonia are, however, the most important of the diseases which affect the Negro's duration of life. The facts here brought together show that these diseases are on the increase and that, too, in contrast with the constant decrease of the mortality from consumption among the white population. In Massachusetts the average annual death rate from consumption was 441 per 100,000 of population for 1851–55, against 334 for 1866–70, 314 for 1881–85 and only 236 for 1891–93. In England the mortality from consumption has decreased from 257 per 100,000 for 1858–60 and 222 for 1871–75 to 164 for 1886–90. The fact, therefore, that the Negro race should show such an enormous increase in the mortality from this cause is one of great significance. The large decrease in the mortality among the white race may permit us to indulge in the hope that a decrease in the mortality for the colored race is also possible. But at present the race tendency is the other way; and a close study of related phenomena will convince the reader that only the most radical changes in the race traits and tendencies of the colored race can accomplish this, if it is at all possible.

Closely allied to consumption are *scrofula, syphilis* and other *venereal* diseases, all of which are more or less constitutional diseases. They are therefore considered together and, much to my regret, less in detail than would have been desirable.

It has often been asserted that scrofula was a common disease among the colored population before the war. Dr. Cartwright has stated that it was extremely common among the colored children.[1] I have found little statistical proof of an excessive mortality from either scrofula or syphilis. In the Charleston mortality reports for 1822–48, mention is made of only two deaths from syphilis among the white and of four among the colored population. Both scrofula and syphilis may, however, have been frequent as diseases but of less fatality. By examining the tables of Dr. Baxter, showing the causes of rejection of white and colored applicants for enlistment into the army, I find that the rate was greater for both diseases among the colored than among the whites.

REJECTIONS FOR SCROFULA AND SYPHILIS.[1]
(Per 1,000 applicants for enlistment into the army.)

	White.	Colored.
Rejected for diseases in general	264.1	170.2
" " Scrofula	2.8	3.8
" " Syphilis	3.8	10.7

[1] Medical Statistics of the Provost Marshal General, Vol. I, Washington, 1875.

The rejections for all causes were less for the colored than for the whites, but the rejections for scrofula were 35.7 per cent. and for syphilis 181.6 per cent. in excess of the white rates. These figures support Dr. Cartwright, and prove that scrofula as well as syphilis was more prevalent among the colored males of military age than among the same class of whites. The medical experience of the army during the war furnishes another series

[1] DeBow, "South and West," Vol. 2, p. 319.

of facts of equal importance as showing for both races the rate per 1,000 discharged for disability from disease.

DISCHARGES FOR DISABILITY FROM SCROFULA AND SYPHILIS.[1]
(Per 1,000 of mean strength.)

	White.	Colored.
Discharges for all causes . . .	82.20	35.30
" " Scrofula. . . .	0.37	0.77
" " Syphilis. . . .	0.74	0.45

[1] "Medical History of the War," Vol. III, p. 27.

We have seen that the rejections for scrofula were 35.7 per cent. greater for the negroes than for the whites, but according to the table now before us the discharges for this cause were more than one hundred per cent. higher. For syphilis the rate is less than that of the whites, due in part, but not wholly, to the fact that a much larger proportion of negroes liable to this disease had already been rejected.

Another important series of facts closely related to those presented in the last two tables is furnished by the medical experience of the army, showing the number of cases under treatment in the hospitals. I presume the former series of cases is in part included in the latter. The table which follows shows the rate of admissions to hospitals for scrofula, syphilis and gonorrhœa per 10,000 admissions for all causes, according to race.

COMPARATIVE PREVALENCE OF SCROFULA AND VENEREAL DISEASES AMONG THE WHITE AND COLORED TROOPS UNDER TREATMENT IN HOSPITALS DURING THE WAR. (1861-66.)[1]

	No. of cases of Scrofula.	Per 10,000[2] patients.	Excess of Col'd rate, per cent.
White troops.	6,022	10.34	. .
Colored troops	2,508	39.85	285.28
	No. of cases of Syhilis.	Per 10,000 patients.	Excess of White rate, per cent.
White troops.	73,382	125.96	27.72
Colored troops	6,207	98.62	.
	No. of cases of Gonorrhœa.	Per 10,000 patients,	Excess of White rate, per cent.
White troops.	95,833	164.57	46.64
Colored troops	7,060	112.18	. .

[1] "Medical History of the War," Vol. I, pp. 636-641 and 710-712.

[2] Total number of white patients under treatment for all causes 5,825,480; colored, 629,354.

We have here substantially the same relative frequency of the three specified diseases as was brought out in the preceding table. The rates are per 10,000 of all admissions to hospitals and for this reason cannot be compared with the rates based on the average mean strength of the army. To afford the means of comparison I reproduce the rates given in a previous table, (page 74), which show the comparative frequency of venereal diseases as well as the consequent mortality.

COMPARATIVE PREVALENCE OF AND MORTALITY FROM VENEREAL DISEASES AMONG THE WHITE AND COLORED TROOPS OF THE U. S. ARMY DURING THE WAR.[1]

(Average annual rates per 1,000 of mean strength.)

	Cases.	Deaths.
White	82.04	0.06
Colored	77.74	0.17

[1] " Medical History ot the War," Vol. III, page 13.

The important fact brought out is, that while venereal diseases were less frequent among the colored troops than among the whites, they were almost three times as fatal; and it will be found on close study of the general mortality of the colored race that for all of the most prevalent diseases the rate of fatality is invariably greater among the colored than among the white patients.

The facts thus far brought together would seem to prove that previous to the war, scrofula was more, and syphilis less, prevalent among the colored males of military age than among the whites; that during the war this condition practically remained the same, but that the mortality from venereal diseases was much greater among the colored, although the general prevalence of this class of diseases was less. With these facts before us we may now consider the comparative prevalence of these diseases among the white and colored refugees and freedmen cared for by the relieving officers of the Freedmen's Bureau.

I have already quoted from Dr. Reyburn, from whose reports the following table has been abstracted, the opinion that scrofula was not more frequent among the colored patients than among the whites. I am at a loss to understand the method by which Dr. Reyburn arrived at this conclusion, since the facts before us, identically the same from which Dr. Reyburn drew his inference, prove exactly the contrary to be true.

COMPARATIVE PREVALENCE OF SCROFULA AND VENEREAL DISEASES AMONG THE WHITE AND COLORED PATIENTS UNDER TREATMENT AT THE HOSPITALS OF THE FREEDMEN'S BUREAU.[1]

	Total No. of Patients under Treatment.	No. cases of Scrofula.	Per 10,000 patients.
White patients	22,053	68	30.8
Colored patients	430,466	6,613	153.6
Per ct. excess in Col'd rate,			398.7

	No. cases of Syphilis.	Per 10,000 patients.	No. cases of Gonorrhœa.	Per 10,000 patients.
White patients	379	171.9	191	86.6
Colored patients	10,887	252.9	5,790	134.5
Per ct., excess in Col'd rate,		47.12		55.31

[1] Type of disease, page 16 *et seq*,

So far as it is possible to judge from this summary it would seem that the two populations as here represented were subject to the same "conditions of life" and were, at least, while in charge of the government relieving officers, subject to the same mode of treatment. The facts brought out are of great value in connection with the previous tables as well as with those that are to follow. For we have here the proof that the rate for scrofula among the colored was 399 per cent. higher than among the whites; for syphilis, 47 per cent; and gonorrhœa 55 per cent. The two last named diseases (and it is diseases we are here dealing with, not deaths) we have previously found to be less prevalent among the colored males in the army, but here among the colored population in general we find that the rate for either is much higher than among the whites. Whether this was brought about by the new "conditions of life" which emancipation brought, or whether it is the effect of a cause long in operation, it will always be extremely difficult to prove. The truth lies probably between the two, but the fact is clearly proven that immediately after the war scrofula, syphilis and other venereal diseases were excessively prevalent among the colored as compared with the white population.

Before we go on to consider the comparative frequency of these diseases at the present time, we may with advantage study their comparative prevalence in the West Indies. The data are few, and hence I shall not consume much space in their discussion. The table below will show the comparative rates of admissions to the hospitals as well as the rates for those who were constantly sick and under treatment for venereal diseases. The table covers the period 1886–92 and the year 1893.

ADMISSIONS TO HOSPITAL FOR VENEREAL DISEASES OF THE WHITE
AND COLORED TROOPS IN THE BRITISH WEST INDIES.[1]
1886–1892 and 1893 (per 1,000 of mean strength.)

	Admissions to Hospital.		Constantly Sick.	
	White Troops.	Col'd Troops.	White Troops.	Col'd Troops.
1886–1892 . .	226.0	312.5	17.74	23.36
1893 . .	251.4	317.9	23.55	31.04

[1] Army Medical Department report for 1893, p. 188 *et seq.*

The colored troops show the larger admission rates, but for the year 1893 the increase in the prevalence of the disease has been greater among the whites. Of those constantly sick the increase was about 6 per 1,000 for the white troops and 8.32 per 1,000 for the colored. The rate of increase for the one year is, however, of very little importance, and in the absence of comparative data, which I have not been able to obtain, I am

not able to show for the West Indies whether there has
been an actual increase in the prevalence of this class of
diseases, or a decrease.   The data for the general population of the West Indies are not sufficiently reliable on
this point, in view of the very large number of deaths
without medical attendance.   For the island of St.
Christopher, however, it has been stated by Mr. Parker,
U. S. Commercial Agent, that " according to the most
trustworthy information, the island had more leprosy[1]
and syphilitic diseases to the number of square miles
than any other territory in the world."[2]   Mr. Parker
adds that " until quite recently the common women of
the island were as a rule prostitutes who spread their
disease throughout the island, but in the last eighteen
months there has evidently been a change."   The
proverbial ' oldest inhabitant,' according to Mr. Parker,
" seems to think that the time is not far distant when
virtuous men and women will be quite common on the
island, and that there will be an end to the profanity
and indecency of women on the streets which now exist."   Consul Carroll formerly at Demerara wrote in
the same way about the colored women of British
Guiana.[3]

These facts regarding the West Indies are of considerable importance, since the colored race in those
islands has practically been removed from the influence
of the white race; and whatever conditions of life, race
traits or tendencies we meet with, are largely the result
of conditions for which the colored race alone is re-

[1] " As regards leprosy, the editor of " Lazaretto" (No. 11) a paper
published in the West Indies, asserts that a careful census carried out
by medical officers would demonstrate that St. Christopher and Nevis
contains more lepers per 1,000 of population than any other British
Possession."   W. Tebb in " Leprosy," page 33.

[2] Consular report, Sept. 1893, p. 25.

[3] Consular Report, Sept. 1892.

sponsible. We have here to consider the fact that in comparison with white males of military age, the colored troops are more affected with venereal diseases than the white, although the difference is not very large. But the data affecting the army in those islands are not sufficient, and as I have said, I have no reliable information regarding the prevalence of these diseases among the general population.[1]

If we now return to the southern states we shall first consider the comparative prevalence of scrofula and syphilis as a cause of death in the state of Alabama, for which fairly accurate information is available for the period 1890–94; also for Charleston, S. C., for 1822–48 and 1889–94.

DEATHS FROM SCROFULA AND VENEREAL DISEASES AMONG THE WHITE AND COLORED POPULATIONS OF ALABAMA.*

	Scrofula.		Venereal Diseases.	
	White.	Colored.	White.	Colored.
1890	10	23	3	37
1891	10	17	3	21
1892	8	12	3	24
1893	8	27	7	33
1894	8	15	6	40

*Annual reports for 1890–94 of the State Board of Health of Alabama.

COMPARATIVE MORTALITY FROM SYPHILIS AMONG THE WHITE AND COLORED POPULATIONS OF CHARLESTON, S. C.

		Deaths.	
Period.	White.		Colored.
1822–48	2		4
1889–94	10		66

Among the white population the number of deaths from either disease is too small to be of any importance. Even for the colored race the number of deaths is not very large, but when we consider that the whites form 55

[1] For more detailed information in regard to the mortality and morality of the Negro in the West Indies, see *Quarterly Publications of the American Statistical Association*, June, 1895, pp. 181–200.

7

per cent. of the total population of the state of Alabama it is significant that the proportion of deaths among them from these causes should be so very small. I have already called attention to the fact that in the city of Charleston the number of deaths from syphilis for the period 1889–94, was 66 among the colored population, as against 10 among the whites. This would show a remarkable preponderance of the disease among the negroes. But we have more exact and important data for the cities of Baltimore and Washington, calculated from the report of Dr. Billings on the vital statistics of those two cities. The table given below shows the mortality from scrofula and venereal diseases for the white and colored population, for the period 1885–90, and the percentage of negro mortality over the white from these causes.

MORTALITY FROM SCROFULA AND VENEREAL DISEASES IN BALTIMORE AND WASHINGTON.—1885–1890.
(Per 100,000 of population.)

	Scrofula.		Venereal Diseases.	
	Baltimore.	Washington.	Baltimore.	Washington.
White	6.12	5.28	3.06	5.89
Colored.	29.09	38.39	13.29	23.89
Per cent. of excess of negro mortality, .	375.3	627 1	344.3	305.6

In both cities, almost to the same degree, the negro mortality from the causes under consideration exceeds that of the white population by 344 to 627 per cent. The table confirms the crude statistics for the state of Alabama and Charleston, and makes plain the fact that the prevalence of these two diseases and the consequent mortality have greatly increased since the war. It can not be consistently argued that because the mortality from these diseases is small, the facts brought out therefore, are of less significance than those for consumption.

It is because the disease is closely related to other diseases, principally consumption, and an excessive infant mortality, that the rapid increase of scrofula and venereal disease among the freed people becomes a matter of the greatest social and economic importance.

For the root of the evil lies in the fact of an immense amount of immorality, which is a race trait, and of which scrofula, syphilis, and even consumption are the inevitable consequences. So long as more than one-fourth (26.5 per cent. in 1894) of the births for the colored population of Washington are illegitimate,—a city in which we should expect to meet with the least amount of immorality and vice, in which at the same time only 2.6 per cent. of the births among the whites are illegitimate,—it is plain why we should meet with a mortality from scrofula and syphilis so largely in excess of that of the whites. And it is also plain now, that we have reached the underlying causes of the excessive mortality from consumption and the enormous waste of child life. It is not in the *conditions of life*, but in *the race traits and tendencies* that we find the causes of the excessive mortality. So long as these tendencies are persisted in, so long as immorality and vice are a habit of life of the vast majority of the colored population, the effect will be to increase the mortality by hereditary transmission of weak constitutions, and to lower still further the rate of natural increase, until the births fall below the deaths, and gradual extinction results.

The diseases which next attract our attention are *malarial and typhoid fevers.* The two classes of disease are here considered together because both have to a large extent the same causes. The comparative immunity of the negro from malarial diseases has often been asserted by medical and other writers. I know of no reliable statistical data to support this assertion. Ferguson, in his paper "On the Nature and History of Marsh Poisons," read before the Royal Society,[1] says: "The adaptation of the negro to live in the unwholesome localities of the torrid zone, that proves so fatal to all Europeans, is most happy and singular. From peculiarity or idiosyncrasy he appears to be proof against fevers; for to him marsh miasmata are in fact no poison and hence his incalculable value as a soldier for field service in the West Indies." This view is held to-day by some who unfortunately have never studied the facts. There is abundant proof that the negroes of today are far more liable to malarial and typhoid fever than the whites.

The earliest records of the comparative frequency of malarial fevers which have come to my notice are for the British army in the West Indies during the period 1817–36. According to the records for this period, the death rate from fevers was 36.9 per 1,000, for the whites, and 4.6 for the colored. The fact is clearly brought out in these reports that while the colored race was less liable to fevers, it was far from being exempt. During the same period the colored troops on the west coast of Africa suffered a rate of only 2.4 per 1,000 or about one-half the prevailing rate in the West Indies. Reliable data are wanting for this country for the period before the war. Most of the early writers who were familiar with the negro stated that he was liable to malarial poison. Dr. Nott, than whom few were more qualified to judge, denied that the negro was less liable to malarial diseases than the white. Dr. Sanford Hunt in his paper on the "Negro as a Soldier," gives it as his opinion, based on practical experience, that "the ratio of malarial and typho-malarial disease was about the

[1] *Transactions*, Royal Society, Edinburgh, Vol. IX.

same in all three classes, whites, northern negroes and southern negroes." Dr. Hunt adds that "this corresponds with the facts reported by African travellers, Barth, Anderson and Reade, who speak of the great mortality from intermittent and bilious fevers of the Africans in their native jungles. . . The weight of evidence seems to place them upon the same level as the white in regard to liability to malarial disease."[1] It is extremely fortunate, in view of these conflicting views, that we have now an abundance of statistical data which will enable us to arrive at the truth. Medical experience in the army during the war, demonstrated definitely that the adult negro male of military age was far more subject to malarial disease than the white soldier. The average rate of admissions to hospitals for malarial diseases was 522 per 1,000 for the white troops and 829 for the colored troops, a difference of 307 per 1,000. The average death rate for malarial diseases was 3.36 per 1,000 for the whites and 10.03 for the colored troops. The fact, therefore, is clearly brought out, that whatever the comparative prevalence of this disease may have been before the war, during the war it certainly prevailed more extensively and proved far more fatal among the colored males of military age than among the white troops. Nor were the former free from any of the various forms of malarial fevers. The following table will show the comparative rates of admissions to hospitals for the various types of malarial and typho-malarial fevers in the army during the war.

[1] *Anthropological Rev.*, Vol. 7, p. 47.

DISEASE PREVALENCE FOR FEVERS DURING THE WAR.[1]
(Per 1,000 of mean strength.)

Form of Fevers.	White.	Colored.
Quotidian intermittent	204.00	349.00
Tertian "	171.00	278.00
Quartan "	18.82	21.39
Congestive "	6.24	13.83
Remittent	130.89	167.10
Typho-malarial	26 15	41.06

[1] "Medical History of the War," Vol. III., pp. 93-94.

It needs, therefore, no further proof that the negro soldier was more liable to malarial fevers in all forms, than the white soldier, and the opinion of Dr. Hunt that " the susceptibility of the race *was the same* as that of the white race," is disproven so far as the colored male of military age is concerned. The army statistics do not answer for the general population, and the comparative frequency of malarial disease among the general white and colored populations, may still have been in accordance with the views of Dr. Nott and Dr. Hunt. If we examine the reports of Dr. Reyburn we shall find that the opinion of these two writers holds good for the general population during and immediately after the war, so far as the conditions are indicated by the experience of the Freedmen's Bureau.

PREVALENCE OF MALARIAL FEVERS AMONG THE WHITE AND COL- ORED REFUGEES CARED FOR BY THE FREEDMEN'S BUREAU.[1]

	Percentage of Malarial cases in total of all cases.	Percentage of Mortality from Malaria in total No. of deaths.	Percentage of case fatality.
White	26.78	7.49	1.34
Colored	26.91	10.74	1.17

[1] "Type of Disease," pp. 6 and 7.

From the facts before us we may conclude that while it is possible and even probable that the colored population during slavery may have been less subject to malarial diseases than the whites, immediately after the war the rates of disease prevalence and mortality were about equal for the two races. The negro soldiers, subject to the hardships of military life, proved themselves possessed of less vital force than the white soldier, and in consequence showed a higher mortality rate while subjected to the same, or perhaps more favorable conditions.

The statistics for recent years would prove that the liability of the colored race to malarial and typhoid fever has largely increased since their emancipation. For the city of Charleston we are fortunate in having an unbroken record of the comparative mortality of the two races from these two causes for the period 1865–1894. According to the reports there were 295 deaths from malarial fever among the white population and 553 among the colored population during this period. On the basis of the mean population this would give a rate of 42.45 per 100,000 of population for the whites and 66.63 for the colored, or 56.9 per cent. higher for the colored. For typhoid fever the corresponding rates are 67.34 for the whites and 100.73 for the colored, the percentage of excess being slightly less than for malarial fevers.

These rates indicate a tendency towards a higher mortality for the negroes than the whites from malarial fevers at the present time. For 23 large cities of the south, according to the reports of the National Board of Health for 1881, the rate for malarial fever was 100.4 per 100,000 for the whites, and 133.0 for the negroes, a smaller difference for the two races than that shown by the statistics for Charleston for 1865–94. These rates may be compared with the mortality from malarial and typhoid fever for Baltimore and Washington for the census year 1890.

MORTALITY FROM MALARIAL AND TYPHOID FEVER IN THREE CITIES.
(Per 100.000 of Population.)

	Malarial Fever.		Typhoid Fever.	
	White.	Colored.	White.	Colored.
Charleston, 1865–1894 .	42.45	66.63	67.34	100.73
Washington, 1890 .	25.21	77.94	74.34	112.29
Baltimore, 1890 .	27.78	29.72	42.49	68.35

The mortality for the colored race exceeds that of the white in all three cities for both diseases, but the greatest difference is shown for Washington, where the mortality from malarial fever is more than three times as great for the negroes as for the whites. As we have seen, the homes of the colored population in this city are better situated as regards the mean elevation than are those of the whites; hence the great excess of negro mortality from malarial disease is remarkable for this city. For Baltimore the excess of negro mortality from this cause is very slight, but if we examine the mortality rates for various ages, we shall find that it is only at the earliest ages, when the mortality from these diseases is very slight, that the rates for the colored race fall below those of the white.

MORTALITY FROM TYPHOID FEVER AND MALARIA FOR WASHINGTON
AND BALTIMORE, ACCORDING TO AGE AND RACE.—1890.[1]

	Ages. 5—15		15—45		45 and over.	
	White.	Colored.	White.	Colored.	White.	Colored.
Typhoid Fever.						
Baltimore . . .	20.11	64.62	59.04	81.62	39.58	28.46
Washington . .	35.09	119.10	99.57	149.80	59.60	41.32
Malarial Fever.						
Baltimore . . .	25.37	15.98	17.87	23.69	58.63	75.90
Washington . .	21.53	87.43	23.95	63.85	32.78	107.44

[1] Vital statistics of Washington and Baltimore, page 28 and 29.

The two tables are very instructive and need little explanation. It is shown that for all age groups the negro mortality in both cities exceeds that of the whites, excepting the age group 5–15 for Baltimore. The proof is therefore complete as regards the greater susceptibility of the colored race to malarial and typhoid fevers at the present time, and the fact brought out is one of considerable economic importance as well as of general value. For with a greater susceptibility to malarial diseases, the economic importance of the negro as a laborer in the alluvial and swamp regions of the South is materially affected. The two following tables will illustrate the importance of this point better than a textual discussion, and at the same time afford proof of another tendency of the colored race which seems to have escaped those who have so frequently discussed the various aspects of the so-called 'race problem,' namely, the smaller increase in the colored population living in the coast swamp regions of the South and in those parts of the country which have an altitude under 100 feet.

WHITE AND COLORED POPULATIONS OF THE UNITED STATES, 1880 AND 1890, IN THE COAST SWAMPS AND ALLUVIAL REGIONS OF THE MISSISSIPPI.[1]

	1890.	1880.	Percentage of increase 1880–1890.
A. Coast Swamp Region.			
White population . . .	1,035,000	867,000	19.38
Colored population . .	774,000	702,000	10.26
B. Alluvial Region of the Mississippi.			
	1890.	1880.	
White population . . .	348,000	275,000	26.55
Colored population . .	537,000	408,000	31.62

[1] Census of 1890, Population, Vol. I, p. xlvi, *et seq.*

WHITE AND COLORED POPULATION OF THE UNITED STATES, 1880 AND 1890, LIVING AT AN ALTITUDE OF LESS THAN 100 FEET.[1]

	1890.	1880.	Percentage of increase 1880–1890.
White population . . .	8,679,000	6,774,000	28.12
Colored population . .	1,708,000	1,499,000	13.94

[1] Census of 1890, Population, Vol. I, p. xlviii, *et seq.*

It will be seen that the white population, while proportionately less in numbers in the low and swamp lands of the country, nevertheless increased at a much greater rate during the decade 1880–90 than the colored population. The larger increase in the colored population on the alluvial lands of the Mississippi is in part due to the migration of colored people from other parts of the country. But the significant fact here brought out is that in just those regions which we have been told time and again were only fit for the habitations of the colored race or of a mixed race, the white race is increasing at a much greater rate than the colored. This progress of the whites we must largely, if not solely, attribute to the increasing power of vital resistance of the white race and its lesser susceptibility to malarial and typhoid fevers than the colored race. The statistics of Charleston prove that even in those sections which years ago were subject to the most excessive death rates the white race can live and increase without immigration. What is true for Charleston is no doubt true more or less, for all the southern states; otherwise it would be impossible to explain the larger increase in the white than in the colored population in the swamp and low lands of the country.

I called attention in the beginning of this chapter to the excessive mortality from fevers among the white troops in the West Indies in the early part of this century. It will be of value to compare the condition at that time with the experience for recent years. The next table of comparative disease prevalence and mortality has been abstracted from the Army Medical Report for 1893 and shows the rates for the period 1886–92 and for the year 1893.

DISEASE PREVALENCE AND MORTALITY FROM MALARIAL FEVERS IN
THE BRITISH WEST INDIES—1886-1893.
Per 1,000 mean strength.

	1886-1892.		1893.	
	Admissions to hospital.	Mortality.	Admissions to hospital.	Mortality.
White Troops,	45.5	1.16	30.1	0.79
Colored Troops,	120.6	2.08	34.7	None.

DISEASE PREVALENCE AND MORTALITY FROM MALARIAL FEVERS IN
WEST AFRICA—1886-1893.
Among the Colored Troops only,

	1886-1892.		1893.	
	Admissions to hospital.	Mortality.	Admissions to hospital.	Mortality.
Colored Troops,	939.1	9.40	757.7	None.

In the beginning it was stated that the mortality from
all fevers per 1,000 of mean strength, for the period 1817
–35, was 36.4 for the whites, and for the colored troops only
4.6. We have here the proof that this condition has radically changed and that at the present time it is the negro
who is most subject to malarial fevers, even in those regions which it has been argued could only be inhabited
permanently by the colored race. The admission rate
to hospitals is nearly three times as great for the colored
as for the whites, while the mortality is more than twice
as high. Surely the "conditions of life" cannot possibly have anything to do with this inordinate mortality
of the negro under the same military conditions as the
white soldier and under the influence of a climate which
we have been told is peculiarly adapted to his needs. If
we examine the mortality records of the colored troops on
the west coast of Africa, we find a still more remarkable
condition, the admission rate being 939.1 per 1,000 for
the period 1886–92 and a corresponding death rate of
9.40.

From the very meagre data at my command it is not

possible to arrive at any intelligent idea as to the influences responsible for such an inordinate disease prevalence and mortality from malarial fevers among the
colored troops in west Africa; but it is possible that owing to the fact that many of the soldiers had formerly
lived in the West Indies, they fell victims to climatic
influences which more than fifty years ago sealed the fate
of countless white soldiers in the same locality. The
subject is deserving of further investigation in view of
the many colonization schemes constantly brought to
the attention of the colored people of the South.[1]

[1] According to the *African Repository* for January, 1892, p. 31,
the total number of emigrants settled in Liberia by the American
Colonization Society, had reached 16,349, yet according to the "States-
man's Yearbook" for 1894, the total Afro-American population of Liberia was only 18,000 in 1894. Hence there does not seem to have been
any natural increase in the emigrant population. I have found it almost impossible to obtain accurate information on the health of Liberia, but am informed by Mr. Wilson, the secretary of the above-named
society, that "the health statistics of Liberia, if it were possible to
obtain them, would compare favorably with those of the colored people in our Southern States." Since the health of the colored people
of the Southern States is far from favorable, we must conclude that
the climate, etc., of Liberia are equally unfavorable to the progress of
the colored race. That the early emigrants to the colony suffered
severely is evidenced by the frequent references to the subject in the
work of Mr. Alexander on the " History of African Colonization "
from which I quote the following passage : " The health of the colonists had suffered much during the year (1834) and the mortality
among the emigrants by the latest expeditions had been unusually
great. Out of six hundred and forty-nine emigrants, one hundred
and thirty-four died. Though all were more or less subject to the
fever, those who came from the northern part of the United States
suffered by far the most. . . . The emigrants were imprudent and
did not sufficiently guard against the exciting causes of fever ; especially those from the southern part of the United States, who supposed that they were not liable to be attacked by the African fever.
And when sick, instead of following the advice of those in the colony
who had experience, they listened to those of their own number who
professed to have skill," (pp. 437 and 438). This experience of sixty
years ago found its repetition in the fate of a party of colonists sent
out to Liberia on the 19th of March, 1895, by the International Emigration Society of Birmingham. According to a dispatch to the

On the basis of all the facts here brought together we may assert that the tendency of the colored race towards a higher death rate and disease prevalence from malaria, is of comparatively recent origin ; that this tendency is to be observed in the South as well as in the West Indies, in marked contrast with the lesser susceptibility of the white race ; and that this favorable condition of the whites cannot be attributed to better conditions in life, but must be attributed to an increasing power of vital resistance. If the claim of Dr. Lewis, the secretary of the North Carolina state board of health,[1] and others, as to the cause of malarial fever be true, and better sanitary conditions be brought about, it is doubtful whether the negro would benefit by such improved conditions of life to the same extent as the white race, for, as we have seen in discussing the effect of altitude and density on the death rate, his inordinate mortality is about the same, proportionally, under the best as under the worst conditions. Any amelioration of his unfortunate condition in this respect would undoubtedly be of the greatest possible value from an economic as well as from every other standpoint ; but the race tendency towards an excessive mortality would only be slightly affected.

Yellow fever is another disease to which it has often been claimed the negro was not liable, or if at all, to only a very slight degree. According to Dr. Cartwright " they are not liable to the dreaded el vomito, or yellow fever, at least they have it so lightly that I have never seen a negro die with black vomit, although I have seen a num-

Evening Post of September 7, 1895, out of 211 who comprised the party sent out in March, only half survived the ravages of the fever, aggravated by privation. Those who were able returned to the United States, while many were too ill or too poor to leave.

[1] 5th biennial report, North Carolina state board of health, pp. 148 *et seq.*

ber of yellow fever epidemics."[1]   Dr. Nott laid down
the proposition that "mulattos, like negroes, although
unacclimated, enjoy extraordinary exemption from yellow fever when brought to Charleston, Savannah, Mobile, and New Orleans."[2]   In Cuba, according to the
United States yellow fever commission of 1879, "many
physicians assert that negroes enjoy an absolute immunity from yellow fever."[3]   Topinard also speaks of the
immunity of negroes and their cross breeds from yellow
fever.[4]

The dearth of statistical material for the early part of
this century makes it impossible to prove that the immunity of the negro from this most dreaded disease ever
existed in fact.   That he was comparatively less liable
to its ravages there is not the slightest doubt, and it is
very likely that this comparative infrequency of the disease among the slaves caused the impression that there
was an absolute immunity.   If we consult the mortality
records of Charleston for the period 1822–48, we shall
find that while the disease was infrequent among the
colored, it was not entirely absent.

MORTALITY FROM YELLOW FEVER IN CHARLESTON, 1822-1848.

	White.	Colored.
1822–30	352	8
1831–40	579	6
1840–48	3	0

There were, therefore, 14 deaths from yellow fever recorded among the colored population of one city alone
during the period 1822–48. This record may be compared
with the record of the same city for the period of 1871–
76.

[1] DeBow, "South and West," vol. 2, p. 319.
[2] "Types of Mankind", p. 373.
[3] National Board of Health Report, 1880, p. 48.
[4] "Anthropology", p. 412.

MORTALITY FOR YELLOW FEVER, CHARLESTON, 1871-76.

	White.	Colored.
1871-76	256	 27

With very slight changes in the proportion of the white and colored populations of the city we find substantially different condition as to the liability of the colored race to this disease.

Since 1877 there has been no yellow fever in Charleston and hence we cannot compare the mortality of the two races for a more recent period for this city. But we may recur again to the mortality experience of the army during the war. The comparative number of cases and deaths from yellow fever among the white and colored troops was as follows:

SICKNESS AND MORTALITY FROM YELLOW FEVER AMONG THE WHITE AND COLORED TROOPS DURING THE WAR.[1]

	White	Colored
Cases.	1181	190
Deaths	409	27

[1] "Medical History of the War," Vol. I, page 636 *et seq.*

There was, therefore, no immunity from this disease among the negro soldiers during the war.

Among the colored refugees under the care of the Freedmen's Bureau there were 512 cases of yellow fever and 38 deaths during the period 1865–72. During the great epidemic of 1878 at New Orleans 383 deaths occurred among the whites and 183 among the negroes, and the same year in South-west Louisiana there were 454 and 154 cases for the two races respectively. It had already been observed, during the epidemic of 1869 at New Orleans, that the colored troops were by no means free from attacks of yellow fever. The experience of the army gave a rate of 866 cases and 256 deaths per 1,000 whites, and 521 cases and 73 deaths per 1,000 blacks. Thus the case prevalence among the

negroes had very closely approached that of the white
population, but still the comparative mortality was very
much lower.[1]   During the Memphis epidemic of 1878
the proportion of deaths from yellow fever to the number attacked was 42 per cent. among the whites and
among the blacks only 11 per cent.[2]   During the epidemic in Decatur, Alabama, the case prevalence and
mortality were as follows :

SICKNESS AND MORTALITY FROM YELLOW FEVER AT DECATUR, ALA.

	White	Colored
Cases	100	30
Deaths	30	5
Percentage of deaths.	30.7	16.7

The Decatur epidemic shows a lower mortality rate
for the whites and a higher mortality rate for the colored
than was observed during the Memphis epidemic.   The
number of cases and deaths, however, is probably too
small for safe deductions.

The most recent experience is furnished by the epidemic of Brunswick, Georgia, of 1893.   From a report
of the surgeon in charge, I abstract the following statistics : [3]

SICKNESS AND MORTALITY FROM YELLOW FEVER IN BRUNSWICK,
GA., 1893.

	White	Colored
Cases	353	717
Deaths	35	10
Percentage of mortality	9.9	1.35

This epidemic shows a still greater case prevalence
but a lower rate of mortality.   The proportion of cases
to the population is not given, but the colored popula-

[1] National Board of Health Report, 1880, p. 149.
[2] First Annual Report, State Board of Health of Tenn., 1877–1880,
page 93.
[3] For the statistics for Brunswick I am obliged to Dr. Walter Wy-
man, Surgeon-General of the U. S. Marine Hospital service, Washington. D. C.

tion was in the large majority. Hence the number of cases does not prove conclusively that the proportion of cases was greater for the colored than for the whites; but the fact is clearly shown that the colored race is to-day as liable as the white to the disease, though still having a lower mortality rate from this cause.

With respect to the negro in the West Indies we have it on the authority of the yellow fever commission of 1879 that "it is not true, as has been so often asserted, that Cuban negroes are immune against the disease."[1] The report also refers to the epidemic of 1802 at Martinique, where "the African negroes acting as nurses in the hospital of Fort de France, were attacked and all died, except some old men."[2]

Yellow fever is becoming less and less the curse of the large cities of the South. In New Orleans, where the disease was a constant menace during the early part of the century and up to comparatively recent times, the decrease in the mortality from this cause will appear from the following summary :

MORTALITY FROM YELLOW FEVER IN NEW ORLEANS, 1845-94.

	Total.	Average per Annum.
1845–55	18,131	1,684
1856–67	8,546	777
1868–78	5,084	462
1879–89	27	2.4
1890–95	None	None

The same diminution in the mortality from this disease is to be observed in Charleston.

[1] Annual Report, National Board of Health, p. 148.
[2] *Ibid.*, p. 148.

8

MORTALITY FROM YELLOW FEVER FOR CHARLESTON, 1799-1895.

	Total.	Average per Annum.
1799–1808	829	82.9
1809–1818	270	27.0
1819–1828	503	50.3
1829–1838	456	45.6
1839–1848	136	13 6
1849–1858	No record	
1859–1868	No record	
1869–1878 [1]	284	28.4
1879–1888	None	None
1889–1895	None	None

[1] 213 deaths in 1871, 30 deaths in 1876.

This remarkable change in the prevalence of this most dreaded disease in the large cities of the south would seem to prove that the susceptibility of the white race to yellow fever has diminished while that of the colored race has comparatively increased. It is not a question whether this favorable condition for the whites has been brought about by sanitation or more scientific methods of dealing with the disease; the point is that the white race has become master of the conditions that produced the disease, and by this means the average duration of life has been considerably increased. The colored population, while indirectly benefitted by this improvement, is not directly concerned in this favorable change in the conditions of life at the South. Much to the contrary the liability of the race to this disease has enormously increased, if we can rely on the records of comparative mortality during the period of servitude.

It is commonly supposed that the colored race suffers more from *small-pox* than the white race. The supposition is fairly supported by statistical proof. The mortality from eruptive fevers among the colored troops in the West Indies during the period 1817–35 was 2.5 per 1,000, while for the white troops it was almost *nil*. In Sierra Leone during the same period the rate for the negroes was 6.9 while among the whites there were no deaths at all from this cause. The records of Charleston, S. C., for the period 1822–48 show a large preponderance of negro mortality from small-pox, there being 45 deaths among the white population and 149 among the colored. The experience of the army with this disease during the war was as follows:

PREVALENCE OF SMALL-POX IN THE ARMY DURING THE WAR.[1]
(Per 1,000 of mean strength.)

	Cases	Deaths
White troops	5.49	1.95
Colored troops	36.62	12.21

[1] "Medical History of the War," Vol. III, p. 624.

The excess of mortality and disease prevalence among the blacks was very large according to the above record. It does not appear, however, that out of the same number of small-pox cases a larger number died among the colored than among the whites. This fact is supported by the statistics of the Freedmen's Bureau, according to which the mortality and disease prevalence were as follows:

PREVALENCE OF SMALL-POX AMONG THE WHITE AND COLORED REFUGEES TREATED AT THE HOSPITALS OF THE FREEDMEN'S BUREAU.

	Whites	Colored
Cases	155	10,299
Deaths	24	1,802
Percentage of mortality.	15.49	17.55

These figures support those previously given and prove that while small-pox is proportionally more prevalent among the colored population it is not for this reason much more fatal proportionally. In the New Orleans epidemic of 1875, the mortality was as follows:

PREVALENCE OF SMALL-POX IN NEW ORLEANS IN 1875.

	Whites	Colored
Cases	415	477
Deaths	131	201
Percentage of mortality	31.53	42.14

In this epidemic the case mortality of the colored was in excess of that of the whites, an excess slightly more than 33 per cent.   In the epidemic of 1874 in the same city the number of cases per 1,000 of population was 4.59 for the white population and 11.30 the colored.

These figures do not show that there is any specific race tendency towards a higher mortality or even towards a greater prevalence of the disease among the negroes than among the whites.   On the contrary the statistics for the last twenty years show that if subjected to vaccination and re-vaccination, the prevalence of this disease can as readily be prevented among the colored as among the white population.   The experience of New Orleans proves this very plainly, for the large number of vaccinations among the colored population have virtually banished the disease from that city.[1]   With the exception of the epidemic of 1884 the city has been comparatively free from small-pox for the last twenty years. For Charleston, S. C., the figures are even more instructive.   The city had a small-pox epidemic in 1865–66 which caused the death of 48 white and 366 colored people.   The next epidemic was during 1872–74, when 12 whites and 122 negroes died; and since 1874 there has been but one death from small-pox among the colored and none among the white population.

[1] During 1895 there were 46 deaths from small pox among the colored population of New Orleans against one death from this cause in 1894.   During the same two years there were vaccinated 30,845 white persons and 22,592 colored persons, the vast majority of whom, however, were vaccinated during the last three months of 1895 when the epidemic had run its course.   An ounce of prevention would have prevented the larger part of the mortality of 1895.

I have not been able to obtain satisfactory statistics as to the comparative mortality among vaccinated and un-vaccinated colored persons. The oldest records on this subject are probably those of Boston for 1752 and 1792,[1] but the number of cases is small and the figures contradict each other. For the same reason the statistics for Philadelphia for 1893 and 1894 are unsatisfactory. It would be of value, however, to obtain trustworthy data on this point, to ascertain whether the colored population, properly protected by vaccination, is more or less liable to small-pox than the white race. The great decrease in the mortality from this dreaded disease among all civilized peoples who have made vaccination compulsory is well known. In England alone the mortality rate from this cause has decreased from 219.3 per million during 1858–60 to 13.2 during 1886–90. The diminishing mortality from this disease among the colored population would therefore prove that in this respect they do not differ materially from the white race. If, therefore, the colored people would subject themselves to vaccination to the same extent as the whites, there is no reason why the mortality for this disease should not become equally as low.

For *measles, scarlet fever, diptheria* and *croup*, the mortality among the colored is undoubtedly less than among the whites. There does not seem to be any tendency towards a change in this fortunate condition affecting child life. There are occasional exceptions to the rule, but if we take into consideration that the prevalence of these diseases is very much influenced by conditions of life, especially overcrowding of the population, and inefficient sanitary supervision of schools, we

[1] Shatuck on the Vital Statistics of Boston, *Journal of the Medical Sciences,* April, 1841.

may account for the occasional excess in negro mortality. The table below will show the comparative mortality among the white and colored populations of Charleston, Washington, and Baltimore.

MORTALITY FROM MEASLES, SCARLET FEVER, DIPHTHERIA AND CROUP IN CHARLESTON, S. C.—1865-1894.

	No. of deaths. White.	Rate per 100,000 of population	No. of deaths. Colored.	Rate per 100,000 of population	Excess of White Mortality rate. (per 100.000)
Measles	84	12.1	111	13.4	1.3[1]
Scarlet Fever . .	124	17.8	54	6.5	11.3
Diphtheria . . .	555	79.9	227	27.4	52.5
Croup	106	15.3	77	9.3	6.0

[1] Excess in rate for Colored.

MORTALITY FROM MEASLES, SCARLET FEVER, DIPHTHERIA AND CROUP IN WASHINGTON AND BALTIMORE—1890.

(Per 100,000 of Population.)

	Washington, D. C. White.	Washington, D. C. Colored.	Baltimore, Md. White.	Baltimore, Md. Colored.
Measles	1.94	3.96	55.56	40.12
Scarlet Fever	7.76	7.93	14.16	10.40
Diphtheria and Croup . .	67.88	114.93	60.19	32.69

COMPARATIVE MORTALITY FROM DIPHTHERIA AND CROUP.

	Age 0-1. White.	Age 0-1. Colored.	Age 0-5. White.	Age 0-5. Colored.	Age 5-15. White.	Age 5-15. Colored.
Baltimore . .	171.00	434.78	405.65	203.38	72 38	None
Washington .	103.66	445.01	421.05	499 79	164 91	296.10

For Charleston there is a slight excess in the mortality from measles, which, however, fell entirely on one year. For the other three diseases the mortality among the colored people was less than that for the whites. For Washington all three diseases are more prevalent among the colored, but as I have said, local sanitary conditions may be largely responsible for this. For in Baltimore we find that the mortality among the whites for all three diseases is considerable above that of the colored. No definite rule seems, therefore, to prevail, but on the whole the colored race would seem to be less liable to these diseases than the white race.

I shall have to deal briefly with the less fatal diseases only a few of which can be considered here. Deaths from *child birth, and puerperal diseases* are about equally frequent for the two races. For Baltimore and Washington the rates were as follows:

DEATHS FROM CHILDBIRTH AND PUERPERAL SEPTICÆMIA.
(Rate per 100,000 women, age group 15-45.)

	White.	Colored.
Washington, 1890	40.64	42.31
Baltimore, "	33.10	27.01

For Charleston the rates for the period 1865–94 were as follows:

DEATHS FROM PUERPERAL FEVER.

	Deaths.	Rate per 100,000 of population.
White	.61	8.8
Colored	150	18.1

The excess of negro mortality from puerperal fevers is almost exclusively the result of the conditions of life under which these people live. The employment of ignorant colored women as nurses and midwives has been so frequently condemned as to need only to be referred to. As a *race,* the colored people do not seem to suffer more from deaths in childbirth than the whites: as ignorant or indifferent *individuals* they do, just as does the foreign population of our large cities in the North. The point is of sufficient interest to permit me to present the following tables for the cities of New York and Brooklyn, for the census year 1890.

DEATHS FROM CHILDBIRTH AND PUERPERAL DISEASES.[1]

(Per 100,000 women, 15-45 years of age.)

	New York.	Brooklyn.
Native whites	49.72	50.21
Native colored	81.54	29.04
Of English parentage	45.56	51.38
Of Irish parentage	85.95	73.62
Of German parentage	96.20	67.08
Of Russian Jewish parentage . .	81.36	89.69

[1] Vital Statistics of New York and Brooklyn, p. 48.

The agreement between the rates of the native whites and those of English parentage is significant. That the rates for those of German parentage should be so high is due entirely to the fact that among the Germans and the Jews, midwives instead of physicians are almost exclusively employed in cases of childbirth, in contrast with the English and native Americans who rarely make use of this class of would-be doctors. The high rates for the Irish, and negroes (excluding Brooklyn for the latter, on account of small numbers of negroes in population), are probably due to the same cause, that is, the employment of ignorant old women as nurses during childbirth. If there is another explanation, it will be of interest and great value to have this point more fully discussed by qualified medical men.

Cancer and *tumor* would seem to be more frequent at the younger and less frequent at the older ages among the colored population, if the statistics of Baltimore and Washington represent fairly the general prevalence of these diseases. In the report of Dr. Billings these two diseases have been combined and the following table will show the comparative mortality from these two causes for two age groups.

MORTALITY FROM TUMOR AND CANCER.
(Per 100,000 persons of corresponding ages.)

	White.	Colored.	White.	Colored.
	15–45		45 and over.	
Baltimore, ...	17.87	39.49	290.22	161.29
Washington, . . .	25.21	31.92	199.67	115.70

According to the reports of the health officer of Washington the average ages at which death occur from cancer have been as follows:

MORTALITY FROM CANCER, WASHINGTON, D. C.
(Average age at death.)

	White.		Colored.	
	Males.	Females.	Males.	Females.
1893, ...	57	55	35	54
1894, ...	60	55	51	53

The above table would indicate a slightly lower average age for the colored persons who died of cancer.

Whether cancer has been on the increase among the colored it is impossible to say, more so in view of the fact that it is a disputed point whether the disease has increased among the whites.[1] The fact that more deaths from cancer are now recognized may be entirely due to better medical diagnosis. The disease has always prevailed more or less among the colored people, and probably to about the same extent. The statistics for Baltimore and Washington would indicate that the mortality is greater among the colored people of middle age than among the whites of the same age. If this condition prevails generally an increase in the mortality from cancer among negroes may be expected. As to the frequency of cancer of the uterus, on which a good deal has been written, it can easily be proven that those who believed

[1] See a valuable paper of Arthur Newsholme, M. D., and George King, F. I. A., on the Alleged Increase of Cancer, *Proceedings Royal Society*, Vol. 54, pp. 209 *et seq.*

this disease to be rare or entirely absent in the negro race
have drawn their conclusions contrary to the facts.   Dr.
Middleton Michel of the South Carolina Medical College
and the Charleston board of health has clearly disproved
the theory of Schroeder that "carcinoma uteri, or any
form of carcinoma seldom affects the negro woman"[1]   According to Dr. Michel there have been 48 cases of cancer
of the uterus among the white and 53 cases among the
colored females of Charleston during the period 1878–91.

These figures are supplemented by the following table
for the same city showing the comparative prevalence of
this affliction during the period 1822–48.

CANCER OF THE UTERUS. CHARLESTON, 1822-48.

	White.	Colored.
1822–30, ...	0	0
1831–40, ...	5	0
1841–48, ...	4	8

The above figures would indicate that the disease was
rare among both races, an indication which is probably
more the result of the failure of physicians to recognize
the disease than of its actual infrequency.

The annual reports of the state health officer of Alabama contain some interesting statistics which may be
of value in connection with those of Dr. Michel.

CANCER OF THE UTERUS IN ALABAMA, 1890-94.

	White.	Colored.
1890, ...	22	15
1891, ...	19	18
1892, ...	26	21
1893, ...	25	19
1894, ...	27	24

[1] *Medical News*, October, 1892.

The statistics for this state would indicate about an equal degree of prevalence of this disease among the two races. The more accurate statistics of Charleston, and perhaps better still, those for the city of Washington for the period 1874–94, prove that cancer of the Uterus is by no means an infrequent disease among colored women. But there would seem to be a distinct difference in the liability of unmarried females of the colored race to this disease, as will be observed in the next table.

DEATHS FROM CANCER AMONG WHITE AND COLORED FEMALES FROM SEPTEMBER 1, 1874, TO JUNE 30, 1894,—WASHINGTON, D. C.[1]

Cancer of	White Females. Conjugal Condition.				Colored Females. Conjugal Condition.			
	Total	Married.	Widowed.	Spinsters.	Total	Married	Widowed	Spinsters.
Breast.	191	77	74	40	89	32	45	12
Uterus	350	217	105	28	166	77	70	19
Ovary	18	11	5	2	5	4	1	
Stomach.	113	40	48	25	57	16	32	9
Liver	64	29	22	13	8	4	3	1
Face, head, neck, mouth and throat	49	16	23	10	14	6	3	5
All other	169	83	48	38	55	26	19	10
Total	954	473	325	156	394	165	173	56

[1] Annual report of the Health Officer of the District of Columbia, 1894, pp. 149–50.

Among the unmarried white females only 17.95 per cent. of the deaths from cancer were from cancer of the uterus, while 33.93 per cent. of the deaths among unmarried colored females were from this particular form of cancer. In contrast with this fact we find that cancer of the breast was more frequent among single females of the white race than among those of the colored. The figures to be trustworthy should be based on the number of those living at the same ages, but it is probable that there would be no material difference, relatively speaking. Dr. Michel deserves much credit for having called attention to the facts as to this interesting phase of the pathological history of the race.[1]

I may here refer briefly to the liability of the negro to *appendicitis*. It has been claimed that this disease is extremely rare among the colored population, some having maintained that the race is not liable to it at all. Dr. Ashmead of New York seems to favor the latter view, while Dr. Gaston of Atlanta, Dr. Hand of Shubuta, Miss., and Dr. Baldwin of Columbus, Ohio, in letters to the *Medical News*[2] bring forward their own experiences, which prove that the disease does occasionally occur among the colored population. I myself have record of twelve deaths of colored persons from this cause, of whom five were females. According to the report of the board of health of New York city, 129 persons died in New York in 1892, from typhilitis, perityphlitis, and perforation of the vermiform appendix, of whom only one was colored. But I am not inclined to attach much value to this apparent immunity, for it is only for a very recent period that these diseases have been extensively recognized. Thus in New York city during the period 1881–92 the deaths from this cause have increased as follows: 1881, 10 deaths; 1884, 10 deaths; 1888, 72 deaths; 1892, 129 deaths. With the exception of the one case in 1892 there is no record of any other death from this cause among the colored in the city of New York.[3] I do not

[1] The disease prevalence and consequent mortality from Cancer among the persons cared for by the Freedmen's Bureau during the period 1868–72 was as follows:

	Cases.	Per 1,000	Deaths.	Per 1,000
Whites	23	1.04	1	0.05
Colored	462	1.07	62	0.14

According to these figures the disease was about equally prevalent among both races, but much more fatal among the colored than among the whites.

[2] Oct. 7, 1893.

[3] No annual report of the New York board of health has been published for the last three years.

know of any trustworthy statistics by which this doubtful matter can be cleared. It is probable that in time, as the disease becomes better recognized, the number of reported cases will increase, which, however, will not prove that the disease did not exist in equal proportions during the past. There is therefore no immunity, as has been claimed, but possibly a less degree of susceptibility to appendicitis, in the colored race.

Desirable as it would be to deal in this manner with all of the important diseases which affect the colored race, it is not possible for me to do so here. I have considered those which I have taken pains to investigate to a limited extent, and on which it is desirable that data should be brought together in order to encourage further research. But before I conclude this part of my work I wish to deal, as briefly as possible, with the prevalence of three diseases which bear on the morbid psychological nature of the negro rather than the purely physical.

Alcoholism, *insanity* and *suicide* are three important phenomena of the sociology of the colored race, to which frequent reference has been made in medical, anthropological and economic literature. But few facts have been brought forward to support one view or the other. This is largely due to a paucity of data; which, however, is no excuse for the expression of unwarranted opinions.

"*Alcoholism* among negroes," we are informed by Dr. Norman Kerr, than whom few have more thoroughly dealt with the subject of inebriety, "differs materially from the same disease in the white and Indian races. The negroes, with their vivacity and enthusiasm, from their nervous sensitiveness, are easily excited. Their drunkenness is more demonstrative than profound, but the anæstethic influence is less lasting. They may be characterized as more readily intoxicated than the white men of western countries but less liable to the diseased condition which I designated narcomania, intoxicate mania or inebriety.[1]"

This view of Dr. Kerr is supported by a considerable body of reliable statistics of which those of the United States Army during the war are the most valuable in view of their completeness.

According to the reports of the Provost-Marshal General the rate of rejections for chronic alcoholism was as follows for the principal nationalities :

REJECTIONS FOR CHRONIC ALCOHOLISM, U. S. A., 1861-65.[1]

United States, white	0.535	per 1,000 examined
" " colored · · ·	0.310	" "
Natives of Germany	0.619	" "
" British N. America . . .	1.848	" "
" England and Wales . . .	2.346	" "
" Ireland	3.779	" "

[1] Report Provost-Marshal General, Vol. II, p. 431, *et seq.*

The rate of rejections for chronic alcoholism was therefore the lowest for the colored race and the highest for the Irish. It will prove of interest to know how far this relation was maintained during the progress of the war.

COMPARATIVE DISEASE PREVALENCE AND MORTALITY FROM INTEMPERANCE.[1]
U. S. Army, 1861-66.

	Whites.		Colored.	
	Cases.	Deaths.	Cases.	Deaths.
Delirium tremens.	3,744	450	12	4
Intemperance	5,589	110	22	2
Chronic alcoholism	920	45	6	1
Total	10,253	605	40	7

[1] "Medical History of the War," Vol. I, p. 636, *et seq.*

This is truly a remarkable record and one which presents perhaps the most hopeful side of the negro char-

[1] "Inebriety or Narcomania," by Norman S. Kerr, M.D., p. 131.

acter. The corresponding mortality rates were one death to every 220 for the white soldiers, and one to every 4,500 colored. The figures therefore prove that while the race had a lower rate of rejections for alcoholism before active service, it did not develop under the influences of the hardships of war times a tendency toward a higher rate of intemperance. The experience of the Freedmen's Bureau brings out this fact with still greater force.

COMPARATIVE DISEASE PREVALENCE AND MORTALITY FROM
INTEMPERANCE.[1]
Persons cared for by the Freedmen's Bureau, 1865-72.

	Whites.		Colored.	
	Cases.	Deaths.	Cases.	Deaths.
Delirium tremens	49	2	65	1
Inebriation	51	0	48	2
Chronic alcoholism	11	1	19	12
Total	111	3	132	42

[1] "Type of Disease," p. 16, *et seq.*

The total number of cases under treatment for all causes was 430,466 for the colored and 22,053 for the whites; hence the figures show largely in favor of the colored race, and support the experience of the army before and during the war. Dr. Reyburn comments on the infrequency of this form of disease among the freed people in the following words :

[1] The small number of cases of delirium tremens met with among the freed people, being only sixty-five, with one death, presents marked contrast in frequency when compared with the large number of cases met with among the white population of our country. This may be partially explained by the fact that chronic alcoholism is not so frequent among the colored people as among their neighbors of the Caucasian race; still, there does seem to be even among those of the freed people who habitually use intoxicating drinks, a marked exemption from this disease. In the Freedmen's Hospital, under my charge, at Washington, D. C., which has had under treatment from 1865 to the present time about 5,000 patients, I remember seeing only one or two cases, and these were mild in type.

My own belief is that the true explanation of this exemption is to be sought for in the want of development of the cerebral hemispheres,

which so often exists among the negroes. Delirium tremens is pre-
ëminently a disease causing disorder of intellection, and hence the
continued abuse of alcoholic drinks in the negro race is more likely
to produce eleptiform convulsions or mania than delirium tremens.

If we now consider the prevalence of this form of
disease at the present time we find substantially the same
infrequency of intemperance among the colored population. For the state of Alabama the records for five
years (1890–94) show 46 deaths among the whites and
14 among the colored from alcoholism. For Washington and Baltimore the death rates for the census year
have been as follows :

DEATHS FROM ALCOHOLISM,[1]
(Per 100,000 of Population.)

	White.	Colored.
Washington	16.81	3.96
Baltimore	10.35	11.89

[1] Census Report of Dr. Billings, pp. 28–29.

The above table shows a larger death rate from alcoholism for the colored population of Baltimore than
for the white, but I am inclined to believe that this rate
is rather accidental and largely due to the small number
of cases on which the rate is based. For during the six
years 1885–90 there were only 27 deaths from alcoholism
among the colored population of Baltimore and 190
among the white population. It is therefore plain that
the rate for 1890 was exceptionally high. The comparative infrequency of the disease among the negroes still
exists.

If it is argued that the mortality from alcoholism does
not fully determine the prevalence of intemperance,
since many other diseases are the indirect consequence
of the intemperate use of alcoholic drinks,[2] I would call

[1] "Type of Disease," p. 14.
[2] See Newsholme, "Vital Statistics," page 215.

attention to the table below which shows the comparative mortality from diseases of the liver, which is commonly accepted as a sequel of intemperance. The death rates are for two age periods and of exceptional interest in view of the preceding tables.

MORTALITY FROM LIVER DISEASES.[1]
(Per 100,000 of same age.)

	Ages 15-45.	
	White.	Colored.
Washington	10.08	17.19
Baltimore	11.92	15.80
	Ages 45 and over.	
Washington	77.48	49.59
Baltimore	70.36	28.46

[1] Census Report of Dr. Billings, pp. 28-29.

This table presents a most interesting phase of the question of the comparative frequency of alcoholism. In both cities the mortality from disease of the liver is higher for the negroes than for the whites for the age period 15–45, while it is lower in both cities for the age period 45 and over, which includes largely the "old stock." If reliance can be placed on these figures, and there is no reason to believe that the conditions in other cities would vary greatly, the mortality from the effects of intemperance is on the increase among the present generation of colored people. It is not possible at present to determine whether this is an actual tendency, and such related facts as I have consulted would rather tend to prove that alcoholism in its violent form is not as frequent among the young colored people at the present time as among whites. Thus the statistics for Charleston show 936 white and 625 colored persons arrested for drunkenness during the three years 1892–94, and for the city of Savannah during the same period the arrests were 300 white to 127 colored. In both cities the colored population is in excess of the white.

9

Thus whatever the condition may be in the North it is not shown that the negro at the South reveals any positive tendency to a higher rate of mortality from alcoholism. The subject, however, needs further investigating before a definite conclusion can be arrived at. Personally I have observed very little intemperance among the older colored people, but have met with many cases among the young men of the present generation. But, while it is probable that the negro indulges in liquor to a considerable extent, there is no doubt that he suffers less from the consequences of over indulgence, and this may account for the low mortality rate from this cause. It is to be hoped that this phase of the subject will be thoroughly investigated by some one more familiar with the facts and with better opportunities for observation. If the race is still as free from alcoholic taint as it was before and during the war and reconstruction period, such exemption will prove of considerable economic advantage in the struggle for life.

Insanity and lunacy are less common among the colored population than among the whites. Accurate statistics on this point, so far as I know, have never been collected and those of the census are mere approximations. According to the census of 1890 there has been a decrease in the rate of insane per million of population, for both races; but it is admitted that the statistics are incomplete. It is the opinion of many writers that insanity is on the increase among both races, but I have been unable to obtain satisfactory proof of this. There are various elements bearing on statistics of insanity and idiocy which are often ignored by those who have discussed the subject from the statistical standpoint.[1] The number remaining in institutions at the

---

[1] For a valuable discussion of the value of statistics of insanity see General Report on the English Census, 1891, p. 74, *et seq.*

end of the year is largely affected by the number of re-coveries and the rate of mortality, while the average number of admissions is largely affected by the amount of hospital accomodation.

With respect to the rate of mortality I find that in Virginia the mortality rate was 6.9 per cent. for the white patients and 8.5 per cent. for the colored, during the year 1894. In Georgia during the same year the mortality of the white patients at the state lunatic asylum was 6.5 per cent. against a colored rate of 11.6 per cent. It requires only a simple calculation to show that this excessive mortality of the colored insane would seriously affect the total number remaining at the end of the year, and that, consequently the actual rate of in-crease would be greater than the apparent rate. With respect to hospital accomodation it is plain to any one who will look into the subject that there is an insuf-ficient accomodation for the insane of both races in many states, and the rate of admission is governed more by changes in political control or the condition of the state treasury, than by the actual increase of the number of insane in the population. The superintendent of one of the largest institutions of the South refers to this point as follows : " The number of patients received was not as great last year, due to the fact that no addition was made to the hospital as was the case the year before."

Mere statistics of cases of insanity and idiocy are also of little value as long as no distinction is made between the different forms of insanity. It is generally admitted that it is extremely difficult to draw the line of distinc-tion between one form and another, yet it is evident that the forms of insanity differ materially for the two races. The broad distinction between idiocy, " in which the pro-cess of mental development has not been carried far enough," and insanity "in which it has been carried in the wrong direction,"[1] is hardly sufficient for the purpose of establishing the traits and tendencies of a race; and in the absence of a thorough study of the statistics of insanity of the negro it is difficult to deal with the question.

The most reliable data are probably those of the army during the war, which have been so frequently made use of in this work. According to the statistics of the Provost-Marshal General the rate of rejections for insanity was 0.808 per 1,000 for the white applicants for enlistment, and 0.503 per 1,000 for the colored. This would give an excess of 60.6 per cent. for insanity among the white males of military age. During the war the discharge rate was 0.34 per 1,000 for the whites and 0.18 for the colored, a difference of almost one hundred per cent. in favor of the colored troops. While the rate of rejections was less among the colored, the rate of discharges for mental diseases was still lower, as compared with the white troops. These statistics support the general opinion that insanity was not a common disease among the colored population before the war.

If we compare this low rate of insanity among the colored men in the army, with the prevalence of this disease among the colored refugees cared for by the Freedmen's Bureau, we meet with a somewhat different condition.

INSANITY AMONG THE REFUGEES CARED FOR BY THE FREEDMEN'S BUREAU.

	Cases of Insanity.	Per 100,000.	Deaths.	Per 100,0000.
White	54	235	3	1.3
Colored . . .	1,171	272	73	16.6

[1] "Sanity and Insanity," by Dr. Mercer, p. 287.

It is here shown that the number of insane patients and the number of deaths from insanity was larger among the general colored population than among the whites during the period immediately after the war. I am not inclined to believe that these figures indicate an actual increase in insanity, since the effect of the war on the general colored population may have been a material factor in the large number of cases. More especially do I believe this in view of the fact that we have no information as to the forms of insanity, and since it is highly probable that insanity of a serious nature was not frequent; for there is no proof of such an increase in the statistics of the Government Hospital for the Insane at Washington, into which colored persons have been admitted almost from the time the institution was opened in 1856. As a matter of fact, the superintendent of the asylum calls attention to the matter in the following words, which apply to both races: " Contrary to the anticipations which history authorized us to entertain at the outset of the struggle, the admissions of civil cases in this institution, situated in the very midst of the perturbations of the war, have been fewer during the last two years than before."[1] It is therefore very doubtful whether the higher rate of insanity among the colored refugees indicated an actual increase of insanity. The table below will show the admissions to the Government Hospital for the period 1856 –1894.

[1] Report of the Sup't of the Gov't Hospital for the Insane, 1860-63, p. 21.

ADMISSIONS TO THE GOVERNMENT HOSPITAL FOR THE INSANE,
WASHINGTON, D. C.—1856-1894.

	Males.		Females.	
	White.	Colored.	White.	Colored.
1856–59	128	9	55	15
1860–64	1,096	25	94	23
1865–69	937	75	119	33
1870–74	731	56	160	42
1875–79	715	84	181	65
1880–84	870	127	214	86
1885–89	977	153	261	108
1890–94	1,129	192	253	141

The increase of colored patients during the period of
1865–69 was almost entirely among males, and of the
75 admissions 34 were soldiers. As I have said before,
it is extremely difficult to reason from the statistics of
insanity, and not having been able to study in detail the
published data, I submit the following tables for Virginia, Georgia and Pennsylvania, principally for the purpose of calling attention to the need of a thorough inquiry into the subject.

YEARLY ADMISSIONS OF INSANE PERSONS TO THE CENTRAL AND
EASTERN HOSPITALS FOR THE INSANE IN THE
STATE OF VIRGINIA.[1] 1888-1894.

	Central Hospital—Colored.		Eastern Hospital—White.	
	Male.	Female.	Male.	Female.
1888	108	98	44	6
1889	99	76	51	20
1890	89	67	65	13
1891	141	102	70	22
1892	44	29	63	33
1893	121	114	35	26
1894	99	77	70	42

[1] Annual reports of the Eastern and Central State Hospitals, 1888-1894.

INSANE PERSONS CONFINED IN HOSPITALS IN PENNSYLVANIA AT
THE END OF EACH YEAR FOR THE PERIOD 1887-1894.[1]

	Males.		Females.	
	White.	Colored.	White.	Colored.
1887	3081	84	2999	65
1888	3231	70	3114	95
1889	3434	76	3268	106
1890	3697	89	3495	118
1891	3803	92	3641	113
1892	3923	98	3725	109
1893	4065	105	3805	129
1894 . . .	4346	127	4013	130

[1] Annual reports of the Pennsylvania state board of lunacy, 1887-1894.

INSANE PERSONS CONFINED IN THE STATE LUNATIC ASYLUM OF
GEORGIA AT THE END OF EACH YEAR FOR THE PERIOD 1890-94.[1]

	Males and Females.	
	White.	Colored.
1890	1089	477
1891	1142	523
1892	1061	509
1893	1146	530
1894	1204	539

[1] Annual reports of the Georgia State Lunatic Asylum, 1890-94.

The statistics of the Government Hospital for the Insane would indicate a considerable increase in insanity among the colored population of Washington; but if the increase in population and the admission of colored soldiers from all parts of the country is taken into account, as well as the possible admission of colored patients from the surrounding country, it remains to be proven whether there has been an actual increase of insanity or not. According to Mr. Bruce, who had exceptional opportunities for observation, lunacy is very uncommon among the colored population of Southside Virginia, and this is true for other parts of the state, as I know from personal observation. The irregular number of admissions to the colored insane asylum do not afford a fair means of estimating the probable increase, and the statistics for Georgia and Pennsylvania are for too short a period to prove a decided tendency towards a

greater prevalence of insanity among the colored population. The following table will show the proportion of
admissions to Virginia state institutions for various age
groups of both races :

NUMBER OF INSANE AT EACH AGE AND PROPORTION TO TOTAL AT
TIME OF ATTACK OF INSANITY.

Age.	Colored.[1]	Percentage.	White.[2]	Percentage.
Under 15	87	2.85	83	3.88
15–20	333	10.89	186	8.69
20–25	386	12.63	302	14.12
25–30	406	13.29	270	12.62
30–35	371	12.14	238	11.13
35–40	365	11.94	228	10 66
40–45	289	9.46	182	8.51
45–50	216	7.07	153	7.15
50–60	207	6.77	190	8.89
60–70	134	4.39	112	5.23
70–80	56	1.83	31	1.45
80 and over . . .	10	.33	1	0.05
Unknown	196	6.41	163	7.62
Total	3056	100.00	2139	100.00

[1] Admissions to the Central State Hospital from the beginning to September 30,
1894.
[2] Admissions to the Eastern State Hospital from 1868 to September 30, 1894.

It would appear from this table that there is a very
slight tendency towards a higher rate of admissions for the
earlier age groups of the colored race. This might indicate an increase of insanity since such increase would
probably appear first in the younger generation. In the
absence of comparative statistics I give the information
for the benefit of those who may wish to pursue this interesting subject farther than it has been possible for me
to do. It must be taken into consideration that insanity
is more frequent among the natives of Africa than might
be supposed. The only statistics which have come to
my notice are those of the lunatic asylum of Sierra
Leone for the period 1843–53. The table abstracted
from Dr. Clark's report may be of enough interest to
warrant its being inserted here.

NUMBER OF LUNATICS UNDER TREATMENT, AND DEATHS, IN THE
COLONIAL HOSPITAL AT SIERRA LEONE, WEST AFRICA—1843-1853.[1]

	Cases.	Deaths.		Cases.	Deaths.
1843 . . .	58	13	1849 . . .	61	19
1844 . . .	54	11	1850 . . .	54	11
1845 . .	54	17	1851 . . .	88	14
1846 . . .	52	19	1852 . . .	111	26
1847 . . .	56	15	1853 . . .	98	23
1848 . . .	43	13		——	——
Total				729	181

[1] *Journal of the Royal Statistical Society*, Vol. XIX, p. 81.

It will be observed that the number of lunatics admitted during the period covered by this table was 727,
which would clearly prove that insanity was not an uncommon disease among the natives of Africa at the time.
The prevalence of the disease at the present time may,
therefore, be as much due to the consequences of heredity
as to the effects of the struggle for life. In the West
Indies, where the colored population leads an existence
free from all mental strain and physical over-exertion, I
find that the rate of insanity is about the same as
the census rate for the colored population of the United
States. The statistics of insanity for the West Indies
are, however, subject to all the objections that have been
advanced against the data for the United States; though
the element of error is probably the same in the English
colonies as in this country.

RATES OF INSANE PER 1,000 OF POPULATION IN THE UNITED STATES
AND THE WEST INDIES—1881-1891.

	1881.	1891.
United States (colored) . .	2.4[1]	2.3[1]
Jamaica.	1.4	1.3
Trinidad	1.8	1.9
Grenada	. .	2.8
British Guiana	. .	2.2
Leeward Island	. .	2.0
Barbadoes	. .	2.6

[1] For 1880 and 1890.

I have diligently searched for more reliable information on the rate of insanity and the tendency of the
colored population with regard to it, and the statistics
here given constitute what seemed to me the most reliable body of facts bearing on the subject. They do
not prove that there has been any decided tendency
toward an increase in the insanity rate of the colored
population—which, however, a more careful inquiry
might disclose.

Suicide among the colored population is very rare
and the most careful examination of the available statistical material fails to disclose any decided tendency
towards a change. There have been frequent statements
to the contrary, and even so careful a writer as Morselli[1]
speaks of "the extraordinary propensity of blacks to
suicide." The New York *Medical Examiner* a few
years ago quoted with approval the statement: "It is
said that before the war suicide among the colored population was very infrequent, but since they have been
compelled to earn their living by their own exertion,
this form of death has become quite common." But, as I
have said, there is no proof for this assertion, and suicide
among the colored population is apparently as infrequent
now as it was before the war. In fact, there have been
times when self-destruction among the slave or freed
colored population prevailed even to the extent of an
epidemic, and suicide among the slave population has
been recorded by many writers on the negro in Africa
and on this continent. One of the earliest references to
negro suicide I find, is in the history of a negro settlement in Brazil, sometime in the seventeenth century.
At the time of the Dutch invasion, some negro slaves
escaping from Pernambuco settled in the forest of Pal-

[1] "Suicide," page 133.

mairas, in the province of Alagoas. Their number soon increased to several thousands and for more than sixty years they maintained their independence, repulsing first the attacks of the Dutch and afterwards those of the Portuguese, and were not subdued till 1679, by an army from S. Paulo. When defeat was certain, several negro chiefs leaped from a high rock to death, which they preferred to slavery.[1] An almost identical case is cited by Bryan Edwards in his history of the West Indies,[2] where some of the Maroons, when defeat was inevitable before the advancing forces of the British, hurled themselves over the precipices and were dashed to pieces on the rocks below.

Epidemics of suicide among negro slaves have been cited by H. W. Bates in his work on "Central America, the West Indies and South America," (London, 1878). The cause of these was a simple resolution on the part of the slaves to die *en masse*, and was not due to any ill treatment on the part of their masters.[3] These epidemics may have been due to a belief that after death they were to be restored to their native land and enjoy their friends' society in a future state.[4] In a report on "The Medical and Miscellaneous Observations Relating to the West India Islands," Dr. John Williams, in 1817, refers to this interesting phase of the subject as follows: "The ill-disposed toward their masters will sometimes be guilty of suicide; or by resolute determination resort to dirt eating and

[1] "Hand Book of Brazil," page 10.

[2] Bryan Edwards, "History of the British Colonies in the West Indies," London, 1801, Vol. I.

[3] O'Dea, "Suicide," page 197.

[4] "They [the negro slaves on the Central American plantations] will form a general resolution to poison themselves all round and will carry it out with the greatest stoicism, and this without being necessarily driven to it by ill treatment." W. H. Bates, quoted by O'Dea, "Suicide," p. 197.

thus produce disease and at length death. It is often necessary to check this spirit, and as negroes imagine that if decapitation be inflicted after death the transition to their native country cannot follow, a humane principle leads the proprietor to have the head of such a negro placed in some prominent situation and such has been found a salutary mode of deterring the rest from conduct so destructive."[1]

The method here applied to check the tendency to suicide is very much the same as that in the case of the Milesian virgins. That dirt eating was resorted to by resolute determination to suicide is very doubtful, however, for clay eating is not infrequent even at the present time and can hardly be connected with a tendency to suicide. If the habit can be called a disease, and it probably is, it is met with among negroes under all conditions. Thus the liberated slaves cared for at the colonial hospital at Sierra Leone were " frequently attacked with *mal d'estomac* or dirt eating."[2] According to Dr. Robert Clark it was induced by nostalgia.[3] According to Cartwright,[4] dirt eating was not uncommon among slaves and was largely due to a depressed mental condition induced by superstitious fears of having been poisoned or

---

[1] DeBow, "South and West," Vol. I, pp. 92-93.

[2] *Journal Royal Statistical Society*, 1856, p. 61.

[3] The prevalence of and mortality from nostalgia among the white and colored soldiers during the war was as follows :

	Cases.	Deaths.	Deaths per 1,000 cases.
White troops	5,213	58	11.6
Colored troops . . .	334	16	49 9

Among the freed people under the care of the Freedmen's Bureau there were 108 cases of nostalgia among the colored and 6 cases among the white refugees, a rate of 2.5 per 1,000 for the former and 2.8 for the latter. While therefore the disease was about equally prevalent, it was much more fatal among the colored soldiers during the war.

[4] DeBow, "South and West," Vol. II, p. 321.

conjured. According to Ribot,[1] dirt eating presents a curious instance of morbid heredity, and according to Humboldt, it is met with in all tropical countries. In Alabama at the present time (Winston Co.) several hundred white families are addicted to this habit and as a cause or effect they are extremely superstitious. Thus it is extremely doubtful whether dirt eating has a direct relation to suicide, unless it creates a morbid state of mind favorable to the act.

In Hayti we have record of the suicide of Christophe and others who preferred death to imprisonment or a worse fate at the hands of their enemies. B. S. Hunt, in his pamphlet on "Hayti and the Mulatto," writes that "suicide, *formerly so common* amongst the slaves is now almost unknown in Hayti. Since 1842 [this was written in 1860] only three instances of it in which Haytians were the subjects, have come to my notice. One, an officer disgraced, hanged himself; a retired citizen, insane, cut his throat; a merchant embarrassed in his affairs took poison. All were men of education and light color."[2] I could give many other instances of this order, but will conclude with a reference to the case cited by Burmeister, of the negro slave who, after building a house for his master, was refused his freedom and in a fit of despondency put an end to his life.[3] Darwin quotes Reade to the effect that even among the negroes on the west coast of Africa suicide was common.[4]

It is therefore plain from the facts before us that suicide was more or less frequent among the negro population under various conditions and as the result of a variety of causes. In no wise does the negro show a

[1] Heredity," p. 88.
[2] Pages 18–19.
[3] Essay on the negro of Brazil, page 15 ; *Evening Post* reprint, 1856.
[4] "Descent of Man," Ch. IV.

special race characteristic. The cases cited could be duplicated by those of other races.[1] Nowhere is there shown a specific tendency towards self destruction. Only under exceptional conditions, such as have at all times induced people to end their own existence, do we find the negro giving way in a moment of despair.[2]

For Charleston, S. C., the record for the period 1822–48 shows that only nine colored persons killed themselves during the twenty-eight years, while 40 whites took their own lives. During the 6 years 1889–94 there were three suicides among the colored and twelve among the whites. This is at the rate of one suicide to every two years, a number too small to have any definite relation to the population in general. For Philadelphia I have the records for 1866–94 which fail to indicate any decided tendency towards an increase in negro suicides.[3]

[1] See article on " Suicide among Primitive Peoples " in the *American Anthropologist*, 1894.

[2] From such statistics as have come to my notice, suicide would appear nearly twice as frequent among the American Indians as among the colored population. The following are the number of suicides as reported to the Commissioner of Indian affairs :

Year.	No. of Suicides.	Year.	No of Suicides.
1882	13	1889	12
1883	6	1890	11
1884	2	1891	14
1885	3	1892	13
1886	6	1893	12
1887	*	1894	14
1888	*	1895	16

* Not reported.

On an estimated population of 250,000 the above figures would give an average rate per million of 52.6 for the seven years 1889-95 in contrast with an average rate of 28.1 for the colored population of eight representative southern cities, during the period 1890-94.

[3] During the war there were only nine colored suicides in the army and during the twenty years since the war (1870-90) only seven. Among the 400,000 patients of the Freedmen's Bureau only three committed suicide, although 1171 were treated for madness.

SUICIDES AMONG THE COLORED POPULATION OF PHILADELPHIA, 1866–1894.[1]

Year.	No. of cases.	Year.	No. of cases.	Year.	No. of cases.	Year.	No. of cases.
1866	None	1873	None	1880	None	1887	2
1867	None	1874	None	1881	None	1888	None
1868	None	1875	None	1882	None	1889	1
1869	1	1876	None	1883	None	1890	3
1870	1	1877	None	1884	None	1891	1
1871	1	1878	None	1885	None	1892	1
1872	1	1879	None	1886	None	1893	2
						1894	2

1864–96.—Sixteen during twenty-nine years.

[1] Annual report Philadelphia Board of Health, 1894, pages 333–334.

According to Dr. Billings the rate for Philadelphia per 100,000 of population over 15 years of age was 3.20 for the colored population, while the rate for the whites was 12.99, and that of the foreign population, 23.57. But if this rate had been calculated on 1891 the relation would have been entirely reversed. Instead of three we had only one colored suicide, and instead of 77 whites there were 107. Hence the futility of reasoning from rates based on too small a number of cases, and the need of taking account rather of the actual numbers. The table which follows shows the actual number of colored suicides for the period 1876–94, with the records for a few years wanting. The table is for the four cities, Washington, Baltimore, New Orleans and Richmond, all representative cities of the South.

SUICIDES AMONG THE COLORED POPULATION OF SOUTHERN CITIES.

	Washington.	Baltimore.	New Orleans.	Richmond.
1876	–	–	†	†
1877	–	–	1	–
1878	–	–	1	†
1879	–	–	1	–
1880	2	–	1	–
1881	–	–	1	†
1882	2	–	1	1
1883	2	–	5	–
1884	1	1	5	–

† No record.

	Washington.	Baltimore.	New Orleans.	Richmond.
1885	–	–	4	†
1886	3	1	4	1
1887	3	2	–	1
1888	–	1	4	†
1889	1	–	3	1
1890	1	–	2	–
1891	3	2	2	–
1892	2	†	3	–
1893	1	†	6	–
1894	4	†	4	2

† No record.

This table does not show that there is any decided tendency towards an increase in the number of suicides. In fact it shows that in proportion to the population there has rather been a decrease. But I would not argue on the basis of the population, for such basis can only be applied when there is an actual relation between the general population and a certain series of observed facts. With the possible exception of New Orleans there is no regularity in the number of cases of colored suicides, and hence, I doubt whether there is any influence in the physical, mental or moral life of the colored people tending to increase the number of suicides. In New York city, where the conditions of life are probably most unfavorable for the negro, only 12 cases of suicide occurred among the colored during the six years 1885–90, an average of about two cases per annum. In Brooklyn during the same period only three occurred, while in Boston only one case was recorded during that period.[1]

The negro commits suicide, as a rule, only in a fit of passion, during loss of self control, or as in most cases, to

[1] During the census year ending May 31, 1890, there were reported 3816 white suicides and 116 colored. In proportion to the population this would give a rate of 69.5 per million for the whites and 15.5 per million for the colored. Hence the white rate is shown to be 348.4 per cent. in excess of the colored rate. We may compare

escape the consequences of his crimes. I have been able during a number of years to collect the facts concerning 18 suicides among colored people and the following is an analysis of the motives that prompted them.

Out of the 18 one was a woman who ended her life at the age of 32 because her husband proved her guilty of adultery with a white man. Another woman killed herself because the man she wanted to marry already had a wife. Of the 16 males, 9 were guilty of crime at the time of their death. Eight had killed either wife or mistress or the wife of some other man before ending their own lives. In one case a man was accused of theft by a railroad company and rather

this calculation, based, as it must be admitted, on incomplete returns, with the statistics for eight representative southern cities for the period 1890–94.

MORTALITY FROM SUICIDE IN EIGHT SOUTHERN CITIES DURING THE FIVE YEARS 1890–1894.[1]
(Per million of population.)

	White.	Colored.
Savannah, Ga.	344.8	16.1
New Orleans, La.	195.1	51.4
Nashville, Tenn.	194.0	36.8
Washington, D. C.	180.2	26.9
Memphis, Tenn.	176.0	24.3
Atlanta, Ga.	104.7	12.7
Charleston, S. C.	91.1	18.8
Richmond, Va.	57.4	11.9
Eight cities	171.3	28.1

[1] Mean population of eight cities 1890–94, White, 573,173
Colored, 335,008
Total number of suicides 1890–94, . . . White, 491
Colored, 47

According to this table, which is as accurate as present registration methods can make it, the white suicide rate was 171.3 per million against a colored rate of only 28.1. There would therefore seem to be no decided tendency on the part of the negro population to commit suicide under the influences of city life, but rather under any exceptionally abnormal condition, not necessarily connected with the struggle for life in the cities.

than stand trial shot himself. Two negroes, one in
New York and the other in Chicago, killed themselves
to escape arrest. Two were apparently insane when
they committed the act, one from the effects of la
grippe, and the other (a teacher) from causes not
ascertained. Another case was that of a man in Alabama, who had once been a prosperous farmer; but bad
crops had ruined him and rather than give up his
mortgaged horses he deliberately drove them over a
bluff, killing the horses and himself. One, a jockey,
killed himself because the woman with whom he was
living in adultery deserted him. The last case was that
of a young colored man who attempted suicide 'because
his mistress had treated him shabbily.'[1] In all of the
instances cited, the underlying motive appears to have
been criminal or ani-social. In none of the cases can
we trace any of the more subtle motives which only too
often prompt the unsuccessful or weak of more cultured
and advanced races.

From the facts given there does not appear to be any
decided tendency toward an increase in the suicide rate;
and this agrees with the facts brought out regarding the
prevalence of alcoholism and insanity. Mr. Bruce in

[1] It may be of interest to give the following facts in regard to the
methods employed in the commission of suicide. The data have
been compiled from the census of 1890 and show the actual numbers
as well as the per cent. of each group in the total for all suicides.

Method.	Whites. Cases.	Per cent.	Colored. Cases.	Per cent.
Shooting	1,035	27.1	31	26.7
Drowning	217	5.7	7	6.0
Poison	829	21.7	29	25.0
Other method	1,735	45.5	49	42.3
Total	3,816	100.00	116	100.00

According to this table there would seem to be no distinct trait in
regard to the means selected, but rather a close similarity to those
made use of by the white population.

his work on the "Plantation Negro as a Freeman," remarks : "As a corollary of their comparative immunity
from insanity for moral reasons, it is found that the
blacks rarely commit suicide, a fact easy of explanation
when a full knowledge of the character of the race has
been obtained. In the first place no cause of anxiety
presses long enough upon the mind of the individual
negro to foster a desire to put an end to life . . . .
then, too, he lacks the coolness and fortitude to destroy
himself : above all he has a peculiar horror of death,
owing to his morbid imagination and not improbably
to his tendency to live wholly in the present."

Suicide, according to Morselli "preponderates in those
states which are most advanced in civilization and above
all in intellectual development. . . . The inferior
races, just because they withhold themselves from the influences of civil progress do not acquire any increased tendency, even amid contact with Europeans, or at least
only by slow degrees and in proportion as they adopt
our civilization." [1]

Now it is true that suicide is most frequent in those
states where intellectual culture has advanced most, but
it is not true that it is intellectual culture which has
caused the increase, but rather the want of it or the mal-
adjustment of the individual to the conditions of life.
As Morselli has said elsewhere, "all transition is painful" and the lesson of life which so few will accept, is
that during individual as well as social evolution we
must have patience and do our duty in whatever manner
it is placed before us. The individual who attempts by
some means or others to overcome by force the obstacles
that hinder him from reaching the level of others will
often, in despair, end his own life, but more often be-

[1] "Suicide," page 118.

cause he violated the common law and lacks courage to face the result.

"It may confidentially be assumed," writes Mr. Humphreys, "that the most important branch of vital statistics is that which deals with deaths and rates of mortality. This is not only the most complex branch of the subject, deserving the most careful study, but the influence of health on the human race is so powerful for good or evil that statistics of deaths, and rates of mortality acquire their greatest value for their acceptation as trustworthy indications of public health." That this conclusion is fully warranted, has, I trust, been proven by the preceding pages, which so far as I know, represent a summary of the most important and reliable data pertaining to the comparative mortality of the two races.

As to the value of the conclusions arrived at, or rather as to the results brought out by the comparative mortality rates, I accept the statistical method as the most useful and reliable which has yet been devised for reaching conclusions more definite and scientific than individual observation or opinions. By the statistical method we have before us a picture of the condition, past and present, of the whole race, and by the comparative method we can obtain information which will present with much accuracy the probable tendencies of one race in comparison with another.

In regard to the statistics of mortality for American cities, it cannot be denied that to a limited degree they fall short of a representation of the actual facts. But, in the words of Mr. Milme, "it may reasonably be presumed that the returned numbers are always in the same ratio to the true, and this is all that is necessary to the truth of the inferences drawn . . . . for it is not absolute numbers, but their relative proportions only that are essential to the calculations.[1]" On the assumption, therefore, that the statistics of mortality represent fairly the actual differences between the viability of the two races, the following conclusions seem warranted:

First. The excess of births over deaths is greater for the white race than for the colored in the southern states.

Second. In the northern states the colored race does not hold its own, for the deaths outnumber the births. The apparent increase in the population is due exclusively to migration.

Third. For ten representative southern cities the mean death rate for five years (1890–94) was 20.12 per 1,000 for the white race, and 32.61 for the colored. The excess of mortality represents a loss of 16,046 lives on the basis of the rate of mortality for the whites during the five years, of 3,209 per annum, in the ten cities. On the basis of Farr's normal death rate of 17 per 1,000, the loss in lives was 35,457 during the five years. On whatever basis we may estimate the value of a life, the economic loss alone must be enormous.

Fourth. The excess of negro mortality is greatest at the age period under fifteen and least at the higher ages. This is largely the result of an excessive mortality of infants and children under five.

Fifth. The number surviving to productive and reproductive ages is in consequence of this excessive infant mortality considerably less for the colored than for the whites, and by just so much their comparative social and economic efficiency is diminished.

Sixth. The expectation of life at birth is from 12.5 to 17.11 years less for the colored than for the white·

[1] "Value of Annuities and Assurance," Vol. II.

population in four cities for which life tables
culated at the census of 1880.

Seventh. The effect of altitude and density of population on mortality is about the same for both races and
the differences in mortality of the two races remain practically the same. The effect of the conditions of life
is, therefore, comparatively unimportant, while to the
effect of race and heredity are largely due the existing
differences in the mortality of the two races.

Eighth. The mortality of the colored race is on the
increase, in contrast with a diminishing death rate for
the white race. This increase in the negro death rate
appears entirely in the period which has elapsed since
emancipation.

Ninth. The colored race is subject to a higher death
rate than the whites from the following diseases :

(1). All diseases of infants, including premature and
still births.

(2). Consumption, at all ages, but most especially for
the age group 15–45. The mortality from this disease
before the war was less for the colored than for the
whites. The present tendency is towards a still higher
death rate among the colored, in contrast with a steady
decrease of the rate among the whites.

(3). Pneumonia, the mortality being greatest at the
early ages. This disease is also on the increase.

(4). Scrofula and venereal diseases. These are much
more prevalent among the colored, and are on the increase.

(5). Malarial fevers, contrary to general opinion, are
more prevalent among the colored population, with a
decided tendency towards an increase.

(6) Typhoid fever is more prevalent at the ages be-

low 45, and less prevalent at the ages above 45. The tendency is towards an increase.

Tenth. The facts for the other diseases may be summarized as follows:

Yellow fever, contrary to general opinion, occasionally prevails among the colored race, though with less severity than among the white race. There is a decided tendency toward an increase in the susceptibility to this disease among the colored population.

Smallpox is more prevalent among the colored, but this is due almost entirely to an unprotected condition. When vaccination is properly attended to the mortality is easily reduced, and there is a decided tendency towards a decrease through this means.

Measles, scarlet fever, and diptheria are as a rule less prevalent among the colored population, and there are no positive indications of an increase. The opinion held by some, that the negro is not liable to scarlet fever, is disproved.

Deaths from childbirth and puerperal fever are more frequent among the colored, but the diseases are subject to control. The high mortality is entirely the result of ignorance and want of proper medical attendance.

Tumor and cancer are less prevalent among the colored, but on the increase among the population below the age of 45. Carcinoma uteri, from which some writers have supposed the negro exempt, is prevalent, though to a less extent, among the colored population.

Appendicitis, another disease to which it was supposed the negro was not liable, is prevalent, though apparently to a less extent than among the whites.

Alcoholism is less prevalent than among the whites and there is no positive proof of a tendency towards an increase.

Insanity is also less prevalent with no positive proof of a tendency towards an increase.

Suicides are rare with no positive indications of an increase of the number.

The general conclusion is that the negro is subject to a higher mortality at all ages, but especially so at the early age periods. This is largely the result of an inordinate mortality from constitutional and respiratory diseases. Moreover, the mortality from these diseases is on the increase among the colored, and on the decrease among the whites. In consequence, the natural increase in the colored population will be less from decade to decade and in the end a decrease must take place. It is sufficient to know that in the struggle for race supremacy the black race is not holding its own ; and this fact once recognized, all danger from a possible numerical supremacy of the race vanishes. Its extreme liability to consumption alone would suffice to seal its fate as a race. That alone would suffice to make impossible numerical supremacy in the southern states. " Sufferers from phthisis," writes Mr. Haycraft,[1] "are prone to other diseases such as pulmonary and bronchial attacks, so that over and above the vulnerability to the one form of microbe, they are to be looked upon as unsuited not only for the battle of life but especially for parentage and for the multiplications of the conditions for which they themselves suffer."

[1] Haycraft, "Darwinism and Race progress."

CHAPTER III.

ANTHROPOMETRY.

In the following pages I shall discuss as fully as the limited material will permit, the anthropometric characteristics of the colored race as compared with the whites. In view of the preceding discussion I shall confine myself almost entirely to data having a direct bearing on the longevity of the two races and consequent social and economic efficiency. The most essential characteristics falling under this restricted class of facts are, weight, play of chest, lung capacity and frequency of respiration.

The close relation of weight to longevity is a fact sufficiently established to need little further explanation. The uniform result of statistical investigations of life insurance companies has been to prove that persons under average weight have a decided tendency towards pulmonary diseases. The elaborate investigations of the medical departments of the New York Mutual Life in 1874,[1] the Washington Life in 1886,[2] the Prudential Insurance Company of America[3] in 1895, and the New York Mutual Life in 1895,[4] prove conclusively that low weight in proportion to age and stature is a determining factor in the susceptibility of an individual to consumption. It is therefore of importance to ascertain whether the colored man, subject to such an inordinate mortality from pulmonary and respiratory diseases, is on the average of lesser weight in proportion to stature than the

[1] "Mortuary experience of the Mutual Life Insurance Co.," New York, 1877 ; Vol. II., page 44, *et seq.*

[2] "Experience of the Washington Life Insurance Co.," New York, 1889, page 148, *et seq.*

[3] Statistics of Consumption, by Edward Hamill, M.D., "Transactions of the Association of Life Insurance Medical Directors," 1889–95, page 95, *et seq.*

[4] "Statistics of Consumption, Mutual Life Insurance Co.," New York, 1895, page 12, *et seq.*

white. I may anticipate the data which follow by saying that he is not; but on the contrary he is on the
average of greater weight in proportion to age and
height than the white.

The most elaborate collection of facts bearing on this
point is in the statistics of the Sanitary Commission[1] and
of the Provost–Marshal General.[2] The former work
deals with recruits at the time of application for
enlistment, while the latter deals with the soldier in the
field. I give below the mean weight of white and colored soldiers according to age and stature. The instances cited will suffice to bring out the fact that the
colored males almost without exception weigh more than
the whites.

MEAN WEIGHT OF WHITE AND COLORED SOLDIERS ACCORDING TO
AGE AND STATURE.[1]

Stature.[2] Inches.	Age 20. White. Lbs.	Colored. Lbs.	Age 25. White. Lbs.	Colored. Lbs.
64.5	130.4	138.8	128.8	136.7
65.5	133.8	137.9	137.7	142.5
66.5	138.5	141.7	142.7	147.1
67.5	142.8	145.0	146 2	152 5
68.5	147.3	150.9	149.8	156.9
69.5	147.4	156.0	157.6	152 5
70.5	154.7	144.8	161.8	166.4
	Age 30.		Age 35.	
64 5	135.0	143.5	131 5	143.6
65.5	136.4	142.6	140.6	137.7
66.5	147.0	142 0	147.0	146.4
67.5	148.2	150.8	149 3	170.0
68.5	152.7	153.9	151.9	148.1
69.5	159.0	160.4	145.4	161.8
70.5	156.5	154.9	157.2	.

[1] Gould, "Military Statistics," pp. 426-433.
[2] For colored soldiers the mean statures are 64.25, 65.25, 66.25, 67.25, 68.25, 69.25 and 70.25 inches.

[1] "Investigations in the Military and Anthropological Statistics of American Soldiers." By Benjamin Apthorp Gould, Actuary to the Sanitary Commission. Cambridge, 1869.
[2] "Statistics, Medical and Anthropological, of the Provost–Marshal General's Bureau," vol. 2. By T. H. Baxter, A.M., M.D., (Washington, 1875).

According to this table the colored males weigh more at all ages and for any stature than the whites. The very few exceptions are of no importance, since the variations from the normal are due to the smaller number of observations for these ages. The above result may be differently presented in a comparative table of weight and stature, in which the element of age is not taken into account. I give below a theoretical table showing the average weights of white and colored soldiers, their stature varying from 60 to 72 inches. The table, abstracted from the work of Mr. Gould, was calculated from actual measurements.

THEORETICAL WEIGHT FOR DIFFERENT STATURES.[1]

Stature, Inches.	Whites, Lbs.	Blacks, Lbs.
60	113 6	118.7
61	117.4	122.7
62	121.3	126.7
63	125.3	130.8
64	129.3	135.0
65	133 3	139.3
66	137.5	143.6
67	141.7	148.0
68	145.9	152.4
69	150.3	156 9
70	154.7	161.5
71	159.1	166.2
72	163.6	170.9

[1] Gould, "Military Statistics," pp. 409 and 417.

This valuable table fully confirms the preceding one and clearly establishes the fact that colored adult males weigh more than white males of the same class. By still another method we may compare the average weights with regard to circumference of the chest; and here again the result is decidedly in favor of the colored race.

MEAN WEIGHT OF WHITE AND COLORED SOLDIERS ACCORDING TO
CIRCUMFERENCE OF CHEST.[1]

Circumference of Chest. Inches.	White Soldiers. Lbs.	Negro Soldiers. Lbs.
32.	118.93	129.05
32.5	123 31	131.02
33.	126.25	133.76
33.5	128.12	135 58
34.	132.03	139 07
34.5	134.18	143.25
35.	137.93	146.21
35.5	140.69	147.84
36.	143.33	150 68
36.5	147.18	152.71
37.	150.01	154.43
37.5	152.04	160 59
38.	156.27	161.94
38.5	158.78	166.79
39.	161.24	174.00
39.5	163.76	166 55
40.	168.30	168.51

[1] Gould, "Military Statistics," pp. 454 and 456,

The excess of weight for the colored soldier is therefore proven, and it remains to be shown whether this favorable condition has been persisted in to the present time.

The data for an investigation of the comparative weight in proportion to age, stature and circumference of the chest, are very limited, and one might hesitate to make use of the published facts did they not so fully confirm one another as to leave no doubt of their accuracy. For the United States Army recent anthropometric statistics have been made public for the three years 1893, '94 and '95. Limited as is the number of observations, and few as are the points covered, they are nevertheless of considerable value.

AVERAGE HEIGHT AND WEIGHT OF ACCEPTED RECRUITS, U. S. A.,
1892–94.[1]

Year.	Height, (inches.)		Weight, (lbs.)	
	White.	Colored.	White.	Colored.
1892	67 42	67.26	145.07	148.08
1893	67.47	67.14	144.10	148.25
1894	67.39	67.21	145.65	149.19

[1] Compiled from the annual reports of the Surgeon General, U. S. A., 1893-4-5.

The above table shows that while the average stature of colored recruits was slightly less than that of the whites, the average weight was invariably greater. This is true for all ages irrespective of stature, as was shown in the tables of Mr. Gould. I have calculated from the data before me the proportionate weight to stature for different groups, that is the number of pounds to an inch of stature. By this method the effect of the smaller stature of the colored soldiers is eliminated.

PROPORTION OF WEIGHT TO HEIGHT ACCORDING TO AGE GROUPS,
RECRUITS IN U. S. ARMY, 1892–94.[1]

Age.	White. Lbs. to an inch in Stature.	Colored. Lbs, to an inch in Stature.
Under 20	2.03	2.06
20–24	2.02	2.17
25–29	2.17	2.21
30–34	2.21	2.26
35–39	2.24	2.33
40- 49	2.27	2.27
50 and over	2.26	2.32
All ages	2.15	2.21

[1] Compiled from the annual reports of the Surgeon-General, U. S. A., 1893-4-5.

This table reads that at the age group 20 to 25, for example, the average weight of a white soldier to every inch of stature was 2.12 pounds, as compared with 2.17 pounds for the colored soldier. The difference is small, but it is important to know that the difference exists. According to life insurance experience " even a moderate variation from the standard of weight is of considerable influence in diminishing or increasing the mortality from consumption." In the experience of the New York Mutual Life Insurance Company, it was pointed out that nearly 80 per cent. of those who died of consumption were below the standard weight. In the experience of the Washington Life Insurance Company it was shown that 'for light weight, coupled with a predisposition to consumption, the rate of mortality from consumption was greatest.' The latest investigation of this point by the Mutual Life Company, of New York, fully confirms this view. On the strength of these investigations, fully establishing the rule that "even a slight excess of weight is almost sufficient to annul a consumptive tendency," it is remarkable that we should find in the colored race an excess of weight coupled with an inordinate mortality from consumption.

It cannot be argued that army recruits, who differ materially from the general male population from which they are drawn, on account of the element of favorable selection, represent an exceptional condition in this respect; for it was ascertained by Mr. McCauley that of the insurance applicants from the West Indies the average weight for the negro applicants was greater than that of the whites, and my own data of fifty measurements of adult colored males support the figures of Mr. McCauley.[1] According to the latter the average weight of the white applicants of 5 ft., 8 in. in height was 153.2 pounds, while the negro applicants of the same average stature weighed 154 pounds. The difference is very small, but as I have pointed out before, it is of value to know that there is any difference at all. The mulatto applicants weighed less than the whites, only 149

[1] *Publications of the American Statistical Association*, June, 1891, p. 292.

pounds. According to Gould the mulattoes weighed on the average as much as, if not more than, the pure negroes.

The table below will show the average weight among fifty colored males, according to girth of chest. For purposes of comparison I add the average weight of white males. The measurements were taken by a physician of exceptional experience and may be accepted as accurate. The numbers are sufficiently large for the purpose of showing that under various conditions there exists a difference in weight between negroes and whites having the same physical proportions.

COMPARATIVE WEIGHT OF NEGRO AND WHITE ADULT MALES ACCORDING TO GIRTH OF CHEST.[1]

Girth of Chest.	Weight, lbs.	
Inches.	Colored.	White.
32.5	121	133
33.	123	136
33.5	145	139
34.	150	141
34.5	155	143
35.	147	145
35.5	154	152
36.5	168	164
37.	176	155
38.	170	167
38 5	175	168
39.5	180	176
40.5	207	188
41.	190	201
44.5	240	230
45.	230	226

[1] Measurements collected by the writer. Colored men examined all lived in New Jersey.

This table is not comparable with the table of Mr. Gould in that the individuals included were weighed in ordinary indoor clothing while the soldiers are weighed either naked or under different conditions than life insurance applicants. But the result is the same as shown in Mr. Gould's table.

I have obtained, through the kindness of Dr. Hamilton D. Wey, of the Elmira Reformatory, the comparative measurements of 12 white and 12 colored juvenile delinquents. According to the measurements furnished me the average weight of the white inmates measured was 127.2 lbs. against 136.6 lbs. for the colored. The average age of the whites was 20.4, while that of the colored inmates was 21.3 years. The average stature of the whites was 64.8 inches in contrast to an average of 65.6 inches for the colored. This excess of height for the colored is exceptional, since as a rule the colored fall below the white in the average height according to age or weight.[1]

I must add to this collection of facts bearing on stature and weight, a table for children compiled by the superintendent of schools of Kansas City, Mo., who deserves the thanks of investigators for his interest in this subject. The table is for the year 1890 and shows for boys and girls the average height, weight and pounds to an inch in stature, for the ages from 10 to 17.

HEIGHT AND WEIGHT OF KANSAS CITY SCHOOL CHILDREN.—1890.[1]
(10 to 17 years of age.)

	Height. Girls.		Weight. Girls.		Relation of Weight to Stature. Lbs. to In. in Stature.	
	White.	Colored.	White.	Colored.	White.	Colored.
Age.	Inches.	Inches.	Lbs.	Lbs.	Lbs.	Lbs.
10 . .	51.7	49.8	65.9	74.6	1.27	1.50
11 . .	52.7	52.8	66.2	79.9	1.26	1.84
12 . .	54.0	54.0	80.6	82.8	1.49	1 53
13 . .	57.4	56.9	91.7	97.2	1.60	1.71
14 . .	60.3	58.8	100.0	103.8	1.65	1.77
15 . .	62.0	61.5	109.4	110.1	1.76	1.79
16 . .	62.5	62.8	111.2	117.0	1.78	1.86
17 . .	62.9	66.0	117.1	128.0	1.86	1.94

[1] Annual report of the Superintendent of Kansas City schools for 1890–91. The tables in full for 1886 and 1890 are reprinted in the bulletin of the Tennessee state board of health, March, 1892.

[1] The excess in stature may be due to the greater average age of the colored inmates, which exceeds that of the whites by nearly one year.

	Height. Boys.		Weight. Boys.		Relation of Weight to Stature. Lbs. to In. in Stature.	
	White.	Colored.	White.	Colored.	White.	Colored.
Age.	Inches.	Inches.	Lbs.	Lbs.	Lbs.	Lbs.
10 . .	52.0	51.0	67.5	72.7	1.30	1.43
11 . .	53.0	53.4	70.9	78.3	1.34	1.47
12 . .	56.0	53.7	78.3	83.0	1.40	1.55
13 . .	56 6	56.0	87.5	89.0	1.55	1.59
14 . .	58.6	58.9	93.5	93.6	1.60	1.59
15 . .	62.4	61.0	111.3	112.0	1.77	1.84
16 . .	63 9	64.4	119.0	121.0	1.86	1.88
17 . .	64.8	65.0	126.6	130.0	1.94	2.00

The tables confirm the others that have thus far been introduced and show that even for the young generation a distinct physical peculiarity of the colored race has remained the same. We have here for the colored children, both boys and girls, a smaller stature and greater weight than for the whites. The table is further confirmed by a similar investigation made by the same teacher in 1886. It is to be hoped that in the future teachers will follow this example, and collect anthropometric data which will be of value to the student of the subject as well as to themselves.

The results from these tables are at variance with the accepted rule that a high mortality from consumption attends a low average weight as proportioned to stature. The negro, therefore, in this respect presents entirely different characteristics from the white race. I am not aware that this exception to a general rule has heretofore been discussed. Yet the result was not wholly contrary to my expectations. It is a fact already referred to by Dr. Hunt,[1] that the negro is a hearty eater; that, well-fed, he is capable of enduring hardships of military service even better than the white, but ill-nourished, he soon falls a victim to melancholy and despair. Yet it is

[1] " The Negro as a Soldier," *Anthropological Review*, 1869, p. 43.

the quantity with him, not quality, and the amount of flesh put on may be of less firmness and more subject to degenerative processes than that of the white race.

However, this would not explain the variation from the rule of lesser susceptibility to consumption as an increase of weight is met with. It only proves that a physiological law may hold good for one race and not for another. Thus, for instance, the Bengalese are of very low weight, so much so that the normal increase in weight with advancing stature is only 3.33 pounds to the inch, in contrast with an average of 4.17 pounds for the white soldiers and 4.35 pounds for the colored during our civil war. Yet we are informed by Surgeon-Captain W. J. Buchanan, of Bhagalpur, India, that "if a man in India reaches this standard, he will be able to perform the severest form of hard labor." A similar difference is met with among the Jews of East London, who with the distinct physiological characteristic of lighter weight than the English, show a much lower mortality, not only from all causes, but from consumption in particular.[1]

Another fact which is brought out by these tables, is that on the whole the conditions of life of the colored people must be fairly satisfactory so long as we meet with proof of better nurture among them than among the whites. Thus among the Kansas City school children the contrast is marked, and the excess of weight clearly proven. At the same time the condition of life of the colored population of Kansas City seem, on the whole, to their disadvantage when measured by the standard of life of the white race. But is it an actual

[1] The mortality of the Jews in comparison with other races has been fully discussed by the writer in the *Spectator*, an insurance journal, for November 7 and 14, 1895. For reprint of the principal tables see *Public Health* for June, 1896.

disadvantage or only an apparent one? The negro mortality of Kansas City is far in excess of that of the whites;[1] yet from the standpoint of the ratio of height and weight the school children, at least, present a better physical type than do the children of the whites.

The effect of weight as a determining factor in the duration of life, and especially as a predisposing cause to consumption, in cases where the individual falls below the average standard, is of less influence on the colored race than it is on the white, and we must seek for other physiological traits in explanation of the excessive mortality of the colored race.

In the second chapter of this work I quoted from Dr. Hunt: "A careful series of weights of normal lungs to contrast with weight of an equal number of whites is a great desideratum. It should be reinforced by measurements of the volume and expansion of the living thorax."[2] On the first point I have knowledge of only one series of measurements, made by Dr. Russel, who in a report to the Sanitary Commission, states that the average weight of the lung of the negro is four ounces less than that of the white.[3] I do not know the number of observations on which this conclusion was founded, but it is probable that a sufficient number of cases were investigated by Dr. Russel before publishing his conclusion. The result confirms the view of Dr. Hunt that "the negro has a small or tropical lung." It remains for me to show how far this view is supported by measurements of the living thorax and the actual capacity of the

[1] Approximate mortality, 1894: whites, 11.5 per 1,000; colored, 20.4 per 1,000.

[2] *Journal, Anthropological Society*, vol. 7, 1869.

[3] "Sanitary Memoirs of the War of the Rebellion," page 333; contributions relating to the causes and prevention of diseases, edited by Austin Flint, M.D., New York, 1867.

lungs. The data on this important point are fairly complete and of greater determining value than those of weight and stature. The following three tables are abstracted from the report of the Provost-Marshal General, and show the relation of girth of chest to increasing stature, weight and age. The last two tables also show the chest mobility, that is, the difference between forced inspiration and forced expiration. The results of the first table are based on measurements of 25,828 colored soldiers, while those of the two following tables deal only with 377 measurements. For the white troops the number of cases in all tables is, of course, much larger.

RELATION OF GIRTH OF CHEST AT EXPIRATION TO INCREASING HEIGHT IN MEN, 18 TO 45 YEARS OF AGE.[1]

Stature.	Native White Troops (315,620.) Girth of Chest. Inches.	Native Colored Troops (25,828.) Girth of Chest. Inches.
Under 61 inches	30.84	31.25
61–63	31.13	31.68
63–65	31.98	32.84
65–67	32.92	33.65
67–69	33.65	34.34
69–71	34.23	34.77
71–73	34.72	35.15
73 and over . . .	35.16	35.56
Mean	33.42	33.69

[1] Report of the Provost-Marshal General of the Army, Vol. I, p. 33.

RELATION OF HEIGHT, GIRTH OF CHEST AND MOBILITY OF CHEST TO INCREASING WEIGHT IN MEN, 18 TO 45 YEARS OF AGE.[1]

Weight.	Native Whites (6359).			Colored (377 men).		
	Height. Inches.	Girth. Inches.	Mobility of Chest. Inches.	Height. Inches.	Girth. Inches.	Mobility of Chest. Inches.
Under 100 lbs.. .	64.00	29.71	3.07	. .	. .	. .
100–120 . .	65.19	30.47	3.15	63.79	30.14	3.33
120–140 . .	66.86	31.99	3.24	65.32	32.05	3.21
140–160 . .	68.42	33.64	3.29	67.07	33.47	3.22
160–180 . .	69.92	34.99	3.29	69.19	35.11	3.27
180– . .	70.22	36.55	3.27	69.75	35.25	3.38
Mean . . .	67.30	32.49	3.24	66.39	32.84	3.23

[1] Report of Provost-Marshal General, Vol. I, pp. 39–46.

RELATION OF HEIGHT, GIRTH OF CHEST AND EXPANSION OF CHEST
TO INCREASING AGE IN MEN, 18 TO 45 YEARS OF AGE.

	Native Whites (6359).			Colored (377 men).		
	Height. Inches.	Girth. Inches.	Mobility of Chest. Inches.	Height. Inches.	Girth. Inches.	Mobility of Chest. Inches.
Under 20 years .	66.49	31.32	3.26	65.56	31.64	3.17
20–25 . . .	67.48	32.49	3.25	66.23	32.73	3.28
25–30 . . .	67.54	32.94	3.22	66.97	33.27	3.25
30–35 . . .	67.59	33.14	3.22	66.59	33.29	3.19
35–40 . . .	67.80	33.30	3.26	67.55	33.95	3.18
40– . . .	67.74	33.63	3.18	65.84	33.28	3.34
Mean . . .	67.30	32.49	3.24	66.39	32.84	3.23

It will be observed that almost without exception the
girth of chest (by which is meant the chest at expiration) is greater for the negro than for the white. The
same fact is brought out in the last two tables, which
show the mobility of the chest in addition to girth.
Neither stature, weight nor age exert an influence on
this condition, and the result is almost without exception in favor of the colored soldier. It must be taken
into consideration that the recruits here dealt with present probably a better type than the average colored
male of the same period; nevertheless the difference is
striking. If we compare this table with the one which
follows we shall find that the recruit of the present day
does not present the same favorable characteristics, but
to the contrary invariably falls below the standard of the
white. The table shows also for both periods, the mean
degree of chest mobility for white and colored recruits.

COMPARATIVE CHEST MOBILITY OF U. S. RECRUITS, 1861–65 AND 1892–94.[1]

Age Periods.	U. S. Army. 1861–65. White.	Colored.	Excess in	U. S. Army, 1892–94. White.	Colored.	Excess in
Under 20 .	3.26	3.17	favor of white.	2.82	2.56	favor of white.
20–24 . .	3.25	3.28	" " col'd.	2.86	2.52	" " "
25–29 . .	3 22	3.25	" " "	2.93	2.62	" " "
30–34 . .	3.22	3.19	" " white.	2.96	2.64	" " "
35–39 . .	3.26	3.18	" " "	2.94	2.57	" " "
40–49 . .	3.18	3.34	" " col'd.	2.84	2.52	" " "
All ages	3.24	3.23	" " white.	2.93	2.58	" " "

[1] Compiled from the report of the Provost-Marshal General (Vol. I) and annual
reports of the Surgeon General U. S. A., 1893–94–95.

If the data here presented may be relied upon, they would prove a lower vital power for the negro of the present time than for the negro of about thirty years ago. The table shows that at the present time the negro is invariably inferior in chest expansion to the white. The dearth of data on this point make it difficult, however, to prove whether there is a decided tendency in this direction,—such a tendency we should expect to find in view of the inordinate mortality of the race from pulmonary and respiratory diseases.

It was proven by Gould that the average lung capacity of the negro was considerably less than that of the white. The result of his investigations are abbreviated in the table below which shows the average capacity of the lungs for both races according to stature and circumference of chest. Both methods bring out the same result.

PULMONARY CAPACITY ACCORDING TO STATURE.[1]

Stature. Inches.	White. Cubic Inches.	Negro. Cubic Inches.	Mean Difference in Favor of Whites. Cubic Inches.
60	138.5	130.5	8.0
61	145.0	136.0	9.0
62	151.0	141.0	10.0
63	157.5	146.0	11.5
64	163.5	151.5	12.0
65	170.0	156.5	13.5
66	176.0	162.0	14.0
67	182.5	167.5	15.0
68	188.5	173.5	15.0
69	194.5	179.0	15.5
70	200.5	185.0	15.5
71	206.5	191.0	15.5
72	212.0	197.5	14.5

[1] Gould, "Military Statistics," p. 480.

PULMONARY CAPACITY ACCORDING TO CIRCUMFERENCE OF CHEST.[1]

Girth of Chest, Inches.	White. Cubic Inches.	Colored. Cubic Inches.	Mean Difference.
30	149.5	124.0	25.5
31	156.5	132.5	24.0
32	163.0	141.0	22.0
33	169.5	148.5	21.0
34	175.5	156.0	19.5
35	181.0	163.0	18.0
36	186 5	170.5	16.0
37	192.0	178.0	14.0
38	196.5	185.5	11.0
39	200.5	194.0	6.5
40	204.0	202.0	2.0

[1] Gould, "Military Statistics," p, 493.

The contrast is very marked and suggests the question why there should be a smaller lung capacity in view of the slight difference in chest expansion. The rule was laid down by Dr. Hutchinson that)" the size of the chest and the quantity of air a man can breathe have no direct relation to each other. The circumference of the chest has also no relation to vital capacity; but it has to weight, increasing an inch for every ten pounds."[1]) We must, therefore, consider both series of measurements independent of each other; but the greatest value must be attached to the comparative degree of vital capacity, for, as has been pointed out by the same writer, " by *disease* the vital capacity decreases by from 10 to 70 per cent." The only data which I have been able to obtain with respect to the negro of the present day are those of twelve inmates of the Elmira Reformatory, furnished me by Dr. Hamilton Wey. According to this authority, the average vital capacity of the colored inmates was 180 cubic inches, in contrast with 196 cubic inches for the white inmates. In respect to weight, circumference of waist and strength of chest, the negro was superior to the

[1] *Medico Chirugical Transactions*, xxix, p. 248.

white, but in respect to vital capacity he proved himself decidedly the inferior to the white inmate.

In consequence of this inferiority the following remark of Dr. Wey is justified : " It has been noted here [the New York Reformatory] as in other institutions, that color exercises an influence in disease resistance. Thus, other things being equal, the white opposes the greatest resistance ; next comes the full blooded negro, or the best type of the blooded negro found in this locality ; while the mulatto is most susceptible, as if the inferior elements of two colors combined in him produced a strain ill-calculated to resist disease." [1]   According to Gould the average lung capacity of white soldiers was 184.7 cubic inches, of blacks 163.5, and of mulattos 158.9.[2]   The mean circumference of the chest was 35.8 inches for whites, 35.1 for blacks, and 34.97 for the mixed races.[3]

The inferior vitality of the mixed race is, therefore, sufficiently proven by both methods.   On the hypothesis that lung capacity differs in man according to age, height, weight and disease, the smaller lung capacity of the colored race is in itself proof of an inferior physical organism, and this assertion is proved by the greater mortality of the race as compared with the white.   The effect of disease on lung capacity is clearly brought out in the table below, which shows for white, black and mulatto soldiers the lung capacity in usual vigor, and with vigor impaired.   The table is very interesting and supports those previously introduced, as well as the rule of Hutchinson that there is a direct relation between lung capacity and disease.

[1] Eighteenth Year Book, New York Reformatory, p. 178.
[2] Gould, "Military Statistics," p. 471.
[3] *Ibid*, p. 316.

AVERAGE LUNG CAPACITY OF WHITE AND COLORED SOLDIERS,[1]
1861–1865.

Color.	In Usual Vigor. (Cubic Inches).	With Vigor Impaired. (Cubic Inches).
White soldiers	187.9	166.3
Full blacks	165.3	149.7
Mulattoes	161.6	145.4

[1] Gould, "Military Statistics," p, 471.

Closely related to lung capacity and girth of chest is the respiratory movement of the chest. On this point the only information I know of is in the statistics collected by Gould. They are admitted to be of less value than those pertaining to other bodily measurements, but on the whole they may be accepted as representing fairly the functional differences of the two races in this respect. The tables which follow give the number of respirations per minute for whites, blacks and mulattoes, between the ages 17 and 35, in usual vigor and with vigor im-

MEAN FREQUENCY OF RESPIRATION ACCORDING TO AGE.[1]

Ages.	In Usual Vigor.		
	Whites.	Blacks.	Mulatto.
Under 17	16.40	18.45	18 32
17	16.55	18.05	17.73
18	16.39	18.43	18.20
19	16.36	19.37	19.50
20	16.41	18.74	19.55
21	16.53	18.15	18.74
22	16.45	17.59	18.55
23	16.47	17.46	18.57
24	16.50	16.96	20.06
25	16.46	17.54	19.91
26	16.36	16.69	19 47
27	16.33	16.87	18.42
28	16.38	17.36	19.29
29	16.51	16.74	18.26
30	16.41	17.03	18.85
31–34	16.37	17.09	19.10
35 and over	16.50	18.04	18 82
Mean	16.44	17.75	19.01

[1] Gould, "Military Statistics," pp. 521–22.

MEAN FREQUENCY OF RESPIRATION ACCORDING TO AGE.[1]

	With Vigor Impaired.	
	White.	Black. and Mulatto.
Under 17	17.32	20.50
17	16.95	20.50
18	16.76	19.62
19	16 55	18.54
20	16 63	19.82
21	16.76	22.59
22	16.60	22.78
23	16.89	21.21
24	16.69	20.91
25	16.92	22.65
26	16.34	19.70
27	17.07	22.54
28	16.40	21.00
29	16.91	21.21
30	17.16	22.60
31–34	16.70	20.21
35 and over	17.16	18.97
Mean	16.84	20.71

[1] Gould, "Military Statistics," p. 522.

paired. The distinction as to vigor is necessary to meet the point raised in the discussion of vital capacity as to the effect of disease. For those with impaired vigor the data for pure and mixed races have not been separated by Mr. Gould on account of the small number of cases, (294).

Under conditions of health and disease the number of respirations is least for the white and greatest for the mulattoes. The number of respirations increases during disease. According to the tables before us, the average number per minute was 16.44 for the whites in usual vigor, and 16.84 with vigor impaired. For the blacks the rate was 17.75 in usual vigor and for the mulattoes 19.01. For the two races combined the rate was 20.71 for those with vigor impaired. The differences in favor of the whites exist at all ages and are fairly constant. Since the accelerated respiration falls almost entirely on the colored race it is self-evident from these figures and those pertaining to lung capacity that on the whole the colored race, even at the time of a favorable rate of mortality, presented characteristics which in part explain the inordinate mortality peculiar to the race at the present time.[1]

Inferior vital capacity is closely associated with slight physical strength. The data collected by Mr. Gould proves this to be true, and as the table below will show, the mean lifting strength is less at nearly all ages for the colored soldiers as compared with the whites. This is contrary to the prevailing notion that the average negro possesses superior physical strength, but in full accordance with the lower power of vital resistance and consequent susceptibility to disease.

I know of no comparative data for the colored male of the present day, with the exception of the twelve measurements of colored boys in the Elmira Reformatory already referred to. The results of Dr. Wey's measurements confirm this point and show that while the average strength of the back and legs are 274.8 lbs. and 369.8 lbs. respectively for the white inmates, the averages for the colored were only 270.4 lbs. and 349.4 lbs. respectively. The dearth of data makes a more accurate comparison impossible.

[1] The same unfavorable condition is to be observed in the rate of the pulse, which increases during disease even in its incipient stage. In the comparison below, the full blacks show the most favorable rate while the least favorable rate is shown by the mulatto both in health and disease.

MEAN FREQUENCY OF PULSE.[1]

	Usual Vigor.	Vigor Impaired.
Whites	74.84	77.21
Full blacks	74.02	76.91
Mulattoes.	76.97	83.12

[1] Gould, "Military Statistics," p. 523.

MEAN LIFTING STRENGTH OF WHITE AND COLORED SOLDIERS.[1]

Age.	White. Lbs.	Colored. Lbs.
Under 17	250.4	258.9
17	292.8	295.0
18	312.6	285.8
19	320.7	297.1
20	331.2	316.2
21	337.4	327.4
22	343.3	329.6
23	358.4	334.8
24	355.8	347.2
25	365.1	349.5
26	363.0	338.9
27	350.1	343.2
28	367.6	354.1
29	365.9	356.9
30	351.2	349.8
31–34	361.9	366.8
35–39	366.0	339.2
40–44	347.0	336.6
45–49	325.7	328.7
50 and over	321.2	297.0

[1] Gould, " Military Statistics," pp. 461 and 465.

There is one more subject concerning which the statistics I have collected may be of value, and that is, vision. I regret that the limited range of data on this important point makes a full discussion difficult, if not impossible; but the subject is one which is well deserving of being more fully investigated. The work of Gould contains considerable information which, however, deals more fully with the eyesight of the white soldier than of the colored. The actual power of vision was greatest for the Indian and least for the full black. The mean distance at which a test object could be read was 47.3 inches for the white, 45.5 for the full black, 46.6 for the mulatto and 51.8 for the Indian.[1] But the small

[1] Gould, " Military Statistics," page 530.

number of observations (253) on mulattoes impairs the value of the figures for this class. The superiority of the vision of the white over that of the negro is, however, clearly shown.

If we consider the comparative prevalence of color blindness we meet with an entirely different result, as 2.2 per cent. of the white soldiers were color blind, and only 1.1 per cent. of blacks and 0.3 per cent. of the mulattoes.[1] There is therefore apparently no distinct relation between power of vision and color blindness.

We are fortunate in having some valuable and reliable data on this point for the present time for the state of Alabama, from the official reports of which I have compiled the following table showing the comparative frequency of cases of color blindness and defective vision in four years.

AVERAGE NUMBER OF REJECTIONS FOR DEFECTIVE VISION BY THE STATE BOARD OF EXAMINERS FOR ALABAMA, 1888–1891.[1]

Color.	No. Examined.	No. of Rejections.	Per Cent. of Rejections.
White	7,403	285	3.9
Black	1,253	24	1.9
Mulatto	265	5	1.9

[1] Annual reports of the Alabama State Board of Health, 1888–1891.

This table presents the results of examinations made during 1888–91 of persons employed or desiring to be employed in the railway service. The class rejected or disqualified includes those with visual defects of all kinds and therefore the results are not strictly comparable with those of Mr. Gould's investigation, which deals with color blindness only. But the result is largely in favor of the colored, and to an equal degree for mulattoes and full blacks. A similar result is brought out by the following table abstracted from the reports of the Sur-

[1] "Military Statistics," p. 554.

geon-General of the army and showing the rejections for
diseases of the eye during a period of eight years.

REJECTIONS FOR DISEASES OF THE EYES FOR 1,000 MEN EXAMINED,
1887–1894.[1]

Year.	White.	Colored.
1887	74.2	50.9
1888	90.0	76.7
1889	89.1	77.5
1890	89.1	55.1
1891	86.7	40.8
1892	88.3	64 5
1893	82.0	51.2
1894	80.7	30.7

[1] Annual reports of the Surgeon-General of the Army, 1888–1895.

Without exception the rejections for diseases of the
eye are most frequent among the whites, and there does
not seem to be any tendency towards a change in this
favorable condition for the colored race.

The conclusions deducible from the preceding tables
of anthropometric statistics may be summarized as
follows:

First. The average weight of the colored male of
military age, and of colored male and female children, is
greater than that of whites of the same classes. This
excess in weight prevails irrespective of age, stature, or
circumference of the chest.

Second. The average stature of the negro is less than
that of the white, and the difference, though slight, prevails at all ages.

Third. The greater weight and smaller stature of the
negro as compared with the white are found to prevail
practically the same today as thirty years ago. The
race has therefore undergone no decided change in respect to these conditions of bodily structure.

Fourth. The average girth of chest of the negro male

of thirty years ago was slightly greater than that of the white, but at the present time the chest expansion of the colored male is less than that of the white. This decrease in the size of the living thorax in part explains the increase in the mortality from consumption and respiratory diseases.

Fifth. The capacity of the lungs of the negro is considerably below that of the white. This fact coupled with the smaller weight of the lungs (4 oz.) is without question another powerful factor in the great mortality from diseases of the lungs.

Sixth. The mean frequency of respiration is greater in the negro than in the white. As accelerated respiration indicates a tendency towards disease, the fact just stated fully supports those regarding inferior vital capacity and lesser degree of mobility of the chest.

Seventh. The mean lifting strength of the white is in excess of that of the negro. The prevailing opinion that the negro is on the whole more capable of enduring physical exercise is therefore disproved. This fully agrees with the facts regarding excessive mortality, which in itself is proof of a lesser degree of physical strength.

Eighth. The power of vision of the negro is inferior to that of the white, but he is less liable to diseases of the eye, especially color blindness.

The facts brought together in the preceding section prove conclusively that there are important differences in the bodily structure of the two races, differences of far-reaching influence on the duration of life and the social and economic efficiency of the colored man. Superficial writers,[1] either ignorant of or indifferent to

[1] Davy "On the Character of the Negro." *Journal, Anthropological Society*, vol. vii, p. clvi *et seq.*

the facts, have maintained that such differences were only trivial and of no importance. All the researches of and investigations from Soemmering[1] to Gould have clearly proven that the differences are vital. Sir Duncan Gibb, in his remarks on the paper of Dr. Beddoe,[2] well said that " the vital energies of a people had a great deal to do with the state of the body, and that the capacity of the chest should count for something very considerable as an indication of national power. He thought that the British people as a race were superior to most other people in consequence of the vigour they possessed in that respect."[3]

The apparent decrease in the vitality of the negro is in marked contrast to the favorable change in the white population. Taking account only of students we have it on the authority of Professor Hitchcock that " The physique of the Amherst student is altered very considerably from what it was in the sixties. The young man now in college has at his entrance less of the simple, flabby, weak appearance than had the young collegian of 1861. . . . There are two facts in our statistical history which illustrate this point. One is the test of actual strength. Almost from the first beginnings of our department we have possessed and used the two well known tests known as the 'dip' and the 'pull up'. . . . The records of tests with these instruments applied to all the colleges, were averaged for the period 1861 to 1888, with the result that the 'dip' stood at 6, and the 'pull up' at 9. For the sake of comparison we have averaged the same

---

[1] S. T. Sommering, "Ueber die körperlichen Verschiedenheiten der Neger von Europaern," Frankfurt a. M., 1785.

[2] "The Stature and Bulk of Men in the British Islands."

[3] *Journal of the Anthropological Society*, Vol. 7, p. ccxxi.

items for the past five college years and find the 'dip' to be 7.1 and the 'pull up' 9.9, that is, we register a gain of 9 and 8 per cent. respectively. Another test is found in our record of time lost on account of sickness. Statistics taken from 1861–65 showed that each student during that period averaged a loss of 2.18 days annually during term time from being too sick to study. The records for 1885–89 show an average loss of 1.75 days, a gain in health of 8 per cent. The deaths during 1861–70, exclusive of those who fell in the war were 6.1 per cent. of the whole number graduated; the deaths during 1881–90 were 3.4 per cent. of this number. This certainly indicates a greater vitality now than twenty-five years ago."[1]

In contrast with this favorable change of physical condition for the white race, we have abundant proof of the physical deterioration of the colored race. Before emancipation he presented in many respects a most excellent physical type, a type even superior to the average white man examined for military service under similar conditions. The opinions as to his fitness for military service were so very emphatic, and so largely in his favor, that I cannot do better than quote a few of the many recorded views of the examining surgeons, who had excellent opportunities for observation. The Kentucky negro of thirty years ago was described by Dr. James Foster, of London, Ky., as follows:

For symmetry, muscular strength and endurance, I do not think the Kentucky negro can be surpassed by any people on earth. The stoutest and most muscular men I ever examined were the negroes I examined at this office. . . . . I think the negro, if he was better informed, and as a consequence, possessed of more moral courage, would be more enduring as he is certainly more muscular

---

[1] Annual report of the Professor of Hygiene and Physical Education of Amherst College, 1891.

12

than the white man. He is, in addition generally better developed in the chest than the white man.[1]

Dr. John C. Maxwell, of Lebanon, Ky., wrote as follows:

I think I may state without fear of contradiction, that the colored man in this locality, if bone and sinew, chest measurement and general physique are the criteria, presents the greatest physical aptitude for military service.[2]

In the eastern states the opinion of the examining surgeon was equally favorable. Dr. John Streeter, of Boston makes the following report:

I have not examined a very large number of colored men, not exceeding 300, consequently I cannot speak from large experience. Those that I have examined compare favorably in intelligence and aptitude for military service with white recruits. In muscular development and freedom from physical disqualifications they are superior to the average white men I have examined. The finest specimens of physical development I have seen were among the colored recruits. I am not aware why the colored race should not furnish as efficient soldiers as ever were in service.[3]

Dr. R. G. McLord, of Norwich, Conn., wrote as follows:

The negro possesses in general a sound and vigorous body, with a powerful development of the thorax and superior extremities, and is in every way physically adapted for garrison duty, assailing earth works, as well as for short marches.[4]

The opinion of Dr. Stevenson, of Camden, N. J., was given as follows:

The negro race physically are well developed, muscular and strong. . . With the exception of a greater tendency to scrofulous disorders, they are quite as free from disease as the whites. The negro then would seem to be well adapted to endure the fatigues of a long march and in those duties where manual labor is required, ought to be superior to the white man.[5]

Finally I may quote the opinion of Dr. H. B. Hub-

[1] Provost-Marshal General's report, vol. I, p. 384.
[2] *Ibid*, p. 370.
[3] *Ibid*, p. 201.
[4] *Ibid*, p. 237.
[5] *Ibid*, p. 285.

bard, examining surgeon of the 2nd Mass. district, who observed the negro in British Guiana :

An experience of some months' practice among this class some years since in Demerara, enables me to give a decided opinion that the negro is generally of good physique . . . and fully as able, (as the white) to support fatigue and endure hardship. I think the negro has every physical qualification for military service. I refer to the pure or nearly pure, black ; for although I have known some muscular and healthy mulattoes I am convinced that, as a general rule, any considerable admixture of white blood deteriorates their physique, impairs the powers of endurance and almost always introduces a scrofulous taint.[1]

This testimony as to the sound physical condition of the negro previous to emancipation, was almost unanimous. Those who disagreed with the favorable opinions in regard to the negro's fitness for military service found fault largely with the lack of muscular development of the calf of the leg, and the extreme flat-footedness, and, among those of mixed blood especially, tendency to scrofula. In regard to the first two objections the opinion of Dr. Sanford Hunt may be quoted, according to whom " the large flat inelastic foot of the negro was at first considered an objection, but consequent experience has not sustained the idea. I have known a command of about 1,500 negroes to march 78 miles in 76 hours with remarkable ease and without increasing the sick list except for blistered feet. The general experience of army officers has decided that the negro marches as well as the majority of the troops."[2]

Hence we have an almost perfect agreement of widely separated authorities and investigators, that the negro of thirty years ago was physically the equal if not the superior of the white, and this view has been fully sustained by the statistics of mortality, which also ranked

[1] Provost-Marshal General's report, Vol. I, p. 199.
[2] " The Negro as a Soldier "; *Anthropological Review*, Vol VII, p. 43.

him the equal if not the superior of the white of thirty years ago. While it is not possible to demonstrate as clearly as is desirable the present physical condition of the colored race, enough facts have been introduced to show that a process of deterioration has been going on in this respect, which is revealed by the inordinate mortality of the race from consumption and respiratory diseases. And the opinion is warranted that if facts were collected in the same comprehensive and scientific manner as was done by Mr. Gould and Dr. Baxter, they would prove that in vital capacity, the most important of all physiological characteristics, the tendency of the race has been downward. This tendency if unchecked must in the end, lead to a still greater mortality, a lesser degree of economic and social efficiency, a lower standard of nurture and a diminishing excess of births over deaths. A combination of these traits and tendencies must in the end cause the extinction of the race.

CHAPTER IV.

RACE AMALGAMATION.

In this work, the terms " colored " and " negro " have been used indiscriminately, but I have made the more extended use of the former, since the type of the pure negro is rarely met with. The race is so hopelessly mixed that it is difficult to arrive at a clear definition, and the term " colored " will probably serve as well as the awkward phrase, " persons of African descent."

Of the original African type few traces remain, and the race is largely a cross between the African and the white male; for no considerable crossing of negroes with white females has ever taken place. The instances where white women have married colored men are very rare and the few cases that occur cannot possibly have affected the traits and tendencies of the race. On the other hand, the infusion of white blood, through white males, has been widespread, and the original type of the African has almost completely disappeared. A small settlement near Mobile, Ala., a few years ago was asserted to have preserved the purity of the race : but I am informed by Dr. D. T. Rogers, the health officer of Mobile, that this is no longer true.[1] It is therefore a

[1] This settlement consisted originally of thirty full blooded Dahomeyans, brought over in the "Clothilde" in 1859, the last cargo of slaves brought to this country. They were exceedingly fine specimens of the native African and in the course of a few years became an industrious, peaceble community. For a considerable period no intercourse with the native colored population took place, but of late years they have mixed and intermarried with the latter. The result of this inter-marriage is given fully in the following extracts from a letter of Dr. Rogers, written from Mobile, Ala., Dec. 18, 1895, who kindly investigated the matter for me. "The settlement is located about three miles from Mobile. Some

question of great importance to know what influence, favorable or otherwise, the infusion of white blood has had on the physical, moral and mental characteristics of the race. It is of further importance to ascertain, if possible, whether there is a decided tendency towards a mixture of the two races, and if so, whether this tendency is in the direction of lawful marriage or of concubinage and prostitution.

It is an open question whether crossing leads to the improvement or deterioration of races. There is no agreement amongst high authorities. Gobineau maintains that intermixture of different races leads to final extinction of civilization. Serres and others maintain that crossing of races is the essential lever of all progress.[1] Topinard holds that crossing of races anthropologically remote does not increase fecundity; while M. Quatrefages holds the contrary opinion. Nott, Knox and Perrier hold that intermixture of races would lead to decay, while M. Bodichon declares that the era of universal peace and fraternity will be realized by crossing. The latter opinion is shared by Waitz, Deschamps, and many others.

But it would seem that the majority of the writers draw their conclusions from insufficient evidence and

years ago they all lived together on their own land, which was given to them, but in the course of time, as they have married, they have moved away from the old place and now are scattered over a section of about two square miles. The old original Africans were fine specimens of the African race, all being tattoo marked and speaking their own language. They are large, well developed and healthy, and in this respect superior to the other colored people. They have largely married among themselves but also among other colored people in this section. The increase in the population has not been greater than that of the native colored people. *The offspring of those who have married native born colored persons exhibit characteristics of an inferior physique to those of the original Africans and they do not enjoy good health.*"

[1] Waitz, " Anthropology," p. 347.

isolated cases of fecundity or sterility, which had little
or no bearing upon the future progress of the races. I
have failed to find in any of the works on Anthropology
a statement of facts which would warrant definite conclusions one way or the other.

The imperfect state of vital statistics, even at the
present time, makes it difficult if not impossible to settle
scientifically the question of increase or decrease in
fecundity. This question would seem to have been the
main object of the many inquiries in regard to the effect
of crossing, and the physiological effects seem to have
been generally ignored. Not one of the many writers
on the subject deals in a satisfactory way at all with the
comparative vitality of mixed races, and although many
statements as to comparative mortality are made, they
are usually based on insufficient evidence. Finally, it
would seem that past inquiries have been directed rather
to establishing one theory or another as to the
unity or plurality of the human race, than to the
far more important end of proving in a scientific way
whether a race has actually been benefitted intellectually,
morally, or physically by crossing. Again, the distinction pointed out by Topinard has not been sufficiently
drawn, that there is or may be a wide difference in the
effects of crossing of races anthropologically remote from
each other, as compared with races which have arrived
at about the same stage of development.

That races of similar culture and physical and psy-
chical development can intermarry to mutual advantage
is too patent a fact to need instances in its support.
That the children of mixed parentage of Indo-Germanic
stock, irrespective of nationality, are superior to the parents, is a fact which we observe in every day life. But it
is an entirely different matter when Germans and Italians,

English and Spaniards, Swedes and Turks intermarry and have children[1]. And it may be said, only with emphasis, that the cross-breed of white men and colored women is, as a rule, a product inferior to both parents, physically and morally. Waitz himself expresses the opinion that "with regard to sexual intercourse and the quality of the offspring there exists both in individuals, as well as between different nations, not exactly antipathy, but incompatibility which though not explicable as to its origin, is sufficiently established."[2]

That such antipathy does exist is sufficiently proven by the fact that white women of this country do not and never have shown a decided inclination to marry negroes, and the most careful inquiry fails to show that there has been developed any tendency towards a change in their attitude. The underlying cause for this antipathy is what Westermark calls "the law of similarity," which, according to this eminent writer "does more than anything else to maintain the separation of the different classes." "A civilized race," he writes, "does not readily intermingle with one less advanced in civilization, for the same reasons which prevent a lord from marrying a peasant girl. And, more than anything else, . . . the enmity, or at least the want of sympathy, due to differences of interests, ideas and habits, which so often exists between different peoples or tribes, helps to keep the races separate."[3]

Again, "Affection depends in a very high degree upon sympathy. Though distinct aptitudes, these two classes

---

[1] *Journal of the Royal Statistical Society*, 1865, pp. 274-75.

[2] "Introduction to Anthropology," by Dr. Theodore Waitz, (London, 1863,) Vol. I, p. 185.

[3] "Human Marriage," p. 282.

of emotions are most intimately connected : affection is strengthened by sympathy and sympathy is strengthened by affection. Community of interest, opinions, sentiments of culture and mode of life, as being essential to close sympathy, is therefore favorable to close affection. The contrast must not be so great as to exclude sympathy." [1] Finally, "want of sympathy prevents great divisions of human beings, such as different races or nations, hereditary castes, classes and adherents of different religions . . . from intermarrying, even where personal affection plays no part in the choice." [2]

There would seem therefore to be in operation a most powerful cause, which for ages to come will make amalgamation of the white and colored races, in this country at least, an impossibility. "Between him (the negro) and the white, the race antipathy seems too strong for any great degree of amalgamation ever to take place while the mulatto has the infertility of a hybrid." [3] But we have to face the fact that the races do mix in spite of the effect of the law of similarity which makes intermarriage of such rare occurrence. The crossing of the white and colored races in this country is, therefore, not within the lawful bounds of marriage, but outside of the pale of the moral law. That an immense amount of concubinage and prostitution prevails among the colored women of the United States is a fact fully admitted by the negroes themselves. It is most prevalent, as is natural, in the large cities, but exists also to a large extent in the rural portions of the country. Of the two evils, prostitution for gain prevails the more widely, and it is but natural that we should find on investigation that the inevitable con-

[1] "Human Marriage," p. 362.
[2] *Ibid*, p. 544.
[3] Charles Morris, "The Aryan Race," p. 316.

sequences of a life of sexual immorality have very seriously affected the physical and moral characteristics of
the colored race.

These consequences fall most heavily on the offspring.
The children of colored women and white men, of
whatever shade of color, are morally and physically the
inferiors of the pure black. It has been stated by Nott
and proved by subsequent experience, that the mulatto
is in every way the inferior of the black, and of all races
the one possessed of the least vital force. I cannot do
better than give in full the opinions of the examining
surgeons of the army during the war, as to the vitality
and general physical condition of the mulatto. The
following are excerpts from the report of the Provost-
Marshal General.

There are few if any pure Africans [in Vermont], but a mixed
race only. They probably lose in vitality what they gain in symmetry
of form by admixture ; they die early of scrofula or tuberculosis. [1]

Although I have known some muscular and healthy mulattoes, I
am convinced that, as a general rule, any considerable admixture of
white blood deteriorates the physique and impairs the powers of endurance, and almost always introduces a scrofulous taint. [2]

I believe a genuine black far superior in physical endurance to
the mulatto or yellow negro ; the last named are with few exceptions,
scrofulous or consumptive. [3]

The colored men, as far as my observation goes, make excellent
soldiers, . . . The mulatto, however, is comparatively worthless,
subject to scrofula and tuberculosis. [4]

The chief disability being, ... among those of mixed
blood, a tendency to scrofula. [5]

The majority of those rejected were of northern birth and gener-
erally mulattoes. [6]

In this country the mixture [of the colored] with the whites con-

[1] Page 192, B. F. Morgan, M. D., Rutland, Vt
[2] Page 199, H. B. Hubbard, M. D., Taunton, Mass.
[3] Page 225, C. G. McKnight, M. D., Providence, R. I.
[4] Page 261, C. L. Hubbell, M. D., Troy, N. Y.
[5] Page 302, J. Rallston Wells, M. D., Philadelphia, Pa.
[6] Page 304, J. H. Mears, M. D., Frankfort, Pa.

tributes greatly to lower their health and stamina and we find comparatively few of mixed breeds who are free from scrofula.[1]

The pure Africans, that is, with no admixture of white blood, as a class were the most muscularly developed of any men examined. The mulattoes have more intelligence . . . but they were scrofulous and consumptive.[2]

The African race, when pure and not mixed with white blood, is more capable of enduring hardships . . . than the white race.[3]

The pure blooded African is in every way physically the equal to the European. . . . Their mixture with the white race deteriorates very much from their physical development.[4]

The conviction arising from an examination of a few hundred of various shades of color is that the negro proper is well adapted for military service, but that the mulatto and all varieties of mixture of black and white blood have degenerated physically, being very often found with tuberculosis and other manifestations of imperfect organism.[5]

In contrast with the foregoing opinions, in only one instance was an opinion given, which was favorable to the mixed type and that was based on only two cases, which make it of no determining value.

These emphatic opinions of qualified medical men, with abundant opportunity for observation, is fully supported by the results of the investigations of Dr. Gould. Some of the data collected by Dr. Gould have already been referred to in the previous chapter, but the following summary of comparative physical measurements of the pure and mixed races may not be out of place at this time. As regards weight, there is very little difference. The average was 141.4 lbs. for the white, 144.6 for the full black, and 144.8 for the mulatto. As I have stated before, I attach less value to this test, as applied to the colored race than to the white race, since the increase in weight is one of quantity only instead of quan-

[1] Page 311, R. H. Smith, M. D., West Chester, Pa.
[2] Page 353, Thos. F. Murdoch, M. D., Baltimore, Md.
[3] Page 394, J. R. Veeter, M. D., Jefferson City, Mo.
[4] Page 403, David Noble, M. D,, Hillsborough, Ohio.
[5] Page 418, L. M. Whiting, M. D., Alliance, Ohio.

tity and quality combined. The average circumference of the chest was 35.8 inches for the white, 35.1 for the full black, and 34.96 for the mulatto. The difference is in favor of the full black, but too slight to be of any importance.

The capacity of the lungs, the most important of all determining factors among physical measurements, was 184.7 cubic inches for the white, 163.5 for the full black and only 158.9 for the mulatto. This low vital capacity is without question the most serious fact affecting the longevity of the mixed races, and one which explains the lower vitality and less resistance to disease than is found in the negro of pure blood. The rate of respiration is also unfavorable for the mixed race, and according to Gould is 16.4 per minute for the white, 17.7 for the pure black and 19.0 for the mulatto in usual vigor.

On the basis of these observations, the conclusion is warranted, that the mixed race is physically the inferior of the white and pure black, and as a result of this inferior degree of vital power we meet with a lesser degree of resistance to disease and death among the mixed population, in contrast with the more favorable condition prevailing among the whites and pure blacks. Morally, the mulatto cannot be said to be the superior of the pure black. In the absence of comparative statistics it is next to impossible to prove this assertion, based largely on individual observation, which may and may not be accurate. This much, however, is probably true, that most of the illicit intercourse between whites and colored is with mulatto women and seldom with those of the pure type. From such instances as have come to my notice, the few white men who have married colored females usually prefer the mulatto, and the same selection no doubt prevails among those who disregard the law of sexual morality.

Intellectually, the mulatto is undoubtedly the superior of the pure black. Of this there is much evidence sufficiently well known not to need presentation in detail. It may, however, be of value to give a few data showing the physiological changes that have taken place in the mixed races as a consequence of the infusion of white blood. In the work of Gould information is given showing the comparative cranial measurements of the pure black and the mixed type, and it is shown that as regards circumference of the head and the facial angle, the mulatto approximates the white race more nearly than the pure black. As regards the former, the average circumference of the head was 22.1 inches for the white, 22.0 for the mulatto, and 21.9 for the full black. The facial angle measured 72.0° for the white, 69.2° for the mulatto, and 68.8° for the full black. These facts are fully supported by the observations of Dr. Sanford B. Hunt, who carefully investigated the weight of the brain as affected by crossing. According to Dr. Hunt, the average weight of the brain increases according to the extent of crossing, so that the type presenting the largest admixture with the white, presents also the heaviest weight of the brain. The table of Dr. Hunt is given in full on account of its great value.

WEIGHT OF THE BRAIN OF WHITE AND COLORED SOLDIERS.[1]
(Grammes.)

No. of Cases.	Degree of Color.	Weight of Brain.
24	whites	1424 grammes
25	three parts white	1390 "
47	half white	1334 "
51	one-fourth white	1319 "
95	one-eighth white	1308 "
22	one-sixteenth white	1280 "
141	pure negroes	1331 "

[1]*Anthropological Review*, VII, " The Negro as a Soldier."

The table clearly proves that there is an increase in brain weight with an increase in the proportion of white blood, and this fact agrees with what we should expect from the greater circumference of the head and the larger facial angle of the mulatto as compared with the pure negro. We have, therefore, the contrast of the mulatto being physically and possibly morally the inferior of the pure blooded negro, while intellectually he is the superior.

This statistical fact could easily be supported by numerous instances of exceptional individual progress, which as a rule has been made by those who had a large proportion of white blood in their veins. But important as these ex. 'onal instances may be, they must not be compared, as they too often are, with the intellectual progress of the whites. I cannot do better in illustration of this point than to quote Vogt's remarks on the well known case of Lille Geoffroy, who was the offspring of a Frenchman and a negro woman of Martinique: "As a proof in favor of the scientific and artistic capacity of the negro, we find cited in nearly all works the instance of Mr. Lille Geoffroy, of Martinique, an engineer and mathematician and correspondent member of the French Academy. The fact is that the mathematical performances of the above gentleman were of such a nature that, had he been born in Germany of white parents, he might, perhaps, have been qualified to be a mathematical teacher in a middle class school or engineer of a railway; but having been born in Martinique, of colored parents, he shone like a one-eyed man among the totally blind. M. Lille besides, was not a pure black but a mulatto."[1]

This distinction, so ably pointed out, is almost always lost sight of in discussions on the intellectual pro-

[1] Vogt, "Lectures on Man," pp. 192–3.

gress, not only of the mulatto, but also of the negro. Yet it is the most important, since it alone will separate the real from the unreal.[1]

I may state here that together with an increase in so-called education there has not been as much progress in morality as would take place if the education were genuine and not, as it is in fact, a mere varnish of questionable value. And for this reason the mere fact that there has been an increase in brain weight, in cranial capacity, is of very little importance as compared with the fact that there has been a decrease in vital force by reason of the infusion of white blood. It is only another illustration of the fact that when a race of a lower degree of civilization comes in contact with a superior race it will first imitate the superior race in the external, I might say the ornamental, characteristics, rather than in the useful and permanent. Thus the long heel of the negro has decreased from 0.82 inches in the black to 0.57 inches in the mulatto, compared with 0.48 inches in the white. The same has been shown to be true as regards the facial angle, which is of no possible value as a vital factor. Other points could be given to show that

[1] The remarks of Vogt are applicable to the numerous recent instances where degrees from colleges and universities, and honors as class orators, have been conferred upon negroes who, had they been white men, would never had been for an instant considered deserving of such exceptional appreciation of their intellectual efforts. Honors thus easily gained by members of the colored race, must in the end prove more of a hinderance than a help to real intellectual progress, since the distinction thus conferred is out of proportion to the efforts or achievements by the person thus distinguished. The consequences of such utterly unjustifiable action on the part of great institutions of learning are met in the excessive laudations of their own intellectual or other efforts on the part of the negro writers themselves, and a want of genuine respect for great learning and hard and unremitting mental labor. And as a result the more subtle and important effects of education and the higher life are lost, and only vanity and foolish pride of race are fostered.

in the least important physical characteristics the mixed race has a tendency to resemble the white, while in the more important, that is in vital and moral characteristics, it is inferior even to the pure black.

On the strength of the foregoing facts and observations, the conclusions would seem warranted that the crossing of the negro race with the white has been detrimental to its true progress, and has contributed more than anything else to the excessive and increasing rate of mortality from the most fatal diseases, as well as to its consequent inferior social efficiency and diminishing power as a force in American national life.

If the above conclusion is accepted, it is of no small importance to ascertain whether the tendency of the race is towards amalgamation or isolation. It was brought out in the first part of this work that there is a positive tendency on the part of the colored population in the rural sections of the South to congregate in counties where the race is most numerous. For the large cities the same tendency was shown in the congregation of the colored population in a few wards, usually the worst sections of the city from a sanitary or moral standpoint. It was also shown, for Chicago at least, that this congregation was towards the section containing large numbers of houses of ill-fame, and the conclusion is inevitable that the majority of the colored living in this section were directly or indirectly connected with this lowest phase of city life. Hence, as regards the large cities, it is doubtful whether the congregation of the negroes into a few wards indicates a tendency towards race isolation and race purity. If in this connection we take into consideration the further fact that in the colored race the females outnumber the males more greatly than is true for the white race, the conclusion seems fairly warranted that large numbers of colored women who drift from the country into the cities, from whatever cause, adopt a life of prostitution for gain. And for this unfortunate social fact, the lower classes of white men are almost entirely responsible. For while irregular sexual relations between the two sexes of the colored race prevail all over the South, it is more in the nature of concubinage than prostitution for gain. That lawful marriage between the two races is rare and of even less frequent occurrence now than thirty years ago, will presently be shown by such statistics as I have been able to collect. Before I consider the available data, I wish to deal briefly with the theory of race amalgamation as it has been advocated with more or less persistency during the present century.

One of the earliest discussions on the subject of the gradual absorption of the colored race of this country by the whites, I have met with in the *Edinburg Review* for 1827, which contains the following statement: " We entertain little doubt that when the laws which create a distinction between the races shall be completely abolished, a very few generations will mitigate the prejudices which those laws have created and which they still maintain. . . . At that time, the black girl who, as a slave would have attracted a white lover, will, when her father gives her a good education and can leave her a hundred thousand dollars, find no difficulty in procuring a white husband."

The laws which made a distinction between the races have been abolished, and at least one generation has passed since then, but the two races are to-day more than ever removed from amalgamation by means of lawful marriage. Even the wealth of a colored girl would not procure for her a *good* white husband. A marriage for

13

a consideration would, of course, be a return to marriage by purchase, which, fortunately, is gradually passing away. A 'lover' who would be attracted by a $100,000 girl would be such in name only.

Lyell, in 1849,[1] expressed a similar opinion in the following words: "This incident [the runaway match of a white man with a mulatto seamstress] is important from many points of view, and especially as proving to what an extent the amalgamation of the two races would take place, if it were not checked by artificial prejudices and the most jealous and severe enactments of law."

But the most determined attempt to create a national sentiment in favor of race assimilation on a large scale was made during the period of the war by a Mr. Croly and others, who brought together in a pamphlet their views on the subject, views which were fully shared by the more zealous advocates of the abolition of slavery. Thus Mr. Wendell Phillips in his Fourth of July oration of 1863, advocated "amalgamation to the fullest extent." Mr. Theodore Tilton, editor of the *Independent*, in a speech expressed himself as follows: "I am not advocating the union of whites and blacks. This is taking place without advocacy. It neither waits for the permission of an argument in favor of it nor stays at the barrier of an argument against it. I am often asked, 'would you marry a black woman?' I reply . . I have a wife already and, therefore, will not. I am asked, 'do you think a white man ought ever to marry a black woman?' I reply, when a man and a woman want to get married, it is their business, not mine or anybody else's." And again by the same writer: "The history of the world's civilization is written in one word—which

[1] "Second Visit to the United States," (New York, 1849), Vol. II, p. 216.

many are afraid to speak—many afraid to hear—and that is amalgamation."

But neither Mr. Phillips nor Mr. Tilton went as far as the authors of "Miscegenation," who advocated complete amalgamation not only of whites and blacks but also of whites and Chinese and all other races of whatever state of culture.

All that is needed to make us the finest race on earth is to engraft upon our stock the negro element, which Providence has placed by our side on this continent. Of all the rich treasures of blood vouchsafed to us, that of the negro is most precious because it is the most unlike any other that enters into the composition of national life.

The white people of America are dying for want of fresh blood. They have bone and sinew, but they are dry and shriveled for lack of the healthful juices of life.

The fact may be startling, but the student of ethnology will be willing to admit that in course of time the dark races must absorb the white.

Let the war go on, until church and state and society recognize not only the propriety but the necessity of the marriage of white and black . . . in short, until the great truth shall be declared in our public documents and announced in the messages of our Presidents, that it is desirable that the white man shall marry the black woman and the white woman the black man. . . . It is only by the infusion into the very system of the vital forces of a tropical race, that the white race may regain health and strength.[1]

It is not necessary to comment on any of the foregoing utterances. They are reproduced for the purpose of showing, that, for a time at least, the complete absorption of the negro by the white race, or of the white by the negro race, was seriously discussed and advocated by some of the foremost men of the day.

The fundamental error, which underlies the argument in favor of race assimilation or absorption, has been pointed out in the beginning. To ignore the law of similarity would, in itself, lead to disastrous consequences. It is, for instance, a well known fact that a

[1] "Miscegenation," by D. G. Croly and others. New York, 1864.

lower fecundity prevails in the case of marriages between Jews and Christians than for marriages among
persons of the same creed.   This is atributed by Walcker[1]
to the dissimilarity of the two contracting parties, the
disappointment which follows such unions on account
of the inability of the Christian to adopt the mode of
living or sympathize with the inner life of the Jew and
vice versa.   That is to say, the barriers which make
marriages of Jews and Christians less fruitful are psychological rather than physiological.   It has been found that
the number of children to a marriage was 4.35 where both
persons were of the same religion (Christian), but only
1.58 where the father was Christian and the mother
a Jewess.   When both were Jews the number of births
to a marriage was 4.21, but only 1.78 where the father
was evangelical, and 1.66 where the father was a Catholic.[2]

After all the centuries of contact of the Jews with
Christians only about five per cent of them marry persons
of any other religion than their own.   In Algeria, inter-
marriages of Jews with Christians are not on the increase
and the same has been said of the Jews in other countries.[3]
Yet the differences that separate the Jew from the Gen-
tile are as nothing compared with the gulf that separates
the white from the colored race.   Frequently as races
have intermixed with one another they have been

---

[1] Dr. Karl Walcker, "Grundriss der Statistik" (Berlin, 1889), p. 138.
[2] *Journal of the American Statistical Association*, vol. III, p. 245.
[3] Marriages of Jewish women to European men, 1888–90, 26 cases ;
1891–3, 20 cases.   Marriages of Jewish men to European women, 19
cases during the first three years ; 15 cases during the last three years.
Only one marriage of a Jewish woman to a Mussulman is recorded
during the six year period and none between a native woman and a
Jewish man.   For further details see "Statistique Générale de l' Al-
gérie," Alger, 1891 and 1894.

usually of types of similar degree of culture and mental development.

Among more recent writers, Dr. Leffingwell has advanced the opinion that " before half a dozen centuries have expired, the African will have as completely merged his race in the three hundred millions of people on the American continent as Phenician and Greek, Saracen, Roman and Norman have blended into the Neapolitan who basks in the sunshine of San Lucia." [1]

The few generations of the editor of the *Edinburgh Review* have been expanded by Dr. Leffingwell into a few centuries. The former have passed and no amalgamation has taken place, nor are there any indications whatever that a few centuries will accomplish what has not been accomplished thus far. The opinion of Dr. Leffingwell, that as a matter of course " the greater part of this change (from pure to mixed races) will be effected by lawful marriage " is not supported by a single statistical fact. Evidence of this will be produced farther on, when it will be shown that intermarriage between the two races is less frequent now than ever before, although it has been at all times of rare occurrence.

Mr. T. T. Fortune, the editor of the New York *Age*, (a paper devoted to the interest of the colored race), at the Africa Congress of the Atlanta Exposition, expressed his view in the following words: " The minority race alongside a majority race is destined to be absorbed by the majority race. If the white race did not want to absorb the black it ought to have left it in Africa. If the white man did not want to be absorbed by the black race it ought to have staid out of Africa."

In contrast with the view of Dr. Leffingwell and Mr. Fortune, we have the opinion of Dr. Alexander, the

[1] "Illegitimacy," p. 75.

author of a history of African colonization, who wrote fifty years ago: "Two races of men, nearly equal in numbers, but differing as much as the whites and blacks, cannot form one harmonious society in any other way than by amalgamation; but the whites and blacks in this country by no human efforts, could be amalgamated into one homogeous mass in a thousand years."[1] Mr. Bruce, in his work, "The Plantation Negro as a Freeman," asserts, that illicit sexual intercourse between the two races has diminished since the war.

A far more remarkable evidence of social antipathy of the white people to the negro is the fact that illicit sexual intercourse between the races has diminished so far as to have almost ceased outside the cities and towns, where the association being more casual, is more frequent. This is due to the attitude of the whites, for the negresses are less modest as a class than they were before the abolition of slavery, since they are now under no restriction at all. In consequence of this reserve on the part of the white men, the mulattoes are rapidly decreasing in numbers with the progress of time, and the negroes as a mass are gradually but surely reverting to the African type. . . . As his skin darkens in its return to that of his remote ancestors, the prospects of blacks and whites lawfully mixing their blood fades to the thinnest shadow of probability. . . . The few white women who have given birth to mulattoes have always been regarded as monsters; and without exception they have belonged to the most impoverished and degraded caste of whites, by whom they are scrupulously avoided as creatures who have sunk to the level of the beasts of the field.[2]

The opinion of Mr. Bruce is accepted by Mr. Bryce, who also holds that there is less intercourse between the white male and the colored female under conditions of freedom than there was under slavery. In the *Scottish Geographical Magazine*, he expresses his opinion, which is in marked contrast with the view of those who believe in the possibility of an extensive race amalgamation.

[1] "A History of Colonization on the West Coast of Africa," (Philadelphia, 1846), p. 17.
[2] Bruce, "The Plantation Negro as a Freeman," pages 53-55.

Nothing better illustrates the assimilative power of a vigorous community than the way in which the immigrants into the United States melt like sugar in a cup of tea, and see their children grow up no longer Germans or Norwegians or even Irish or Italians or Czechs, but Anglo-Americans. With the negroes, on the other hand, there is practically no admixture; and so far as can be foreseen they will remain, at least in the sub-tropical part of the South, distinctly African in their physical and mental characteristics for centuries to come. The same remark holds true of the white and black races of South Africa, where the process of blood mixture, which went on to some extent between the Dutch and the Hottentots, has all but stopped. [1]

According to Mr. Bryce there is therefore to be observed not only a decrease in the tendency towards mixture of the white and colored races in this country, but also as between the whites and blacks of South Africa. Hence, neither do the whites absorb the negroes of this country, nor the negroes of Africa the whites who have settled there.

Instances where two or more races have dwelt together for ages without amalgamation are frequent and need not be dwelt upon at length here. According to Mr. Westermark, "marriages between Lapps and Swedes rarely occur, being looked upon as dishonorable by both peoples. They are equally uncommon between Lapps and Norwegians and it rarely ever happens that a Lapp marries a Russian." Count de Gobineau, according to Westermark remarks that "not even a common religion and country can extinguish the herditary aversion of the Arab to the Turk, of the Kurd to the Nestorian of Syria, of the Magyar to the Slav." [2]

An interesting instance is presented in the case of the Ainos of Japan, who are a distinct race from the Japanese, and who, after centuries of close association, are as

[1] "Assimilation of Races in the United States," etc., Professor James Bryce in *Scottish Geographical Magazine*, 1892. Reprinted in Smithsonian Report, 1893, page 586, *et seq.*
[2] "Human Marriage."

distinct in their character and habits of life as if they had never come in contact with the superior race of Japanese. It is said that the Ainos, being unable to affiliate more closely with the Japanese, are doomed to extinction. The half castes die out with the third or fourth generation and the children of Japanese and Ainos are never vigorous and healthy.[1]

The Eurasian race of India present almost identically the same problem as the negroes of this country. According to Sara J. Duncan there is no remote chance of its ever being re-absorbed by either of its original elements, the prejudices of both Europeans and natives being far too vigorous to permit intermarriage with a race of people who are neither one nor the other. I may be permitted to give here the consequences of such intermixture of Europeans with Indians in Calcutta, where some 20,000 of Eurasians live.

> It is a hard saying, but it suffers little contradiction, that morally the Eurasians inherit defects more conspicuously than virtues from both races from which they spring. Drunkenness is not common among them, nor is brutality. . . . But their indolence and unthrift are proverbial, as are their cupidity and instability of character. . . . The social evil among the lower classes is very hideous. They seem to have a code of their own, which is capable of infinite infraction, and they touch a level of degradation which is far lower than any reached by the pure heathen about them. This is apparently an ineradicable thing, for it has its root in physical inheritance and its reason is racial.[2]

In the West Indies the coolies of Trinidad do not mix with the negro or the mulatto. According to Froude they are proud and will not intermarry with the African.[3] According to the registrar-general of Trinidad "very few East Indian women have intermarried with the

[1] "The Ainos of Yezo, Japan," by Romyn Hitchcock, report of the National Museum, Smithsonian Institution, 1890.

[2] *Popular Science Monthly*, Nov., 1892.

[3] "The English in the West Indies," p. 74.

native colored population in which the gradations from white to black are so fine that no census enumeration by complexions has been attempted." [1]

Intermarriage of the negro with the Indian of this country has also been infrequent, although there has at all times been a considerable intermixture of the Indian with the white race. Of the evil effect of such marriages the agent in charge of the Crow agency of Montana wrote as follows :

One great drawback to the advancement of these people [Crow agency, Montana] is the intermarriage of white men among them. As a rule, any white man who will marry an Indian woman is unfit to associate with the Indians. The presence of such men is a great detriment to the Indian. The average Indian is far superior to the majority of whites who marry Indian women. . . . As a rule, the full blooded Indian stands a much better chance to become a man than the half-breed. The presence of these men causes more trouble in the management of the Indian than all other causes combined. [2]

This severe condemnation of intermarriage of whites with Indians is fully confirmed by the investigations of Dr. Holden, who lived for a good many years among the Indians as Agency physician : "Tribes who have been isolated, or who have held aloof from the whites, retained their tribal relations and declared for non-intercourse with the whites, are chaste and free from taint. The tribes who have opened their arms to receive the white man have been subdued by him, have been debauched and inoculated with venereal poison. [3]

There is therefore abundant proof that there is a natural aversion between some races and that attempts to cross this natural barrier, determined by the 'law of similarity' have invariably lead to the most disastrous consequences. It is largely to the frequency of illicit

[1] Census of Trinidad, 1891, p. 18.
[2] Report of the Commissioner of Indian Affairs, 1874, page 261.
[3] *American Journal of Obstetrics*, 1892, p. 58.

intercourse between white males and colored females
that we must attribute the wide prevalence of syphilis
and scrofula among the mixed population, as well as the
excessive mortality, the lower fecundity, the increasing
tendency to consumption and other tubercular diseases,
the smaller chest expansion and vital capacity. All are
the consequences of a union of two races in violation of
a natural law—a law which superficial writers have
hoped to see overcome by legislative enactment.

The following facts will prove that such marriages
are becoming more and more infrequent in this country
as well as in the West Indies. The table below will
show for the state of Michigan the marriages that have
taken place between whites and colored of both types,
that is, pure black and mixed. The table covers a
period of 20 years and is of exceptional value as indicating the tendency of the race in the direction of amalgamation by lawful marriage.[1]

INTER-MARRIAGES OF WHITE AND COLORED IN MICHIGAN.—1874-1893.

Periods.	White Males Married to		White Females Married to		
	Black Females.	Mulatto Females.	Black Males.	Mulatto Males.	Total.
1874–78	2	5	8	7	22
79–83	1	2	8	12	23
84–88	1	4	21	14	40
89–93	2	1	10	13	26
20 years, 74–93	6	12	47	46	111

According to the table before us, during a period of
twenty years only 18 white men married colored females,
while 93 white females were married to colored men.
On the basis of the number of persons married during
the first ten years, there was one mixed marriage to
every 6,220 persons married, as compared with a rate

[1] For this table I am under obligations to the Hon. Washington
Gardner, secretary of state of Michigan.

of one to every 7,931 during the next ten years.   It is a matter of some surprise to find that the numbers of blacks and mulattoes who married white women were almost equal, indicating no decided preference on the part of the white woman for colored persons of mixed parentage; but among the white men who married colored women, the larger number selected mulattoes. This fact supports my observation that for purposes of prostitution and concubinage women of mixed blood are preferred to those of the African type.

The next two tables give the same information for the state of Rhode Island, the city of Providence and the state of Connecticut.

INTER-MARRIAGES OF WHITES AND COLORED IN RHODE ISLAND.
1881–1893.

	Rhode Island.	Providence.
1881	No return	5
1882	No return	5
1883	6	1
1884	2	3[1]
1885	7	6
1886	7	4
1887	7	7
1888	4	4
1889	5	4
1890	3	2
1891	10	5
1892	4	3
1893	3	3
13 years	58[2]	52

[1] In 1884 more mixed marriages were reported in Providence than in the state of Rhode Island. I have not been able to ascertain the cause of this error, which is probably a clerical one in favor of Providence.
[2] Eleven years, 51 white females, 7 white males.

INTER-MARRIAGES IN CONNECTICUT.—1883–1893.

Year.	No. of Cases.	Year.	No. of Cases.
1883	7	1889	6
1884	4	1890	8
1885	6	1891	7
1886	6	1882	6
1887	3	1893	4
1888	8		
11 years, 1883–93, 65 cases.[1]			

[1] Mixed marriages, 1894, 10.

In the table for Rhode Island, which has been combined with the data for Providence, a numerical as well as relative decrease is shown. The rate of intermarriages was one to every 1,012 persons married, for the period 1884–88, and one to every 1,327 for the period 1889–93.[1]

For the city of Providence, in which the large majority of such marriages in the state of Rhode Island are shown to occur, the rate of mixed marriages to total of persons married was one in every 579 persons married during 1881–85, one in every 612 during the five years, 1886–90, and one in every 1,030 during the period 1891–94. For Connecticut the ratio was one to every 1,951 persons married during 1883–88, and one

---

[1] For Boston, I have not been able to obtain a complete record, but the table below, compiled from the reports of the city registrar of Boston, 1855–1890, will show that while mixed marriages increased to the period 1873-77, they have since remained almost stationary in numbers, and in proportion to the increase in the population they have materially declined. The registration reports for very recent years no longer contain information on this point, for, in the words of the registrar, "it cannot possibly interest anyone to know how many white persons marry colored individuals." It is a fact, not generally known, that a few years ago a bill was introduced in the Massachusetts legislature by the only colored member of that body, by which the use of the word "colored" was to be prohibited in all public documents. Considerable opposition was necessary to prevent the passage of this uncalled for measure.

MIXED MARRIAGES IN BOSTON, MASS., 1885-1890.

	Total.	Average Per Annum.
1855–1859	50	10.
1862–1866	45	9.
1867–1871	88	17,6
1873–1877	172	34.4
1878–1882	121	24.2
1883–1887	124	24.8
1890	24	24.

It is not at all improbable, however, that in some of these cases the woman were octoroons, passing as white when obtaining their marriage certificate.

to every 2,036 in 1889–93. On the basis of these figures, therefore, the conclusion seems fully warranted that in this country lawful marriage between whites and blacks is on the decrease.

As will be seen from the table below for Bermuda, the same holds true for the West Indies.

MIXED-MARRIAGES IN BERMUDA, W. I., 1872–1895.[1]

Year.	No. of Cases.	Year.	No. of Cases.
1872	5	1884	2
1873	10	1885	1
1874	11	1886	6
1875	11	1887	3
1876	21	1888	8
1877	6	1889	4
1878	10	1890	4
1879	11	1891	4
1880	10	1892	8
1881	5	1893	9
1882	1	1894	2
1883	8	1895	7
12 years	109	12 years	58

[1] Compiled from the reports of the registrar general of Bermuda, W. I., 1872–1895.

In Bermuda mixed marriages have decreased from 107 during the twelve years 1872–83, to 58 during the twelve years 1883–95. The rarity of such marriages in the West Indies is referred to by Mr. Froude, who cites the case of a Scotchman, the keeper of the reservoir of the water works of Port-of-Spain, who had married a colored woman, as " a remarkable exception to an almost universal rule."

That the whites of the West Indies are leaving the islands and that the proportion of whites to colored is gradually decreasing is a well known fact. It is, therefore, no surprise that in some of the islands the mixed element should gradually decrease and revert to the original type, if we accept the theory that the mixed type of the negro can only maintain itself by constant infusion of new blood. In Barbadoes the proportion of those of mixed blood has decreased from 24.5 per cent. in 1871, to 24.1 per cent. in 1891, while at the same time the proportion of pure blacks has increased from 65.5 per cent. in 1871, to 67.3 per cent. in 1891. The whites decreased during the same period from 10.0 per cent. in 1871, to 8.6 per cent. in 1891.[1] That is to say, the loss in white population was made good by the pure blooded negro and not by the mulatto. Hence, neither in this country nor in the West Indies is there any decided tendency towards the amalgamation of the two races by lawful marriage.

It is an open question whether there is a decrease in sexual intercourse outside of matrimony between the males of the white and the females of the colored race. Mr. Bruce maintains, and Mr. Bryce seems to accept the conclusion, that there is less intercourse between whites and blacks now than formerly. It will always be difficult to prove this point. My own investigations indicate that there is an immense amount of prostitution for gain prevailing among the colored women in large cities. Mr. Bruce dealt entirely with the country negro as he knows him in Southside, Virginia. In such large cities of Virginia, as Richmond, and Norfolk, the conditions in the past cannot have been worse than they are at the present time. Even in the Capitol City the number of illegitimate births is more than ten times as large for the colored as for the whites. The comparative percentages of illegitimates in the total number of births were as follows:

[1] Census of Barbadoes, 1891.

ILLEGITIMATE BIRTHS IN WASHINGTON, D. C.

	Percentage of illegitimate among total births	
	White.	Colored.
1879	2.3	17.6
1883	3.6	19.0
1889	3.6	23.5
1894	2.6	26.5
Average for 16 years .	2.9	22.5

Making an allowance for an improvement in the registration of births, it is nevertheless clear that there is no tendency towards a decrease in the illegitimacy, but very probably the reverse tendency. As I have stated before, the larger amount of illicit intercourse prevails between mulattoes and whites, and hence the figures as regards the rate of illegitimacy are of some value. They are fully supported by similar information from Knoxville, Tenn., and Mobile, Ala., but want of space forbids my giving the figures here. Statistics for the West India Islands prove that there, too, immorality, as shown by the rate of illegitimate births, is on the increase, and the hopeful view of those who expected that emancipation would speedily change the former condition of excessive immorality and vice into one of virtue and chastity has not been fulfilled.[1] On the contrary, we are reliably informed that never at any time in the past was vice so flagrant and marriage treated with such indifference as at the present time.

The fact that lawful marriage between the races is not on the increase, so rare, indeed, as to have no influence whatever on the destiny of the race, does not, therefore, prove that intermixture through prostitution is less frequent now than formerly. It is my firm conviction that unlawful intercourse between the two races

[1] "The Negro in the West Indies" *Publications of the American Statistical Association*, Vol. IV, p. 195, *et seq.*

is excessively prevalent at the present time in the large cities as well as in the rural sections of the country.

The question may be asked, among what class of white women is marriage with colored men most frequent, and what class of white men marry colored women? It is not easy to reply to this question in a satisfactory manner. So far as I know, no one has taken the trouble to investigate this point in a scientific way, but perhaps my own investigation, based unfortunately on a very limited number of cases, may prove a stimulus towards a more elaborate inquiry.

I have been able during a number of years to collect information of a fairly reliable character in regard to 37 mixed relations of which 8 were those of white men who lived with colored women and 29 those of white women who lived with colored men.

Of the eight white men, four were lawfully married while the other four were living openly in concubinage. Three of the men were criminals or under suspicion of being such; one man had killed another for insulting remarks concerning his negro wife, one killed his mistress in a fit of jealousy, one was stabbed and horribly burned by vitrol by his colored mistress, one killed his colored mistress by slow poison to obtain possession of her property, the ill gotten gains from a house of ill-fame. The others were more or less outcasts. One was a saloon keeper, one had deserted his family for his negro mistress, two were men of good family but themselves of bad reputation.

Of the twenty-nine women, only nineteen were lawfully married to the colored men with whom they were living, while ten lived in open concubinage. So far as my information goes only five of the nine were of foreign birth, one English, one German and three Irish.

Of the nineteen that were married, four were known prostitutes, two were guilty of bigamy, four either sued for divorce or had deserted their husbands. Five were apparently of respectable parentage and living in content with their husbands; while for four the information is wanting. Of the ten who were not married, eight were known prostitutes, one was insane and only one was known to be the daughter of respectable parents.

Of the twenty-nine colored men who married or lived with white women, only one, an industrious barber, was known to be of good character. Five were of fair repute; nine were idlers, loafers or drunkards; eleven were of proven criminal and anti-social tendencies; while for three the character could not be ascertained. Of the eleven criminals, two were murderers, three were thieves, three were guilty of bigamy, one was the keeper of a house of ill-fame, while the last two were arrested for inhuman cruelty to their own or foster children. The result of the twenty-nine cases of race mixture prove that of the women, twelve were known prostitutes, three were of ill repute, charged in addition with cruelty and abuse of children, two were murdered by their colored husbands, one committed suicide, one became insane, two sued for divorce, two deserted their husbands,[1] five

[1] In the first of these two cases the woman when leaving her colored husband wrote him a letter from which I give the following excerpt: " It is just two years and five months since we were united to love and obey each other, but time has changed us and I have not the least love for you any more. I have learned to love another man who wants to marry me and I hope you will give me my freedom in black and white. The love I had for you was only a childish fancy. . . . . I am tired of knocking about this hard world and want to get a home, as I want to travel up the ladder and not fall down as I did. I am going on twenty years old and want to make a true and upright woman for this man that wishes to make me his wife and give me a home." (New York *Sun*, March 24, 1896.)

14

were apparently satisfied with their choice, while for
four the information could not be obtained. Thus out
of twenty-nine instances only five gave any indications
of not having been absolute failures and of the five in
only one instance is the proof clear that the marriage
was a fair success.

Comment on these cases is hardly necessary. They tend
to prove that as a rule neither good white men nor good
white women marry colored persons, and that good
colored men and women do not marry white persons. The number of cases is so small, however, that
a definite conclusion as to the character of persons intermarrying is hardly warranted. However, it would
seem that if such marriages were a success, even to a
limited extent, some evidence would be found in a collection of thirty-six cases. It is my own opinion, based
on personal observation in the cities of the South, that
the individuals of both races who intermarry or live
in concubinage are vastly inferior to the average types
of the white and colored races in the United States ;
also, that the class of white men who have intercourse
with colored women are, as a rule, of an inferior type.

Hence the conclusion is unavoidable that the amalgamation of the two races through the channels of prostitution or concubinage, as well as through the intermarrying of the lower types of both races, is contrary to
the interest of the colored race, a positive hinderance to
its social, mental and moral development. But aside
from these considerations, important as they are, the
physiological consequences alone demand race purity
and a stern reprobation of any infusion of white blood.
Whatever the race may have gained in an intellectual
way, which is a matter of speculation, it has been losing
its greatest resources in the struggle for life, a sound

physical organism and power of rapid reproduction.
According to Herbert Spencer "sexual relations unfavorable to the rearing of offspring, in respect either of
number or quality, must tend to degradation or extinction."[1] All the facts thus far brought out in this work
prove the truth of this assertion. All the facts obtainable which depict truthfully the present physical and
moral condition of the colored race, prove that the underlying cause of the excessive mortality and diminishing
rate of increase in population is a low state of sexual
morality, wholly unaffected by education.

This condition can be improved only by the development of a higher morality. Amalgamation with whites
by means of lawful marriage is a remote contingency,
which needs no consideration on the part of those who
concern themselves with the amelioration of the condition of the colored race. The conclusion of Mr. Tucker
that, "Seventeen years since the war have brought great
changes to the colored race, great improvements in many
things to some of them, but no change in morals,"[2] is
fully applicable to the race of the present day, thirty
years after the war. The fact that more than one-fourth
of their children, are admitted to have been born out
of wedlock, in the Capitol City of the country,
where opportunities for moral advancement have been
better than elsewhere, fully justifies the application of
Mr. Spencer's condemnation of unchastity as "tending
towards the production of inferior individuals and, if,
prevailing widely, as a cause of decay of society." Unchastity, "conflicting as it does with the establishment
of normal monogamic relations . . . is adverse to

[1] "Principles of Ethics," Part II, page 448.
[2] "The Relations of the Church to the Colored Race," (Jackson,
Miss., 1882,) p. 18.

those higher sentiments which prompt such relations.
In societies characterized by inferior forms of marriage,
or by irregular connections there cannot develop to any
great extent that powerful combination of feelings . .
affection, admiration, sympathy, . . . which in so
marvelous a manner has grown out of the sexual instinct.
And in the absence of this complex passion, which mani-
festly pre-supposes a relation between one man and one
woman, the supreme interest in life (the raising up of
members of a new generation) disappears, and leaves behind relatively subordinate interests. Evidently, a prevalent unchastity severs the higher from the lower com-
ponents of the sexual relation : the root may produce a
few leaves, but no true flower." [1]

[1] "Inductions of Ethics," p. 463.

CHAPTER V.

SOCIAL CONDITIONS AND TENDENCIES.

Man, since we first encounter him, has made ceaseless progress upwards, and this progress continues before our eyes. But it has never been, nor is it now, an equal advance of the whole of the race. Looking back we see that the road by which he has come is strewn with the wrecks of nations, races and civilizations that have fallen by the way, pushed aside by the operations of laws which it takes no eye of faith to distinguish at work amongst us at the present time as surely and as effectively as at any past period.[1]—*Kidd.*

[1] " Social Evolution."

The social tendencies of the colored race are fairly depicted in the statistics of religion, education, crime, pauperism and immorality. The material for a study along these lines is abundant, but much to my regret I shall have to confine myself in this part of my work to a very few of the more important social phenomena. Want of space forbids any extended comment on the various statistical tables which will be given, but most of them will be sufficiently clear to need but little textual explanation.

No exact data as to the religious condition of the colored race at the time of emancipation are in existence, but sufficient evidence is at our command to show that the growth of religious associations among the colored people has been very great indeed. In 1860, according to Mr. H. K. Carroll, special agent of the census on church statistics, the great majority of the colored population were either members of the Methodist Episcopal church South, or Regular Baptists. It is estimated that there were 275,000 of the former, and 250,000 of the latter, a total of over half a million out of a population

of 4,442,000.[1]   During the thirty years following 1860,
the membership of the Methodist Episcopal church
South increased among the colored to 1,190,860, while
the Baptists increased to 1,403,559.   The latter denom-
ination therefore shows the larger increase.   In 1890
the census gave a total of 23,462 organizations, with 23,770
churches and 2,673,977 members, of whom 2,594,419
were members of the Baptist or Methodist church.   A
summary of the number of members of the various denominations is given in the table below, which has been
abstracted from the report of Mr. Carroll.

DISTRIBUTION OF THE MEMBERSHIP OF THE PRINCIPAL RELIGIOUS
DENOMINATIONS OF THE COLORED RACE.—1890. '

COMMUNICANTS.	
Aggregate number of communicants	2,673,977
Regular Baptists	1,348,989
African Methodist Episcopal	452,725
African Methodist Episcopal, Zion	349,788
Methodist Episcopal	246,249
Colored Methodist Episcopal	129,383
Regular Baptists North	35,221
Disciples of Christ	18,578
Primitive Baptists	18,162
Presbyterian (Northern)	14,961
Roman Catholic	14,517
Cumberland Presbyterian	12,956
All other denominations (17)	34,448

This table gives in detail the various denominations
in the order of their numerical importance.   The very

[1] According to Mr. Edward Ingle, "It was estimated, in 1854, that
one-fourth of the slaves in South Carolina were Methodists, that one-
third in the synod of South Carolina were blacks, and that more than
half of the Baptists in Virginia were of the same race.   In 1859, of
468,000 negro church-members in the South, 215,000 were classed as
Methodists, and 175,000 as Baptists.   For benevolent purposes 5,000
slaves in South Carolina contributed $15,000 in 1853 ; and one-third of
the negro population in Savannah supported three pastors at salaries
ranging from $800 to $1,000 a year."—"Southern Sidelights," (New
York, 1896,) pp. 273-4.

small number of Roman Catholics is surprising, but may be due, in part to the fact that the larger number of colored communicants of Catholic churches would be classed as white, since few separate Catholic churches for colored people exist. A statement in the Kansas City *Catholic* gives the number of colored Catholics at about 200,000, a wide variation from the census figures. According to another newspaper waif, "of the many [?] colored Catholic congregations, all with one exception have white priests. The exception is Chicago." A tendency towards individual preference is shown in the fact that 265 colored persons were members of the sect known as "Old-Two-Seed-in-the-Spirit Predestinarian Baptists," while 211 were members of the "Lutheran Synodical conference," and 94 of the "Lutheran United Synod in the South."

The reports show one communicant to every 2.79 of the negro population, and one to every 3.04 of the white population, indicating proportionally a larger church membership for the colored than for the white race. The amount of church property of the colored population is estimated at $26,626,448 for 1890, most of which has of course been accumulated since emancipation. It must, however, be taken into consideration that the race has been materially assisted by the various religious associations, and to a large extent the vast sum just given has been the result of generous aid on the part of the large religious bodies and generous philanthropists of the white race.

The tendency would seem to be rather favorable for the church, although the complaint is not infrequently made that the young people take less interest in the church than the old. The Augusta, Ga., *Sentinel* speaks of "the monstrous indifference manifested by our young educated colored people to the church and religion. . . . Many come from school wedded to forms of ritualistic ceremonies and are led off from the masses, believing that education has placed them above people."

The education of the colored race has formed the subject of so many essays, speeches and discussions that it might be assumed that little remained to be added to the mass of information and statistical data pertaining to the subject. But this work would be incomplete did I neglect to bring forward some data as to the past and present condition of the race from the educational standpoint. Abundant as the statistics of education are, they fail in many respects to afford a true picture of the intellectual progress of a race. It is more in the effects, or rather in the expected results of education, that we must look for the value of educational processes applied to the elevation of a race from slavery to citizenship.

Previous to emancipation efforts to educate the colored race were made only in isolated instances and on a small scale. In most of the southern states education of slaves was forbidden by law. In Georgia a law had been in force since 1770, which read as follows : " All and every person and persons whatsoever, who shall hereafter teach, or cause any slave or slaves to be taught to write, or read writing, or shall use or employ a slave as a scribe in any manner of writing whatsoever, every such person and persons, shall for every offence, forfeit the sum of twenty pounds sterling."[1] In 1829 another law was passed which substituted a fine and whipping and imprisonment in the common jail as punishment for the education of slaves. Attempts to educate the slaves and instruct them in religious principles had, however, been made since 1705 by the Society for the Propagation of

[1] Cobb's Digest of Georgia laws, p. 981.

the Gospel in Foreign Lands, and in 1752 it was reported in the proceedings of the Society that "a flourishing negro school was taught in Charleston by a negro of the society under the inspection and direction of the worthy rector, Garden, by which means many poor negroes were taught." [1]

But such exceptions were rare and, on the whole, without effect on the race, which at the time of emancipation was almost wholly illiterate. The first systematic effort to educate the colored people was made by the American Missionary Association in 1861, through the opening of a school for 'contrabands' at Hampton, Va. By June, 1862, 86 teachers were at work in various parts of the South. In 1863, General Grant placed the duty of superintending the colored people of the region included in the army operations, in the hands of Rev. John Eaton, who in 1866 had over 770,000 of these people under his charge. But in 1865 a change was made in the educational work, and the Freedman's Bureau was organized under General Howard. The Bureau continued in existence from January 1, 1865, to August 31, 1871, and over five million dollars, it is estimated, were expended through it for the education of the freedmen.

During the past twenty-five years the education of the race has been largely in the hands of the state govern-

---

[1] Among the freed negroes, however, considerable progress in education had been made, as is evidenced by the table below, abstracted from the census reports for 1850 and 1860 and reprinted in Mr. Ingle's "Southern Sidelights."

ILLITERACY AMONG FREE NEGRO ADULTS 20 YEARS AND OVER.
1850 AND 1860.

	Population.	Illiterates.	Percentage.
1850, South	115,231	61,031	52.96
North	104,289	33,594	32.30
1860, South	126,803	62,492	49.36
North	120,303	33,369	27.73

ments, all of which provide to the extent of their ability for primary and even higher education. The efforts of the southern states have been materially aided by money and individual efforts on the part of various religious and philanthropic bodies, of which the Slater and Peabody funds are the most important.

Some attempts have been made to estimate the total amount expended on the education of the negro since emancipation, and the total is indeed a vast sum. It is therefore a question of importance to ascertain whether the race has made intellectual progress in proportion to this expenditure, and if so, whether the education thus acquired has been of benefit to the *race* and not merely to a few isolated individuals.

In the matter of attendance at the common schools there was a greater increase among the negroes during the last census period than among the whites, as the following table will show.

NEGRO PUPILS IN COMMON SCHOOLS IN THE UNITED STATES
IN 1880 AND 1890.[1]

1880.	856,123
1890.	1,416,202

[1] Report on Education and Institutions, census of 1890, pp. 50 and 51.

WHITE AND COLORED PUPILS IN COMMON SCHOOLS IN THE SOUTH-
ERN STATES.—1880-1890.

	1880.	1890.	Increase Per Cent.
White pupils	2,301,804	3,409,061	48.10
Colored pupils	797,286	1,288,736	61.64

PERCENTAGE OF POPULATION ENROLLED AND AVERAGE AT-
TENDANCE.—1890.

	Percentage of Enrollment in Population.	Perentage of School Attendance.
White pupils	21.84	63.3
Colored pupils	18.67	62.4

According to the above figures the increase in school attendance has been 61.64 per cent. for the colored and 48.10 per cent. for the white race. While the percentage of population in schools is greater for the whites by a small fraction, the average attendance at school is almost the same for both races.

The higher education of the race is provided for by a large number of institutions, denominational or non-sectarian under state control, covering practically all the higher branches of learning. The number of pupils attending institutions of this kind was 22,963 in 1885–6, against 34,129 in 1891–2, showing a substantial increase during the short period of only 6 years. The following table will show in detail the various branches of learning selected by the more ambitious of the colored race. The table is incomplete in that it does not show the number of colored students who have been admitted to the colleges and universities for the whites, the number of which, however, cannot be very large.

INSTITUTIONS FOR THE HIGHER EDUCATION OF THE COLORED RACE.[1]—1885-86 AND 1891-92.

	No. of Instructors.		No. of Pupils.	
	1885–86	1891–92.	1885–86	1891–92.
Normal schools	281	324	6,207	8,042
Institutions for secondary education .	270	396	9,970	16,237
Universities and colleges.	238	369	5,119	8,116
Schools of theology[2]	110	65	1,297	577
Schools of medicine and dentistry . .	22	51	208	457
School of law	16	16	98	119
Schools for the deaf, dumb and blind,	40	146	139	581
Total	977	1,367	23,038	34,129

[1] Annual report of the Commissioner of Education, 1885-86, pp. 652-64; 1890-91, pp. 1234-37.

[2] In the 1886 report many students were classed as theological students when they should have been reported as college, normal or secondary students. Hence the apparent decrease is largely due to the correction of the erroneous classification of 1886.

By far, the larger number of students in institutions of higher education select teaching as a profession, although medicine attracts quite a number. The general opposition in the South to white teachers in colored schools has opened a vast field for the educated negro, of which he has not been slow to take advantage, even at the temporary disadvantage of lower wages than those paid to white teachers. The matter of lower wages will be dealt with in the succeeding part of this work, on the subject of the economic tendencies of the race.

The few facts here brought together show that the colored race has not failed to take advantage of the opportunities for intellectual advancement in the higher as well as in the lower branches of learning. Towards the expense of these great educational opportunities the race has contributed only an insignificant fraction.[1] The larger part of it was a free gift to those who cared to take advantage of it, and it is something to the credit of the race that it has not been behind the white race in patronizing the schools established for its own use. But it remains to be shown whether the educational process which the race has undergone during the past quarter of a century and the additional efforts and opportunities for religious instruction have materially raised the race from its low social and economic condition at the time of emancipation.

The main object of education is stated to be "the eradication or modification of undesirable tendencies and their development into favorable ones." From the

[1] According to an estimate of the Bureau of Education, the Southern States have expended from 75 to 80 million dollars for the education of negro children since 1876. Of this large sum, raised almost entirely by direct taxation, the negro has paid but a very insignificant part.

standpoint of this definition we should expect a gradual transformation of anti-social tendencies into such as make for the general well-being and happiness of the individual and the society of which he is a member. Crime, pauperism, and sexual immorality are without question the greatest hindrances to social and economic progress, and the tendencies of the colored race in respect to these phases of life will deserve a more careful investigation than has thus far been accorded them.

During slavery the negro committed fewer crimes than the white man, and only on rare occasions was he guilty of the more atrocious crimes, such as rape and murder of white females. Whether from cowardice or respect and devotion to his master, he respected the persons of his master's household, and few indeed are the recorded attempts at insurrection and revolt on the part of the southern slave. Criminal statistics of the colored population previous to emancipation are difficult to obtain, and on account of the abnormal condition of servitude would have little value for purposes of comparisons with the wholly different conditions of freedom.[1] In dealing with statistics of crime and pauperism I shall, therefore, have to confine myself more especially to a statement of present conditions, which, however, may be contrasted with the well-known fact that neither crime nor pauperism prevailed to any extent among the colored population during slavery.

According to the census of 1890, the total number of colored prisoners in the United States was 24,277, of

---

[1] Otken, in his work on "The Ills of the South," gives some valuable statistics of crime among the free negros in the northern states, which show without exception an excess of criminality on the part of the negro as compared with the white race in the same sections. (See "The Ills of the South," pp. 228-29.)

which 22,305 were males and 1,972 were females. The comparative figures for both races are given below, together with the respective proportions of colored prisoners to the total, and the proportion of the colored to total population. This method of comparing the number of criminals with the proportion of the colored to the total population has been employed throughout this part of the work. Wherever possible, I give the population over fifteen years of age, but as the census figures have not all been published, this has not always been possible.

PRISONERS IN THE UNITED STATES IN 1890.

	Aggregate.	Male.	Female.
White	58,052	53,519	4,433
Colored	24,277	22 305	1,972
Total	82,329	75 924	6,405
	Per Cent.	Per Cent.
Proportion of negro criminals to total .	29.38	30.79
Proportion of negro population to total,[1]	10 20	11.09

[1] Population over 15 years of age.

This table shows, that of all the male prisoners in the United States, 29.38 per cent. were colored, as compared with a proportion of 10.20 per cent. of negro males in the total male population. Of female prisoners 30.79 per cent. were colored, while only 11.09 per cent. of the total female population were of African descent. For both sexes therefore there is about the same excess of negro criminality. The table which follows will show similarly for both races and sexes the proportions according to specified classes of offenses, thus bringing out the specific criminal tendencies of the colored race.

SUMMARY OF OFFENSES COMMITTED BY PRISONERS IN THE UNITED
STATES IN 1890, ACCORDING TO COLOR AND SEX.

	MALES.		
	Total No. of Prisoners.	Colored Prisoners.	Colored Prisoners. Per Cent.
Offenses against the government . . .	1,823	176	9.65
" " society	15,033	2,577	17.14
" " " person	16,511	6,308	38.21
" " " property	36,382	10,924	30.03
Offenses of a miscellaneous character .	6,175	2,320	37.95
Aggregate	75,924	22,305	29.38
Proportion of colored population over 15 years of age in total (males) . . .			10.20
	FEMALES.		
Offenses against the government . . .	16	2	12.50
" " society	3,832	683	17.58
" " person	770	432	56.10
" " property	1,325	655	49.43
Offenses of a miscellaneous character .	462	200	43.29
Aggregate	6,405	1,972	30.79
Proportion of colored population over 15 years of age in total (females) . . .			11.09

It has been stated that the proportion of colored males
in the total male population is 10.20 per cent. It is
shown in this table that of the total number of male
prisoners charged with crimes against the person, 38.21
per cent. were colored, and of the female prisoners, 56.10
per cent. That is to say, as regards the most serious of
all crimes the number of negro criminals is out of all
proportion to the numerical importance of the race.
The same holds true for all other groups, with the exception of crimes against the government,—a group which
however, furnishes only a comparatively small number
of offenders. More detailed information is given below,
where I have arranged the particular offenses for the two
principal groups of crimes—those against the person and
against property.

SPECIFIED OFFENSES COMMITTED BY PRISONERS IN THE UNITED
STATES IN 1890.

Crimes Against the Person.	MALE PRISONERS.		
	Total No. of Prisoners.	Colored Prisoners.	Per Cent. of Colored.
Homicide	6,958	2,512	36 10
Rape.	1,387	567	40.88
Abduction	140	32	22.86
Abortion.	25	2	8.00
Assault.	8,001	3,195	39 93
Crimes Against Property.			
Arson	806	372	46.15
Burglary.	9,647	2,710	28.09
Robbery	2,350	555	23.62
Larceny	7,978	3,126	39.18
Grand larceny	6,411	1,774	27.67
Petit larceny	3,475	1,055	30 36
Percentage of colored in total population over 15 yrs. of age (males)			10.20

Crimes Against the Person.	FEMALE PRISONERS.		
Homicide	393	227	57 76
Assault.	346	198	57.23
Crimes Against Property.			
Arson	80	49	61.25
Larceny	425	225	52 94
Grand larceny	320	159	49.69
Petit larceny	266	99	37.22
Percentage of colored in total population over 15 yrs. of age (females)			11.09

The table fully explains itself and needs little comment. Of homicides the colored prisoners formed 36.1 per cent. For the most atrocious of all crimes, rape, 40.88 per cent. of the prisoners convicted were colored, and for assault 39.98 per cent. The proportion of colored females charged with homicide was even greater than that of males and the same is true for the cases of assault. The large proportion of colored among prisoners charged with arson attests the wisdom of the recognized policy of fire insurance companies in restricting the amount of fire insurance obtainable by colored persons. For all crimes against property, the proportion of colored criminals far exceeds the proportion of colored in total population.

The facts brought out in these tables are so significant that the following supplementary tables for various states and cities may prove of value in that they confirm the census figures, while of course they were largely derived from the same official sources. The table below will show for the state of Pennsylvania the proportion of colored inmates in the two penitentiaries for the years 1886 and 1894.

CONVICTS IN PENNSYLVANIA PENITENTIARIES 1886 AND 1894.[1]

	Males.			Females.		
	Total.[2]	Colored.	Percentage of Col'd.	Total.	Colored.	Percentage of Col'd.
1886 . .	1,730	244	14.10	41	14	34.15
1894 . . .	2,312	384	16.61	52	18	34.61
Percentage of col'd in total population over 15 years of age, 1890, ...			2.23			2.09

[1] Annual reports of the State Board of Charities and Lunacy, 1886 and 1894.
[2] Remaining on Sept 30.

The table shows that in Pennsylvania in 1894, 16.61 per cent. of the male inmates and 34.61 per cent. of females were colored ; yet in the whole population of the state over 15 years of age only 2.23 per cent. of the males and 2.09 per cent. of the females were persons of African descent, showing an excessively high proportion of colored convicts. The figures are confirmed by the statistics of arrests in the city of Philadelphia for 1888–94, which show that 6.04 per cent. of the males arrested, and 12.17 per cent. of the females were colored ; while only 3.78 per cent. of the total male, and 5.04 per cent.

of the total female, population over 15, were colored. The table below has been furnished me by Robert J. Linden, superintendent of police, Philadelphia.

ARRESTS IN PHILADELPHIA, 1888-1894.

	Males.			Females.		
	Total.	Colored.	Per cent. Colored.	Total.	Colored.	Per cent. Colored.
1888	40,305	2,340	5.81	6,594	570	8.64
1889	37,565	2,074	5.52	5,108	540	10.57
1890	43,605	2,480	5.69	5,441	687	12.62
1891	47,343	2,847	6.01	5,841	697	11.93
1892	47,143	2,729	5.79	5,801	702	12.10
1893	51,467	3,239	6.29	5,830	839	14.39
1894	55,136	3,856	6.99	6,342	949	14.96
1888-94 . . .	323,665	19,565	6.04	40,957	4,984	12.17
Percentage of colored in total population over 15 years of age, .		3.89				4.25

It is significant that in the state at large as well as in the city of Philadelphia the proportion of arrests and convictions of colored people has increased during the period under observation. Almost identical conditions as regards the disproportion of colored criminals in the total population are met with in New Jersey during the period 1890–94.

CONVICTS IN NEW JERSEY PENITENTIARY, 1890-94.[1]

	Males.			Females.		
	Total.	Colored.	Percentage of Col'd.	Total.	Colored.	Percentage of Col'd.
1890	877	143	16.30	35	12	34.28
1891	960	175	18.22	29	8	27.58
1892	918	167	18.19	29	9	31.03
1893	936	154	16.45	32	12	37.50
1894	992	166	16.73	34	14	41.17
1890-94 . . .	4,683	805	17.19	159	55	34.59
Percentage of col'd in total population, over 15 years of age,		3.40				3.46

[1] Annual reports of the keeper of the N. J. State Prison.

The proportion of colored among the male convicts during the five years was 17.19 per cent., in contrast with 3.40 per cent. of colored in the total population over fifteen years of age. For females the rate is 34.59 per cent., against 3.46 per cent. of colored females in the total female population over fifteen years. Comparing the results of this table with the results of the table for Pennsylvania, it will be seen that the proportion of colored male convicts was 16.61 per cent. for Pennsylvania and 17.19 per cent. for New Jersey; for colored females, 34.61 per cent. in Pennsylvania, and 34.59 per cent. in New Jersey.[1]

In some of the western cities, especially Chicago, the disproportionate number of colored criminals in the population is even more marked. The fact that in Chicago as well as in most of the other large cities of the country, the colored people live in the slum sections, must be taken into account in estimating the tendency of the race in the anti-social direction. Bearing in mind the fact so forcibly brought out in the "Hull House Maps and Papers," that in the section of the city where the

[1] The increase in crime among the colored population of Pennsylvania during the past forty years is shown for decades in the following table compiled from the 66th annual report of the inspectors of the Eastern Penitentiary of Pennsylvania at Philadelphia. The table also shows the colored population of the state at the census year of the period.

AVERAGE NUMBER OF CONVICTS IN THE EASTERN PENITENTIARY OF PENNSYLVANIA.—1856-95.

Period.	Colored Population.	Census of	Average No. of Convicts.
1856–65	56,949	(1860)	79.5
1866–75	65,249	(1870)	137.0
1876–85	85,535	(1880)	183.9
1886–95	107,596	(1890)	275.0

SUMMARY.

Increase in population, 1860–90, ... 88.9 per cent.
Increase in convicts in Eastern Penitentiary, 1856–95 . 245.9 per cent.

larger per cent. of the colored population live, houses
of ill-fame and dives of the lowest order abound, the
table below will be more fully understood.

ARRESTS IN THE CITY OF CHICAGO, 1880-1894.

	Total Arrests.	Colored Persons.	Per cent. Colored.	Percentage of Col'd in Total Populat'n.
1880-84	165,614	8,429	5.09	1.29[1]
1885-89	230,315	16,826	7.31	
1890-94	407,912	40,120	9 84	1.30[2]

[1] Census of 1880.
[2] Census of 1890.

With only 1.29 per cent. of colored in the total population in 1880, the percentage of colored among the persons
arrested during the five years, 1880–84, was 5.09. This
rate increased to 7.31 per cent. during the next five years,
and to 9.84 during the period 1890–94. At the same
time the proportion of colored in total population remained practically the same during the decade 1880–90.

This increase agrees with the results of the table for
Pennsylvania and Philadelphia. The proportion of
negro arrests is, however, much greater in Chicago than
in Philadelphia, due probably to the more unfavorable
congregation of the colored population of Chicago in the
worst section of the city. But it is not all a result of
the "conditions of life." The colored people are not
alone in their tendency to congregate under conditions
of vice and crime. The Italians are as densely crowded,
if not more so, in the immediate vicinity of the negro
colony, and so are other foreign nationalities. But the
extent of crime among the foreign elements is almost
always, excepting for the Irish, in proportion to the
population.

I have abstracted data from the police reports of the
city for 1890, and compared the same with the percentages of population for the purpose of showing whether

the conditions of life, which are without question more severe for the Italians, Polanders and Russians than for the negroes, affect the other nationalities to the same extent as the colored element. The table below will show that this is not the case, but that on the contrary, the colored race shows of all races the most decided tendency towards crime in the large cities.

PERCENTAGE OF ARRESTS ACCORDING TO NATIONALITY, AND PRO-PORTION OF EACH NATIONALITY TO TOTAL POPULATION (1890).

Nationality or Race.	Percentage of Total Population.	Percentage of Total Arrests.
Irish	6.4	10.3
Germans	14.6	11.1
Norwegians.	2.0	1.3
Swedes	3.9	2.5
Russians	0.7	0.8
Bohemians	2.3	1.2
Polanders.	2.2	1.7
Italians.	0.5	1.2
Negroes	1.3	9.8
SUMMARY.		
Principal foreign nationalities	32.6	30.1
Negroes.	1.3	9.8
All others	66.1	60.1
	100.0	100.0

Of the various nationalities enumerated in this table, the Irish and Italians show a percentage of arrests decidedly above the average, yet small when compared with that of the colored element. If all the leading foreign nationalities are combined, we have 31.1 per cent. of the arrests for 32.6 per cent. of population, a showing decidedly in favor of the foreigner when contrasted with the negro. If it is further taken into consideration that the proportion of males of "criminal age," that is over 15 and under 60, is greater among some of the foreign nationalities than among the native whites and negroes, the showing is even more favorable for the foreigner. Unfortunately the reports of the police department do not give the ages of those arrested, hence nothing but a crude comparison could be made.

In southern cities the excess of negro criminality is less marked on account of the larger proportion of the colored element living in the cities. I leave the method employed in the previous tables unchanged, although a different method of comparison would bring out more clearly the disproportion of crime to population among the colored in the cities of the southern states. The table below is for Louisville, Ky., and covers the five years, 1890–94.

ARRESTS AND COMMITTMENTS TO THE WORKHOUSE, LOUISVILLE, KY., 1890-1894.

Years.	Arrests (Males and Females).			Commitments to the Workhouse (Males and Females).		
	Total.	Colored.	Per Ct. of Colored.	Total.	Colored	Per Ct. of Colored.
1890 .	7,621	2,862	37.55	1,580	653	41.32
1891 .	6,938	3,113	44.86	1,499	581	38.75
1892 .	7,133	3,247	45.52	1,628	651	39.98
1893 .	7,079	3,536	49.95	1,431	524	36.61
1894 .	8,390	3,901	46.49	2,438	985	40 40
1890–1894 .	37,161	16,659	44.83	8,576	3,394	39 58

Percentage of colored in total population	17.78	Percentage of colored in population . .	17.78

The proportion of colored in the total population is 17.78 per cent., but the percentage of the arrests was 44.83 for the colored, and of commitments to the work house, 39.58 per cent. In Charleston, S. C., where the colored population forms 56.39 per cent. of the total, the proportion of colored among the male criminals was 65.58 per cent., and among the female criminals, 79.19 per cent.

ARRESTS IN CHARLESTON, S. C., 1890–1894.

	Males.			Females.		
	Total Arrests.	Colored.	Per Cent. Colored.	Total Arrests.	Colored.	Per Cent. Colored.
1890 . . .	2,758	1,745	63.27	527	434	82.35
1891 . . .	2,752	1,754	63.73	549	437	79.59
1892 . . .	2,961	1,913	64 57	514	385	74.90
1893 . . .	2,579	1,771	68.67	413	327	79.17
1894 . . .	3,098	2,093	67.55	506	404	79.84
1890–1894 . . .	14,148	9,276	65.58	2,509	1,987	79.19
Percentage of colored in total population, both sexes . .			56.39			56.39

The criminal statistics of Charleston are given in sufficient detail to enable me to prepare an abstract for the six years, 1889–94, showing the proportion of crimes due to specified causes. The percentage of colored criminals must not be compared with that for the country at large, since the proportion of negroes in the total population is nearly four times as great in Charleston as for the United States at large.

CAUSES OF ARREST IN CHARLESTON.—1889–1894.

Crimes Against the Person.	Total.	Colored.	Percentage of Colored.
Homicide	67	55	82.09
Rape.	18	17	94.45
Assault.	942	765	81.21
Wife beating	60	58	96.67
Crimes Against Property.			
Larceny	1,581	1,489	94.18
Grand larceny	351	310	88.32
Gambling	546	510	93.41
Percentage of colored in total population			56.48

The negroes are responsible for 82.09 per cent. of the homicides, while they form but 56.4 per cent. of the whole population. They are responsible for practically all the cases of rape, and for other crimes against person and property largely out of proportion to their number in the total population. As a fact of possible interest I have added the arrests for wife-beating, which were almost entirely confined to the negroes. Gambling is also largely prevalent among them, but the small number of arrests of whites on this charge is no proof that in its less flagrant form, betting and private gambling are not as prevalent among the whites.

All the tables for various states and cities confirm the census data, and show without exception that the criminality of the negro exceeds that of any other race of any numerical importance in this country. Only a very searching inquiry can fully disclose the most important phases of this subject, but it has been shown that in this respect education has utterly failed to raise the negro to a higher level of citizenship, the first duty of which is to obey the laws and respect the lives and property of others.

One fact, however, must not be overlooked. Owing to his characteristic negligence the negro when guilty of capital crimes is more easily apprehended than the white criminal. As has been pointed out by Mr. Bruce, "The final detection of the parties to such crime is always assured, not only because there are so many clues that set the officers upon the proper track, but also because the parties generally confess, in their terror, the moment they are accused." "The guilty companions," Mr. Bruce remarks in another place, "do not attempt to remove the various traces of their crime; the act is committed with awkward but relentless coolness and ferocity, the booty is collected, and then the spot is deserted, being left with every evidence of the fatal struggle, including the corpse itself, to bear silent testimony to the awful details of the tragedy of which it has recently been the scene."[1]

[1] "The Plantation Negro as a Freeman," pp. 82-83.

This fact, however, does not materially affect the proportion of colored to white criminality, and rather confirms the conviction of those who know the race by years of personal contact, that while few of the guilty escape, there are few who are convicted when innocent.

Some reference has been made to rape in the preceding tables. It was shown that 567 colored persons were in United States prisons waiting trial for this crime. In the city of Charleston during six years eighteen men were arrested for rape, of whom seventeen were colored. This would prove that not all of the negroes charged with this crime have "met with summary punishment" at the hands of an infuriated mob.

The lynching of colored men is usually for rape, but occasionally also for murder, robbery, miscegenation, etc. The evidence on this point is not such as would recommend itself to an investigation of this kind, in which official data are the main reliance. In the absence of an official investigation or report on the subject, I have to rely almost entirely on newspaper evidence. During the past few years I have been able to collect information of 129 attempts at lynching, of which 83 were successful. By attempts I mean instances of mob violence where colored or white men charged with rape or other crimes were in imminent danger of summary justice. Of the 129 persons thus charged, 102 were colored and 27 white; 102 of the attempts occurred in the southern states and 27 in the North and West. The details are summarized in the table below:[1]

[1] In addition I have collected information in regard to eight attempts at lynching by colored men. In four cases the mob was successful. The cause was rape in three cases and murder in five. Of the persons

ANALYSIS OF 129 ATTEMPTS AT LYNCHINGS IN THE UNITED STATES, 1891-1895.[1]

Colored.	No. of Attempts.	Successful Attempts.	Per Cent. Successful,	No. of Persons Lynched.
Southern states	90	65	72.2	78
Northern states	12	3	25.0	3
White.				
Southern states	12	6	50.0	9
Northern states	15	9	60.0	14

		Causes of Lynchings.		
Colored.		Rape.	Murder.	All Other.
Southern states	90	58	22	10
Northern states	12	6	5	1
White.				
Southern states	12	1	5	6
Northern states	15	7	6	2

It will be observed that out of the 129 attempts at lynching, 72 were for rape, and in 64 of these cases the crimes were the acts of colored men. Of the other crimes 38 were homicides and 19 of a miscellaneous character. The result of this investigation agrees with the statistics previously given, which brought out the large proportion of negroes connected with crimes against women and chastity. With only about 10 per cent. of the population over 15 years of age, they are responsible for 40 per cent. of the cases of rape in the country at large.

The fact is fairly proven that lynchings at the South are not the result of race antipathy, but are due to crimes which meet with summary justice in cases of whites and blacks alike. That the crime is on the increase is the opinion of those most competent to judge. From data collected by the Chicago *Tribune* which has for years made a specialty of collecting criminal statistics not officially reported, it would seem that the crime is increasing at an alarming rate. The table below may be

whose lives were in danger three were white and five were colored. Those actually lynched were all colored.

accepted as substantially correct, since few public lynch-ings fail to be reported in the newspapers, on account of the peculiar horror attached to such occurrences.

LYNCHINGS IN THE UNITED STATES, 1886–1894.

1886	133
1887	123
1888	144
1889	175
1890	125
1891	236
1893	200
1894	165[1]

[1] Nine months only.

Of course not all of the above cases were those of colored men lynched for rape, but the majority undoubt-edly were, and the rate of increase in lynchings may be accepted as representing fairly the increasing tendency of colored men to commit this most frightful of all crimes. In the words of Mr. Bruce, "Their disposition to perpetrate it has increased in spite of the quick and summary punishment that always follows; and it will be seen that this disposition will grow in proportion as that vague respect which the blacks still entertain for whites declines. . . . There is something strangely alluring and seductive to the negro in the appearance of a white woman; they are roused and stimulated by its foreignness to their experience of sexual pleasures, and it moves them to gratify their lust at any cost and in spite of any obstacle. . . . Rape, indescribably beastly and loathsome always, is marked, in the instance of its perpetration by the negro, by a diabolical persistence and a malignant atrocity of detail that have no reflection in the whole extent of the natural history of the most beastial and ferocious animals. He is not content

merely with the consummation of his purpose, but takes
that fiendish delight in the degradation of his victim
which he always shows when he can reek his vengeance
upon one whom he has hitherto been compelled to
fear.   .   .   His invariable impulse after the ac-
complishment of his purpose, is to murder his victim,
that being the only means suggested to his mind of
escaping the consequence of the act, and this impulse is
carried into effect with the utmost barbarity, unless he
is accidentally interrupted and frightened off." [1]

Mr. Bruce, from whose admirable little work on the
"Plantation Negro" the above quotations are taken,
had exceptional opportunities for observation, and few
writers on the negro have so thoroughly grasped the intricate details of their subject.   In all the endless discussion on the subject of lynching, few of those who
write in bitterness against the South and its people,
take into account the peculiar horror of the crime, a
horror which can only be understood by those who, after
years of residence in the South, are thoroughly familiar
with local conditions.   The true sentiment of the southern people is perhaps nowhere better expressed than in
the following passage of an editorial in the Atlanta *Constitution.*

> We advise our northern contemporaries to deal as gently as they
> can with the manifestations of human nature which take place in the
> South and are duplicated at the North whenever the opportunity offers.
> That they are deplorable is not to be denied.   But the cause that leads
> to them—the situation out of which they are developed—is more de-
> plorable still.   It is no light thing, may it please your honor and
> gentlemen of the jury, for the women and girls of the whole country
> side to live in practically a state of seige—to be afraid to venture to a
> neighbor's or a school house lest some black beast shall leap from the
> bushes and give them over to a fate worse than death.   Let us think
> of these things when we become critical enough to take on judicial
> airs.

[1] Bruce, "The Plantation Negro as a Freeman."

Attempts to stop lynchings have been made in many of the southern states where such crimes have become only too frequent. In South Carolina the new constitution of that state provides that "In all cases of lynching where death ensues, the county where such lynching takes place shall, without regard to the conduct of the officers, be liable in exemplary damages of not less than $2,000 to the legal representative of the person lynched." In the Virginia Senate a bill has been introduced which provides that "Whenever a lynching occurs in any county, city, or town, it shall be the duty of the Supervisors or the Council of the city or town as the case may be, to lay a tax levy of $200 for every thousand inhabitants, which is to be collected as other county taxes are collected, the proceeds to be paid into the treasury by the treasurer of the county." In Mississippi the attorney general in his last annual report makes commendations of the same character for the suppression of the crime.

At various times the militia of the state has been called out and large expenses have been incurred to prevent lynchings of men of whose guilt there was not the slightest doubt. Yet there has been no abatement of the crime and no decrease in the number of lynchings, the due consequence of the crime, in spite of all that has been done and said and written about the subject, and in spite of the fact that all over the South the best people are fully agreed that 'lynchings must be stopped.'

Lynchings rarely occur more than once in the same community or section, but they are met with in all sections of the South, especially in remote districts. In Florida, for instance, where in 1895, 12 negroes were reported as having been lynched, the crime of rape has been most frequently committed by negroes from the phosphate mines, which seem to have attracted the vagrant elements from South Carolina and other adjoining states. The commission of the crime seems to be largely confined to this vagrant and worthless element, but the race as a whole suffers greatly from the resulting antipathy of the whites.

Mr. Moncure D. Conway, agent for an English committee, has expressed the opinion that " In some of the southern states the crime seems nearly to have disappeared, and the curious phenomena has appeared that in these orderly states such as Virginia, Maryland and South Carolina, with their large negro population, no suggestion is ever heard of the negro propensity to rape." This statement is not at all warranted by the facts ; for not only have lynchings increased in these three states from 7 in 1891 to 12 in 1895, but the police statistics of Charleston alone show that in six years 18 colored men were arrested for rape, proving that there is neither an absence of propensity to rape, nor a decrease in the number of lynchings in that state.

The crime of lynching is the effect of a cause, the removal of which lies in the power of the colored race. Rape is only one of the many manifestations of an increasing tendency on the part of the negro to misconstrue personal freedom into personal license, and this tendency, persisted in, must tend towards creating a still wider separation of the races. The fact that lynchings should be frequent is a natural consequence of a social and political condition under which the frequent commission of the crime of rape is possible. Until the negro learns to respect life, property, and chastity, until he learns to believe in the value of a personal morality operating in his everyday life, the criminal tendencies brought out in the foregoing tables will increase, and by so much the social and economic efficiency of the race will be decreased.

The low state of sexual morality among the colored population is a fact which, it would seem, has been inadequately treated by those who have written on the subject of negro morality. In this work reference has been made to the subject in the statistics of syphilis and other venereal diseases; but the following table of illegitimate births in Washington will show more emphatically the tendency of the race towards a low level of sexual immorality and vice.

ILLEGITIMACY IN WASHINGTON, D. C., 1879–1894.[1]
(Percentage of illegitimate in total number of births.)

	White.	Colored.
1879	2.32	17.60
1880	2.43	19.02
1881	2.33	19.42
1882	2.09	19.73
1883	3.14	20 95
1884	3.60	19.02
1885	3.00	22.88
1886	3.28	22.86
1887	3 34	21.27
1888	3.49	22.18
1889	3.59	23.45
1890	3.34	26.50
1891	2.90	25.12
1892	2.53	26.40
1893	2.82	27.00
1894	2.56	26.46
Average 1879–94 . . .	2.92	22.49

SUMMARY 1879–94.

	White.	Colored.
Total births, 1879–94	34,803	27,211
Illegitimate births, 1879–94	1,032	6,186
Percentage illegitimate births . . .	2.92	22.49

[1] Report of the health office of the District of Columbia, 1894, page 152.

The average rate of illegitimacy is 22.49 per cent. for the colored population and 2.92 per cent. for the whites.

The rate of increase for the earlier years of the period
1879–94 is affected by a more perfect registration during
the latter part of the period; but even if allowance is
made for this probable element of error, and we assume
that in the earlier part of the period the same amount of
unchastity prevailed as at present, the results are scarcely
less significant.   That under a civilized government
one-fourth of the children of one race should bear "*the
bar* sinister" is a fact which is fraught with far-reaching
consequences.

I have given the statistics of the general progress of
the race in religion and education for the country at
large, and have shown that in church and school the
number of attending members or pupils is constantly increasing; but in the statistics of crime and the data of
illegitimacy the proof is furnished that neither religion
nor education has influenced to an appreciable degree the
moral progress of *the race.*   Whatever benefit the individual colored man may have gained from the extension
of religious worship and educational processes, *the race*
as a whole has gone backwards rather than forwards.
While it is not possible to prove by statistics that the
moral condition of the slaves was exceptionally good, all
the data at my command show that physically the race
was superior to the present generation, and no physical
health is possible without a fair degree of sexual morality.   It is true that the sexual relations were as lax as
they are now, but they were lax in the nature of concubinage or irregular sexual intercourse, in which affection played at least a small if not an important part.   In
the irregular sexual relations of the present day prostitution for gain is the prevailing rule, and one of the
determining causes of the inordinate mortality and high
degree of criminality.

In Washington the colored race has had exceptional educational, religious and social opportunities. Even in an economic sense the race is probably better off there than anywhere else. According to the census there were in Washington in 1890, 77 churches for colored people, valued at $1,182,650, with 22,965 communicants. There were 250 colored teachers in charge of 13,332 colored pupils; but there were also during the year 483 young mothers, whom neither education nor religion had restrained from open violation of the moral law.

In Delaware the low moral condition of the colored population in this respect, is perhaps best illustrated by the following newspaper report, clipped from the Baltimore *American* of recent date.

A wholesale marriage ceremony was performed in Odd Fellows' Hall at Hockessin, a few miles from Wilmington, Del., on Sunday afternoon. Eight couples of colored people were married simultaneously by the Rev. William Jason, president of the State College for Colored Students. The ceremony was witnessed by more than three hundred people. Explaining the circumstances which brought about the wedding, Mr. Jason said: "God must know that when I went among these people and tried to bring them to God, they were a bad lot. At first I did not get much encouragement, but after I had labored with them for several months, I saw that even the hardest of them were touched. In nearly every instance where a man and woman were living together, no marriage ceremony had been performed between them. I told them that it was wrong and sinful; that it was a violation of the civil law and an offence against divine law. That's why I performed this wholesale marriage. At first they objected, but when one couple who had been living together for four years consented to let me marry them, the others gave in and I hope in time that all the rest will follow in their footsteps."

For other states similar information could be given, but it would be merely cumulative evidence. The condition is everywhere the same. In Mobile and Knoxville, as well as in Washington, the rate of illegitimacy is about 25 per cent. of the total births, against an average of about 2.5 per cent. for the whites. The figures here

16

given are only those of births *admitted* to be illegitimate. The actual number if known would of course, give a much higher rate, but the margin of error is probably about the same for both races. The facts brought out show a state of immorality such as does not often prevail in a community claiming even a moderate degree of civilization.

What is true of the negro in the United States is even more true of the colored population in the West Indies. I have elsewhere dealt fully with the social statistics of the negro in the West Indies, and need here to give only a few data to round off this picture of the lowest phase of the social life of the American negro.[1]

It was a favorite argument of the opponents of slavery that freedom, education and citizenship would elevate the negro to the level of the white in a generation or two.   One writer in a report to the Anti-Slavery Society, which was widely circulated, made use of the following language in regard to the effects of the emancipation of the slaves in the West Indies : " The abolition of slavery gave the death blow to open vice. Immediate emancipation instead of opening the floodgates was the only power strong enough to shut them down. Those great controllers of moral action, self respect, attachment to law and veneration of God, which slavery destroyed, freedom has resuscitated."

The West India slaves were completely emancipated in 1838. About 30 years later *The American Missionary* in commenting upon the people of Jamaica used the following language : " A man may be a drunkard, a liar, a Sabbath breaker, a profane man, a fornicator, an adulterer, and such like and be known to be such, and go to

[1] "The Negro in the West Indies," *Quarterly Publications of the American Statistical Association*, Vol. 3.

chapel and hold up his head there, and feel no disgrace from those things, because they are so common as to create a public sentiment in his favor."[1] About 25 years later James Anthony Froude wrote of the negro in the West Indies in the folllowing severe terms :

"Morals in the technical sense they have none, but they cannot be said to sin, because they have no knowledge of a law and therefore cannot commit a breach of the law. They are naked and not ashamed. They are married, as they call it, but not parsoned. The woman prefers a looser tie that she may be able to leave the man if he treat her unkindly. A missionary told me that a marriage connection rarely turned out well which begins with legal marriage. The system is strange, but it answers. There is evil, but there is not the demoralizing effect of evil, they sin but they sin only as animals sin, without shame because there is no sense of wrong doing ; they eat the forbidden fruit, but it brings with it no knowledge of the difference between good and evil—in fact these poor children of darkness have escaped the consequences of the fall, and *must come of another stock after all.*"[2]

The statements of the various writers on the social condition of the West India negro are supported by reliable statistical evidence. The table below, compiled from the annual reports of the registrar-generall of Jamaica bears mute testimony on this point.

ILLEGITIMACY AND ILLITERACY IN JAMACIA.

	Percentage of Illegitimate Births.	Percentage of Females Signing Marriage Register With Mark.
1880–81	57.7	66.8
1881–82	58.2	67.7
1882–83	58.9	68.6
1883–84	58.9	68.8
1884–85	59.9	67.7
1885–86	59.6	64.0
1886–87	59.8	64.8
1887–88	60.6	64.8
1888–89	60.5	65.5
1889–90	61.7	64.9
1890–91	60.7	63.7
1891–92	60.6	61.6
1892–93	60.1	60.0
1893–94	60.6	59.4
1894–95	60.8	57.1

[1] Seaman, "Progress of Nations," p. 518.
[2] "English in the West Indies," pp. 49–50. (The italics are mine.)

After fifty years of educational and religious influence under conditions of freedom, sixty out of every hundred births are acknowledged to be illegitimate.[1] On the other hand, education has progressed at such a rate that in the year 1894 only 40 per cent. of the women who married could not write their own names. The progress of education is shown by the table below:

PROPORTION OF POPULATION OF JAMAICA OVER FIVE YEARS OF AGE WHO ARE ABLE TO READ AND WRITE.[1]

	Per Cent.
1861	31.3
1871	35 0
1881	45.7
1891	52.5

[1] "The Negro in the West Indies." *Publications of the American Statistical Association.*

One of the most recent reports on the condition of the negro in Jamaica was published in the New York *Evening Post* in November, 1895, and contains the fol-

[1] On this point the registrar general, Mr. S. P. Smeeton, in his annual report for 1895, writes as follows: "The subject, (illegitimacy) is not a savoury one, and when discussed 'time' and 'education' are generally mentioned as the remedies to be relied upon. It may, however, be pointed out that the published registration figures for 17 years past show no improvement in the matter, and that *an ever increasing educational force has been for that same period in operation without, apparently, any sign of cleansing away this social cancer.* From time to time great and praiseworthy interest is shown for the development of the material concerns of the island and extensive organizations are formed for the benefit of these, but is there any island product of more value, from any point of view, than the *population* one? What are all others if this be uncared for, and 60 per cent. of it be allowed, as we say in Jamaica, to 'run into bush'? I have in a previous report quoted the words of Cardinal Manning: 'On the domestic life of a people the whole political order of human society reposes. If the foundation be ruined what will be the superstructure?' and they will bear repetition here, for, while it is beyond question that the people of Jamaica are capable of reaching a high state of civilization, it is equally certain that this goal cannot be reached so long as the very root element of social progress is lacking, viz., a morally healthy family life." (The italics are mine.)

lowing: " We have seen such sights as one of their naked voodoo priests standing in the middle of a stream holding a rod in one hand and the other outstretched over the water apparently without moving a muscle for upwards of three hours, while thousands of naked men and women crowded into the stream below him. But this is tame compared to their horrible midnight orgies carried on in their mountain homes, which the white man is not allowed to witness. We can only form an idea of their barbarity from the rumors that come to us from time to time or the reports of some of their more enlightened brethren."

The same condition is met with in other islands: everywhere we find the evidence of grossest immorality, and nowhere do we meet with the anticipated effects of education and political freedom. The main purpose of education, " the eradication or modification of undesirable tendencies and the development of favorable ones," has, according to these facts, not been accomplished. After nearly sixty years of freedom in the West Indies and after thirty years of freedom in this country, during which the most elaborate efforts have been made to improve the moral and social condition of the race, we find that its physical and moral tendency is downwards. A low degree of social and economic efficiency must result from such anti-social conditions. A race living under such conditions can hardly be expected to develop the essential virtue of Indo-Germanic races, thrift. Pauperism with all its consequences is the natural and inevitable result of crime and immorality.

Thrift is the result of self help. It is developed under the most adverse circumstances and once acquired forms the most persistent virtue of a race. It is the result of self-denial and self-sacrifice, developed in races only after a struggle against adverse conditions which would have reduced a race less sturdy to barbarism and savagery.

All attempts to ameliorate the condition of the lower races in which the vital element of self-help is ignored, must in the end, prove a failure. A system of philanthropy that is based on the notion that easy conditions of life are essential to human development must fail in its effort, honorable and unselfish as the motives may be. No system of state socialism will benefit a *race*, much as it may occasionally prove of benefit to the *individual.*

The violation of this fundamental principle of economics on the part of the state or an association of individuals, or individuals working alone for the amelioration of the condition of the lower classes must in the end produce the very effects and tendencies shown to be in operation among the colored population, namely, an increasing mortality, decreasing vitality, and increasing immorality, criminality and pauperism. Such, in the words of Mr. Francis A. Walker, " may be the effects of foolish laws. The legislator [or the philanthropist and social reformer, I would add] may think it hard that his power for good is so closely restricted ; but he has no reason to complain of any limits upon his power for evil. On the contrary, it would seem that there is no race of men, whom a few laws respecting industry, trade and finance passed . . . in defiance of economic principles could not in half a generation transform into beasts."[1]

This principle is as applicable to general social conditions as to those which fall strictly within the domain of economics. Even political liberties, granted with disregard for natural inequalities or stages of human

[1] "Political Economy," p. 362.

progress, must affect injuriously, in the end, the race
on which they were thus conferred. " Self-govern-
ment," writes Mr. Froude, " is a beautiful subject for
oratorical declamation. If the facts corresponded to the
theory and if the possession of a vote produced the elevating effects upon the character which are so noisily
insisted upon, it would be the welcome panacea for
political and social disorder. Unfortunately the fact
does not correspond to the theory. The possession of a
vote never improved the character of any human being
and never will." [1]

We may, in conclusion, consider the facts relating to
pauperism and general dependency. The table below
will show for ten northern and ten southern states the
number of negro paupers per million of population, as
compared with the white population. The table also
shows the average age according to sex.

WHITE AND COLORED PAUPERS IN ALMSHOUSES IN 1890, PER MIL-
LION OF POPULATION.[1]

	Southern States.		
	Whites.	Colored.	
Virginia	1,117	1,658	Colored in excess
North Carolina.	886	992	" "
South Carolina.	794	306	Whites "
Georgia	545	428	" "
Florida	76	42	" "
Kentucky	788	1,208	Colored "
Tennessee	756	1,239	" "
Alabama	386	443	" "
Mississippi	376	388	" "
Louisiana	204	14	Whites "
	Northern States.		
Massachusetts	2,097	3,352	Colored in excess
New York	1,696	3,045	" "
New Jersey.	1,846	2,895	" "
Pennsylvania	1,604	3,599	" "
Ohio.	1,968	3,931	" "
Illinois.	1,406	1,659	" "
Indiana	1,316	2,212	" "
Kansas.	372	1,603	" "
Missouri	834	1,785	" "
Michigan.	906	1,809	" "

[1] Census report on Crime, Pauperism and Benevolence.' Part II, pp. 654-658.

[1] " The English in the West Indies," p. 166.

AVERAGE AGES OF WHITE AND COLORED PAUPERS IN ALMSHOUSES
IN 1890.[1]

Southern States.	Males.		Females.	
	White.	Colored.	White.	Colored.
Virginia	44.08	51.28	43.30	46.11
North Carolina	49.28	48.06	48.22	48.30
South Carolina	52.40	48.77	54 45	58.75
Georgia	52.22	58.85	51.60	54.36
Florida	55.11	39.75	45.20	77 67
Kentucky	49.05	44.07	40.46	41.82
Tennessee	46.40	45.72	41.53	46.81
Alabama	51.35	52.43	47.47	61.04
Mississippi	49.75	54.48	48.93	61.50
Louisiana	62.76	57.80	67.04	56.33
Northern States.				
Massachusetts	53.08	41.25	51.09	41 59
New York	56.64	56.75	54.78	49.77
New Jersey	48.51	51.91	46.75	44.34
Pennsylvania	51.68	42.92	48 53	43.57
Ohio	53.31	46 25	48 63	42.48
Illinois	48.73	38.36	44 28	38.71
Indiana	48.36	39.62	42.52	34.39
Kansas	46.70	40.97	42.82	36.23
Missouri	46.70	41.39	42.21	47.75
Michigan	53.35	50.10	47.09	46.00

[1] Census report on Crime, Pauperism and Benevolence. Part II, pp. 819-20.

It will be observed that with only four exceptions, the
ratio of colored paupers is greater than that of the whites.
The exceptions are Georgia, Florida, South Carolina and
Louisiana, all of which are in the extreme South—sections where indoor pauperism is met with to only a very
limited extent.   In all the northern states the colored
paupers outnumber the whites, which contradicts the
statement frequently made that while the negro race furnishes more criminals, it furnishes fewer paupers than
the white race.

Pauperism, North and South, cannot be compared, on
account of the difference in prevailing relief methods.
In the South the need of indoor relief is very small; the
conditions of life are much easier and outdoor relief is

usually sufficient. Able-bodied paupers, such as we meet with in the alms-houses in the North are rare. The accommodations furnished by almshouses are, on the whole, not such as would encourage pauperism, even among the negroes. With the increase in wealth and general economic progress, the South is making better provision for its dependent classes, and an increase in the number of paupers would prove rather a shifting from outdoor to indoor relief than an actual increase in pauperism.

It will also be observed that the average age of paupers in the South is on the whole about the same for the colored as for the white. But in the northern states, the average age of the colored is, with only two exceptions, considerably below that of the whites. In Massachusetts, for instance, the average age of the white male paupers was 53, as against 41 for the colored. This would clearly indicate that the colored in the northern states become paupers at an earlier age than in the South, where conditions of indoor relief are less encouraging to chronic pauperism.

Outdoor relief to colored persons is exceedingly common in the southern states. It is not given in the form of money, but in the form of free fuel, free fruit, free land for cultivation, free medical attendance and, most of all, free burial in the potter's field. In addition there is an almost unseen agency of outdoor relief, perhaps of all the most pernicious, which furnishes the family of a negro servant with the remnants of the table of the employer.

The difference in the extent of outdoor and indoor relief is illustrated in the table for Cincinnati, in which a comparison is made between the indoor and the various kinds of outdoor relief. The method of comparison is the same as that made use of in the criminal statistics, and the proportion of colored paupers to total is compared with the percentage of colored in total population.

CHARITY AND PAUPERISM IN CINCINNATI.—1894.

	Indoor (Almshouse) Relief.	Out-door Relief. Provisions.	Fuel.	Coffins, Etc.
Total number receiving relief. . . .	450	2,391	1,932	197
Colored	22	488	369	64
Percentage of colored	4.89	20.41	19.09	32.49
Percentage of col'd population in total	3.93	3.93	3.93	3.93

The proportion of colored in the total population of
Cincinnati was almost four per cent. in 1890. The proportion of colored paupers in almshouses was almost five
per cent., an excess amounting to one-fifth of the percentage of population. The percentage of outdoor relief
for the colored was, for provisions 20.41, for fuel 19.09;
while for pauper funerals the rate was 32.49 per cent. of
the total. That is to say, with only 3.93 per cent. of
the population, the negroes were the beneficiaries of one-
fifth of the out-door relief and one-third of the expenditures for pauper funerals.

Pauper funerals, as I have stated, are extremely frequent among the colored population and nowhere else
does absence of thrift so clearly manifest itself as in the
indifference to a burial in the "potter's field." Whoever
has witnessed the pauper funeral of a negro, the bare pine
box and the common cart, the absence of all that makes
less sorrowful the last rites over the dead, has seen a
phase of negro life and manners more disheartening perhaps than anything else in the whole range of human
misery. Perhaps only the dreary aspect of the negroes'
"potters field," the low sand hills, row after row, partly
washed away by the falling rains, unrelieved by a single
mark of human kindness, without a flower and without a

cross, only the pauper lot itself, may be more sad and gruesome than the display of almost inhuman apathy at the funeral. By this I do not wish to be understood as saying that the negro is entirely indifferent, for he is not, and often mourns the loss of a near one as sincerely as the member of any other race, but his indifference is to a condition imposed upon him not on account of his poverty, but on account of his lack of thrift.

In the two tables which follow I give the white and colored pauper funerals in Washington and Charleston for a period of seven years. The table also shows the percentage of colored in total pauper burials and the proportion of colored in total population.

PAUPER FUNERALS IN WASHINGTON, D. C.—1888-1894.

	Total.	Colored.	Percentage of Colored.
1888	391	331	84.65
1889	428	368	85.98
1890	411	375	91.24
1891	487	404	82.95
1892	506	406	80.23
1893	512	424	82.81
1894	527	444	84.25
1888-1894	3,262	2,752	84.36
Percentage of colored population in total			32.89

PAUPER FUNERALS IN CHARLESTON—1888-1894.

	Total.	Colored.	Percentage of Colored.
1888	375	366	97.60
1889	368	356	96.73
1890	336	331	98.51
1891	327	304	92.96
1892	377	366	97.08
1893	351	339	96.58
1894	395	385	97.46
1888-1894	2,529	2,447	96.76
Percentage of colored population in total			56.48

The above tables show, that in Washington 84.36 per
cent. of the pauper funerals were those of colored persons, while only 32.89 per cent. of the total population
were colored. In Charleston 96.76 per cent. of the
pauper funerals were those of negroes, with only 56.48
per cent. of colored in the total population. The tables
must not be compared with each other on account of the
difference in the distribution of the two races in the two
cities. A comparison is made however in the following
summary, in which the percentage of pauper funerals in
the total number of burials is shown for each race, in
both cities.

PROPORTION OF PAUPER FUNERALS IN TOTAL NUMBER OF DEATHS.

	CHARLESTON.			WASHINGTON.		
	Total Burials.	Pauper funerals.	Percent-age.	Burials.	Pauper funerals.	Percent-age.
White	3,672	82	2 23	21,979	510	2.32
Colored . . .	9,388	2,447	26.07	18,086	2,752	15.22

According to this table the proportion of colored pauper funerals in the total number of burials was 26.07
per cent. for Charleston and 15.22 per cent. for Washington. That is to say, while one out of every four negroes
dying in Charleston was buried at public expense, only
one out of six was buried in this way in Washington,
showing a decided improvement in this respect for the
colored people of the latter city. But it is a question
not easily answered, whether this lower rate for Washington may not be due in part to local conditions which
make pauper burials more difficult. For in Cincinnati
it has been shown that one-third of those who were
buried at public expense were colored, and similar rates
are met with in other cities, data for which would only
burden this work with cumulative evidence. The
rational explanation would seem to me to be the de-

velopment in the Capitol City of a higher degree of social pride, which, while not a strictly moral element, is nevertheless of high social and economic value. The principle of association for benevolent purposes, assistance in sickness and insurance at death, has also, without question, largely affected the colored population of Washington, more perhaps than that of any other city.

The beneficient effect of this change is, however, more developed in the seen than in the unseen, and the attention paid to ceremonial matters has had no influence in developing the more important regard for sexual morality and monogamic marriage. Improved economic conditions have therefore affected the less important phases and tendencies of life, rather than the more important; they have affected changes in the surface conditions, but have failed to go to the root.

I cannot do better than close this chapter with the timely words of M. Leroy-Beaulieu, which are as applicable to the colored race as they are to the white or any other race,—and even to a greater degree, since the downward tendencies are so much more distinctly recognizable among the colored than among other races:

We need hardly point out that it is far from our intention to condemn either education in general or that of women [negroes I would add] in particular, but it is rather our desire to point out what appears to be necessary to improve and modify its tendencies. Every age is characterized by its peculiar craze. The present craze is for education, unlimited and injudicious, and for philanthropy equally unlimited and injudicious, both absolutely superficial. By their aid we have succeeded in producing a mental condition and creating social circumstances which are most unfavorable to the growth of the population.[1]

[1] *Journal of the Royal Statistical Society,* 1891, p. 384.

Chapter VI.

Economic Condition and Tendencies.

The general economic condition of the negro race is a subject on which much has been written from the standpoint of the casual observer, or the interested investi-.gator; but no attempt has ever been made by government, national or local, to deal with the subject in a comprehensive manner. This is the more to be regretted since much that is now done in behalf of the race is the result of investigations and observations naturally limited and inadequate. If, instead of the numerous investigations into phases of social life, (with which the government could not interfere even if it desired), an annual or quinquennial investigation were made by a competent commission to ascertain the moral and material condition of the race, in the same way that the government of India prepares its annual and decennial summary reports on the moral and material condition of the people of India, a most important step toward a more scientific view of the needs and wants of the negro would be gained. As matters stand, it is difficult to discuss the subject in a satisfactory way, and this attempt to bring together the most important facts is rather in the nature of a contribution to a more comprehensive study than an attempt to deal comprehensively and exhaustively with the economic condition and tendencies of the colored race. I have confined myself to a few points on which the necessary data were fairly reliable and complete enough to permit a discussion as to the probable future tendency of the race in the direction of material well being, and its influence as an economic factor in the development of the nation.

The Negro as an Agricultural Laborer.

The vast portion of the colored population of the southern states are still agricultural laborers, and the observed tendency of the negro population to drift into the cities has not affected a very large proportion of the total colored population. The attempts made to migrate to the western states or to emigrate to Mexico, Liberia, or other foreign countries, have had very slight influence on the population at large. The fact that of this vast population the majority are tillers of the soil, productive factors in the highest economic sense, invests the probable tendencies of the race with an unusual degree of public interest. Does the negro as an agricultural laborer produce as much as a white man under the same conditions? Does he as a free man produce as much as, or more than, he did under the régime of slavery? To these two questions at present no satisfactory answer can be given, for the reasons stated at the beginning of the chapter. Yet some data are available which may be worth recording, and may serve at least the purpose of showing the dearth of data for this part of my investigation.

The difficulty in deciding as to the comparative efficiency of white and colored labor is enhanced by the conflict of opinion even among those most competent to judge of the negro as an agricultural or industrial worker. " I know of no subject," said the late General Armstrong, " on which you hear such diametrically opposite opinions as you do about the colored people. I have heard two men in the same town, each of them a large employer of colored labor, and each of them with equal experience, say the direct opposite, the one claiming that the colored race might be developed to any extent, the other that there was nothing to be done for them."[1] This difficulty is emphasized in two letters to the Chattanooga *Tradesman* from southern planters. The first, from Mr. Alf. Stone, of Greenville, Miss., maintains that "the negro as a field hand is a failure," and advises planters to substitue "the thrifty foreigner, Italians, Germans, Norwegians." A Mr. Massey, of Friars Point, Miss., replies that "the negro is the most docile and tractable of all laborers and under proper management the most contented and profitable. The thriftlessness generally ascribed to the negro is more the fault of the employer than of the laborer."[2]

In the *Country Gentleman* a few years ago, a Connecticut farmer gave his experience with negro labor, mostly from Virginia, concluding his remarks with the following words: "In the course of several years others came to our town from the same region, and I cannot recall a single instance in which they did not prove efficient and reliable workmen. . . . Those whom we employed were pure-minded and honest-hearted and possessed skill and judgment to a degree which has seldom been equalled by any workman on our farm." The experience of a Virginia planter, Col. Henry Stokes of Prince Edward county, showed that "under the direction of a level head, . . . 20,000 hills of tobacco to the hand were cultivated, in contrast with only 10,000 hills under slavery, demonstrating that a free man is worth just twice as much as a slave."[3]

These favorable views of experienced farmers are in

[1] L. D. Powles, "Land of the Pink Pearl," (London, 1888), p. 193.
[2] *Tradesman*, January 15, 1892.
[3] Farmville *Journal*.

contrast with the opinion of the former commissioner of agriculture of Tennessee, Mr. Killebrew, who, in the *Tradesman* of January 1, 1895, writes as follows: "The great and leading differences between white and colored labor is this, the first has ambition, calculates possibilities, and looks forward to the future; the latter enjoys the present, is indifferent of what is to come, and is utterly incapable of that self denial which makes thrift and prosperity possible."

Reference has been made to the value of free labor in the cultivation of tobacco in Virginia. Mr. Bruce, who studied the negro in the section of Virginia where tobacco is extensively cultivated, writes of the present day negro as follows: "In all those counties of the tobacco region of Virginia in which the crop is cultivated and prepared for market entirely by negroes, there has been a notable decline in the quality of the staple as well as in the character of its manipulation, now that the majority of the hands who were trained for many years under the eye of their master or the overseer are fast dying off. . . . Tobacco requires the most thorough information and the most discriminating skill from the hour that the plant expands in the patch, to the moment the leaf is prized in the hogshead. Under the old system each plantation had its circle of slaves who were carefully educated from childhood to do general or special work, and the individual of that circle attained to much expertness in the various tasks of the barns and fields; but under the present system this is impossible and the result is that labor of the new regime is generally inferior in character."[1]

The production of tobacco in the counties in which

[1] "The Plantation Negro as a Freeman," p. 183.

17

it was most extensively produced previous to the war, was less in 1889 than thirty years ago. If we select five representative counties, as has been done in the table below, it is shown that the product has very materially decreased since 1859.

TOBACCO PRODUCTION OF FIVE SELECTED COUNTIES OF VIRGINIA, 1859 and 1889.

| | Population, 1890. | | Tobacco Production, (Lbs.). | |
	White.	Colored.	1859.	1889.
Albermarle	18,133	14,245	5,429,390	557,364
Charlotte	5,714	9,363	5,666,600	1,762,000
Halifax	14,891	19,533	8,544,500	5,432,500
Mecklenburg . . .	9,192	16,167	6,631,800	2,737,600
Prince Edward . . .	4,750	9,944	4,231,800	1,633,800
Five Counties .	52,680	69,252	30,504,090	12,123,264

The production for 1859 was 30.5 million pounds ; the production for 1889 was only 12.1 million pounds. Leaving out of consideration the increase in the population during this period, the falling off is remarkable. It will be observed that in these five counties the colored are greatly in the majority. Only one county of the state, Pittsylvania, reported a larger production in 1889 than in 1859 (I am speaking here only of those counties the total product of which in 1859 was in excess of four million pounds.) In 1859 the production of tobacco in this county was 7.9 million pounds, against 12.3 million pounds in 1879 and 10 million pounds in 1889. But in this county the whites exceed the colored by a small majority (31 to 29), the former having increased at a higher rate than the latter during the period 1880–90. Hence, the possible argument that the large production of the period previous to the war exhausted the soil and caused an overproduction per acre, hardly holds good. At least it would seem difficult to account for the falling off on this ground, in view of the statement of the correspondent of the Farmville *Journal* that a laborer now takes care of twice the number of plants that was customary previous to emancipation.

We may compare, however, the five counties of Virginia with four counties of Kentucky having a colored population of less than five per cent. The four counties produced about 90,000 pounds of tobacco in 1859 as compared with more than 10 million pounds in 1889. It must be taken into consideration that the large proportion of laborers in these counties must necessarily be white.

TOBACCO PRODUCTION OF FOUR COUNTIES OF KENTUCKY, 1859-1889.

	Population.		Tobacco Production, (Lbs.).	
	White.	Colored.	1859.	1889.
Lewis	14,618	185	35,595	2,340,984
Campbell.	43,496	712	40,520	1,733,227
Bath	11,228	1,585	4,542	4,555,912
Mercer	11,924	3,110	9,681	1,414,733
Four Counties. .	81,266	5,592	90,338	10,044,856

It is of course an open question whether the increased production of tobacco in these counties is not the result of cultivation of new soils not previously exhausted; but that is immaterial for our purpose. The point to be observed is that in counties containing a great majority of negroes the production is falling off, while in other sections of the country containing only a small proportion of colored population, the production has greatly increased. This is true of the production per acre as well as of the total yield. The average product per acre was 396 pounds for the five Virginia counties as compared with 879 pounds for four Kentucky counties.

It is therefore apparent that Mr. Russell was in error when he declared [1] that "tobacco cannot be cultivated in the Free States by hiring and employing laborers, it

[1] "North America: Its Agriculture and Climate," (Edinburgh, 1857), p. 141.

is only cultivated there by small farmers," and that
" free labor cannot successfully compete with slave
labor in the production of tobacco, for among other
reasons, slave owners can always command the quantity
as well as quality of labour that are required to raise
this crop economically."[1] In Virginia, with 38.7 per
cent. colored in the total population, the tobacco crop of
the state has fallen off from 121.8 million pounds in 1859
to 48.5 million pounds in 1889. In Kentucky, where
the colored population forms only 14.7 per cent. of the
total, the production has increased from 108.1 million
pounds in 1859 to 221.9 million pounds in 1889.[2]

In view of these facts, it would seem that the opinion
of Mr. Bruce as regards the deterioration of colored
labor in the production of this staple was justified, and
that the falling off in the tobacco production of the
five selected Virginia counties is more the result of a
diminishing economic efficiency in the negro in this
branch of agriculture than of changes in the productive-
ness of the soil, or the substitution of other crops, etc.
I am fairly familiar with the conditions of one county,
and have had opportunity to observe the effects of the
migratory tendency of the race on the changes in the
agricultural condition of a given locality. In Charlotte
county, for instance, where previous to the war a crop of
over five million pounds was raised, almost exclusively
by slave labor, many of the farm hands have migrated
to the new cities of Roanoke, Newport News, etc.
Hence the valuable special knowledge, so much insisted
upon by writers on the subject, is largely wasted and
the planter has to face the serious question of either
educating constantly a new number of hands, any one

[1] "North America : Its Agriculture and Climate," pp. 140-41.
[2] Extra census bulletin, No. 13. Washington, D. C., 1891.

of whom may leave the locality the next year, or of abandoning the cultivation of this particular crop. On the other hand, the farm laborer in the new cities has to meet new conditions in which his ignorance handicaps him from the beginning, and while thousands of mechanics are imported from the factories and ship yards of the North, earning excellent wages, he fills only a menial position and earns only the wages of unskilled labor.

The economic disadvantage of this tendency to deteriorate in efficiency in a branch of agriculture which is constantly opening up new sections of the country, is perhaps nowhere better illustrated than in the case of South Carolina, where the almost exclusive production of cotton and rice of the ante-war period is gradually giving way to the production of other staples, of which tobacco is today considered one of the most promising. A writer in the Columbia *State* of a recent date, in dealing with the subject of changes in the agricultural condition of the state, refers to the subject as follows : " The tobacco business will not be overdone in South Carolina until the quantity produced is quintupled. For the present it is the best money-making crop in the state, for here the yield is greater and the quality is better than in Virginia or North Carolina." The production has increased from 104,000 pounds in 1859, to 223,000 pounds in 1889 and more than three million pounds in 1894. Hence a field in which this special knowledge of the cultivation of a valuable crop would have been of very great advantage to the colored race, is gradually being abandoned and left to the white race.

In South Carolina the negro has at all times been an indispensable factor in the production of another staple,

rice ; and it may be of value to add the statement of
one who has made this a subject of scientific investigation.   Mr. Milton Whitney, M.S., in a chapter on
"Rice Soils of South Carolina," forming part of a
special report by Mr. Amory Austin, B.S., to the Department of Agriculture, refers to the subject of negro labor
in the rice lands of South Carolina as follows :

> There are at present in South Carolina, and doubtless the same
> conditions hold good in other rice growing states, thousands of acres
> of the finest rice lands, which have been abandoned and are now lying
> idle. . . .   The principal cause which has brought about the exist-
> ing conditions of things and has caused the abandonment of so much
> rice land is the lack of capital due to heavy losses sustained by the
> planters during the late war. . . .   Another fact which has brought
> about the present condition of affairs and explains in part why so
> much rice land has been abandoned, is the scarcity of negro labor, by
> which practically all the field work has been done.   The phosphate
> industry along the coast in South Carolina and Florida has drawn
> large numbers of these negroes away from the rice fields, attracting
> them by higher wages and what they consider a more independent
> life.   It is difficult to secure enough labor to handle the crops and the
> negroes who remain on the plantations are not as steady, as efficient
> or as reliable as the older generations were before the war.   With the
> phosphate works almost in sight of their dwellings, and an abundance
> of fish and game, and a mild climate making it easy to live, they are
> so irresponsible that it is difficult to control labor.   They are very un-
> willing to work in the ditches and canals, and it is almost impossible
> to keep the ditches and canals clean and of a proper depth by the
> available negro labor . . . [1]

This despondent view of the present value of negro
labor in the rice fields is met with in most of the references to the future of rice culture.   It is clearly supported by the statistics of rice production in South
Carolina and Georgia where the annual production since
the war has been considerably below the normal yield
of previous years under the régime of slavery.   The

[1] "Rice: Its Cultivation and Distribution," (Department of Agriculture, 1893), p. 77 *et seq.*

summary below will show the production of rice in three states during the period 1850–89.

Year.	South Carolina. Lbs.	Georgia. Lbs.	Louisiana. Lbs.
1850	159,930,000	38,950,000	4,425,000
1880	52,077,000	25,369,000	23,188,000
1889	31,689,000	14,057,000	76,221,000

The increase in Louisiana is in part explained on the ground that large areas of former sugar plantations near the delta of the Mississippi have been utilized in the cultivation of rice. The method of cultivation, however, does not seem to be such as would insure the same degree of permanency as prevailed in South Carolina previous to the war. The replacing of sugar culture by rice culture is at the same time only a quasi-public benefit. In recent years, so far as I have been able to ascertain, there has been some improvement in the production of rice in South Carolina. The annual product for 1894 is estimated by the South Carolina Agriculture College at 70 million pounds. This is still less than one-half the production of 1850. The annual production of the United States was 215 million pounds in 1850 and only 115.5 million pounds in 1894. In this industry therefore, as well as in the tobacco production, we must attribute a decreasing production more to the growing inefficiency of negro labor than to other economic causes.

In the testimony of Mr. John Schreven before the ways and means committee of the Fifty-first Congress, having under consideration the change of the duty on rice, the statement was made that "since the emancipation of the slaves the cost of agricultural labor in the South has been largely increased. In the rice districts of Georgia and the Carolinas, field labor ranges from 40 to 60 cents, and the best expert (not mechanical) labor to one dollar per diem . . . this without the efficiency to be expected from free labor. The laborers frequently refuse to undertake tasks, easy under a sterner system and essential to nice cultivation. A day's labor is commonly reduced to six hours instead of ten. The consequences of these conditions are reduced production, and commonly, minimum crops."[1]

In the report of Amory Austin, already referred to, the statement is made in regard to rice culture in Georgia, that the decline in the culture of rice is due to "the dislike of the negro to the work upon the marshes."[2]

In the production of cotton, in which it is commonly assumed the negro participates more largely than in the production of any other southern staple, it would seem that the tendency is in the same direction, that is, the work is slowly drifting from the negro into the hands of the whites, both in the states which contain the largest proportion of colored population and in Texas where the whites predominate.

Texas, according to the last census, contained a proportion of 28 colored to every hundred of white population. In 1860 the proportion was 43 to 100. Hence we have for this state a larger increase in white population, the majority of which are of foreign birth or are native settlers from other states.[3] Now, it was one of the dictums of the believers in the value of negro labor in cotton production that "where the greatest amount of

[1] Hearings of ways and means committee, Fifty-first Congress, p. 931.

[2] "Rice: Its cultivation" etc. Washington, 1893.

[3] According to the census of 1890, Texas had a total population of 2,235,523, of which 1,745,935 were white. Of the latter 1,408,-880 were native whites of native parentage, but only 825,280 had been born in Texas. Hence, only 47.8 per cent. were natives in the restricted sense of the word.

cotton is produced there will be found the greatest negro population, and as the one decreases the other does also, though not necessarily in the same ratio."[1] This is no longer applicable in the production of cotton as a southern staple. We may compare the two states Mississippi and Texas to illustrate this point.

COTTON PRODUCTION OF MISSISSIPPI, 1860-1894.

	Colored Population.	Cotton Bales.	Average Net Weight of Bales.
1860	437,404	1,202,507	461 Lbs.
1890	747,720	1,154,725	478 "
1894	. . .	1,167,881	474 "

COTTON PRODUCTION OF TEXAS, 1860-1894.

	Colored Population.	Cotton Bales.	Average Net Weight of Bales.
1860	182,921	431,462	461 Lbs.
1890	303,384	1,471,242	478 "
1894	. . .	3,073,821	474 "

With less than one-half as large a colored population as Mississippi, the state of Texas produced in 1894 almost three times the cotton crop of the former state. With almost twice the colored population of 1860, Mississippi in 1894 produced less cotton than 34 years ago. Thus it is seen that it is not merely the presence of a large colored population to which the cultivation of a large cotton crop must be attributed. For other states similar results could be shown, but the instance cited will suffice.

It is therefore a question to what extent white labor enters into the production of cotton. In the uplands the whites have always cultivated their own cotton. In the alluvial lands along the Mississippi river, of course, the larger part of the crop is grown by negro labor.

[1] Report on internal commerce, Washington, D. C., 1886, p. 560.

The only investigation of which I have knowledge in which it was attempted to ascertain the proportion of the cotton crop raised by colored and white labor respectively, was made in 1876, and is reported by the Commissioner of Agriculture. The results of this investigation were a surprise to many who up to the time held the belief that the whites participated but slightly in the production of this, the greatest of southern crops.

PROPORTION OF COTTON CROP GROWN BY WHITE AND COLORED LABOR. (1876.)

	Colored. Per Cent.	White. Per Cent.
North Carolina	65	35
South Carolina	68	32
Georgia	66	34
Florida	72	28
Alabama	59	41
Mississippi	68	32
Louisiana	77	23
Texas	38	62
Arkansas	40	60
Tennessee	59	41

In 1880 it was estimated that of the total cotton crop, 2,553,000 bales were grown by white labor, against 3,212,000 bales grown by colored labor. In other words over 40 per cent. of the total crop was the result of white labor. In Mississippi, according to a report of the board of immigration and agriculture in 1880, out of a total of 955,800 bales, 328,568 bales, or over 34 per cent., was grown by white labor. It is an open question whether this proportion of cotton production by whites in the states formerly the main producers of this staple, has increased during recent years.

The elaborate investigation of the Senate committee into the condition of cotton growers, failed to deal with the problem of labor in an adequate manner. Only one decided opinion was given in regard to the present value of negro labor, in connection with this industry, and on account of its exceptional value I give the quotation in full.

Of all causes mentioned as contributing to the financial depression of the cotton raiser, the want of reliable labor is perhaps the most important and most difficult to remedy. As stated previously, our crops are mainly cultivated by negro labor. For several years after the close of the war, the manumitted slave was, from previous training and force of habit, a very desirable laborer, but as the generation of the ex-slave passed away and a new generation sprang up, they became more lazy, thriftless and unreliable, until they will soon attain a condition of total depravity and utter worthlessness. . . . The negro laborer, notwithstanding he gets one-half of the crop, and is subjected to no expense, will, upon an average not work more than four hours a day, nor more than three days per week. I can only suggest one remedy for this state of affairs and that I admit is impracticable, if not impossible. That is, for the government to deport and colonize the negro in Liberia or the Sandwich Islands. If such a thing could be accomplished we might suffer some temporary inconvenience and pecuniary loss but the place of the negro would soon be filled by active, honest and industrious whites from the middle, northern and western states, and Europe. Relieve us of this incubus and your name shall be blessed, even unto the tenth generation.[1]

In this statement the same complaint is made, that "the negro will work only a few hours a day, and only a few days out of the whole week." In the production of the great staples as well as in agriculture in general, nothing is more important than continuous application of labor until the crop is harvested. The uncertainty as to the permanency of this labor supply has induced many planters to discontinue cultivation on a large scale. Of the labor in Louisiana, Mr. Henry G. Foster, U. S. Treasury expert, of New Orleans, wrote ten years ago as follows: "The labor in parts of Louisiana is inclined

[1] Report of the Senate committee on agriculture, Vol. I, p. 362, (Washington, D. C., 1895). The quotation is from a letter to the chairman, Senator George, by Mr. I. A. Wimbish, of Cuerro, DeWitt County, Texas.

to be nomadic ; many of them quit the plantation after
the crop is picked and baled, and work during the
winter months on the steamboats, in the cotton yards or
on the levee of New Orleans. This irregular mode of
life demoralizes them and injures their usefulness. They
rarely return to the same plantation which they quitted,
and they become less reliable as steady laborers."[1]

This view is again supported by the results of an elaborate investigation made into the wages of farm labor
in 1892.[2] The investigation was conducted by the regular correspondents of the Department of Agriculture, and
nearly every important county in the South was covered
by the report. From all sources the complaint was made
that the present labor supply was not of a satisfactory
quality, oftentimes insufficient in quantity. A few of
the most emphatic statements are given as follows :

[Mississippi, Perry county]. "Labor abundant but of an exceedingly unreliable character. As a rule no crop can be wholly made by
colored labor, we have no other kind." . . . [Alcorn county].
"Farm labor is scarce because of the tendency of the negroes to
move westward to the Mississippi and Yazoo bottoms and to Arkansas."

[Louisiana, Franklin parish]. "Farm laborers very scarce . . .
many, both men and women have drifted into little hamlets and vil-
lages, where they eke out a precarious living." . . . [West Feli-
ciana parish]. "Laborers are gradually leaving the hills and concen-
trating near rivers and town."

[Georgia, Randolph county]. "An increasing scarcity each year,
as the colored people move to towns." . . . [Habersham county]
"We have no difficulty in procuring farm labor, although the negro
is uncertain, he is indifferent about work if he has a little ahead."
. . . [Lincoln county]. "Farm labor scarce, owing to the vagrant
disposition of the negro."

[South Carolina, Georgetown county]. "Farm labor scarce because the young negroes do not like field work and go to cities, and
the women who constitute the strength of the work in the rice fields

[1] Report on Internal Commerce, 1886, p. 511.
[2] "Wages of Farm Labor in the United States, 1866-1892." Washington, D. C., 1892.

are lazy and do not more than six hours work in a whole day, so that forty cents may be said to be paid for six hours work.

[Virginia, York county]. Farm labor plentiful but very unreliable. . . . . [Charles City county]. Farm labor is more and more uncertain and indifferent. . . . [Accomack county]. " Farm laborers abundant in numbers could they be induced to work. After earning a few dollars they quit work until it is gone.

In none of the hundreds of reports have I found any evidence that colored farm labor is improving in quality, least of all in quantity. The great majority of the correspondents agree that the negro is drifting from the farm into the new industries of the South, that the higher wages paid in railroad building and public works, coal, copper and sulphur mining, saw-mill and general timber industries and turpentine works, are attracting large numbers. To this may be added the demand for labor in the oyster industries of Maryland and Virginia and the phosphate mines of Florida and South Carolina. The women are attracted by such work as picking strawberries, peanuts and green peas and the gathering of sumach.

In view of these facts it is not at all surprising that the negro should be paid less for his labor than the white man under the same conditions, but rather that the difference should be so small as it is. No accurate separation was made of colored and white farm labor in the report of the Agricultural Department, but from the returns made the approximate wages were $23.75 per month, (without board), for white labor, and $14.25 for colored. With board the rates were $16 for white labor and $9.75 for colored. Since the negro lives in comfort on much less than the white laborer, the lower wages inflicts no hardship.

To low wages for farm labor is generally attributed the tendency of the negroes to drift into the cities or to leave the farm for the saw-mill or coal mine. But it is a question whether the change has been an economic advantage to the race. In many directions it undoubtedly has not. In the building of railroads, in public works, in the development of southern cities, or better, the "boom" towns, he was drawn into work of only a temporary character. Railroad building in the South during recent years has come almost to a standstill. Since 1887 the number of miles constructed has steadily fallen off. During the year 1895 only 82 miles of road have been built in Georgia, 53 in Alabama, 32 in Arkansas, 25 in Kentucky, 43 in Virginia. In the timber industry the work is also less steady than in general agriculture and truck farming, and the negro is generally employed only for a small part of the year.

In the report of the Commissioner of Agriculture, already referred to, an attempt was made to ascertain to what extent the freedmen had secured the ownership of individual homes. The report states that "so far as reported the proportion of freedmen occupying their own land is 4 per cent. in Tennessee and Alabama, 5 per cent. in South Carolina and Texas, between 4 and 5 per cent. in North Carolina and Georgia, between 5 and 6 per cent. in Mississippi, Louisiana and Arkansas, and 8 per cent. in Florida. The average, if it fairly represents the unreported cotton area, indicates that nineteen out of twenty have no homes"[1] [of their own]. Since 1876 no attempt has been made by the general government to ascertain the proportion of the colored population of the agricultural sections who own and cultivate their own land.

So far as I know, the only state in which the information is collected and published in a form permitting its

[1] Report of Commissioner of Agriculture, 1876, p. 137.

use in a work of this kind, is Virginia.[1] In this state
the appraisements of real estate for 1891 and 1895 give
in detail the proportion of land owned by whites and
colored ; also the value of the land, the value of the buildings on the land, the value of city lots and the value of
buildings on city lots. As will be seen in the following
brief abstract from the valuable reports of the state
auditor, the number of acres and the aggregate value of
lands owned by negroes has increased considerably during the five years, while the contrary is true for the
white population.

ASSESSED VALUATION OF LAND AND LOTS OWNED BY WHITE AND
COLORED PERSONS IN VIRGINIA IN 1891 AND 1895.

Year.	Acres of Land.	Assessed Valuation.	Assessed Value Per Acre.
		Owned by Whites.	
1891	25,285,981	$123,882,236	$4.88
1895	25,154,781	113,129,317	4 50
		Owned by Colored.	
1891	698,074	2,938,064	4 21
1895	833,147	3,450,247	4.14

It will be observed that the number of acres owned
by negroes has materially increased during recent years.
This increase is in part due to the shrinkage in values,
as a result of which the negro has been enabled to
buy land at low prices. The possession, by negroes
of more than three-fourths of a million acres of land
in one state is an economic fact of much significance.
The question is whether they will make use of their
land to the same extent that the whites do,—a ques-

[1] Through the kindness of Col. Wm. Wright, the state comptroller
of Georgia, I am enabled to give the following facts in regard to
negro ownership of land in that state which are not published in the
regular annual reports on the finances of the state :

No. of acres of land owned by colored persons, . 1,038,824 acres
Aggregate assessed value of land, ... $4,159,960
Value of horses, mules, sheep and other stock, . 2,288,850

tion that has not as yet been satisfactorily answered. From all the available facts it would seem that as a proprietor the negro produces only enough for his own wants, thus curtailing the general production.

An editorial in *The Progressive South*, May 1, 1894, indicates the view held by those who are not in favor of negro ownership of land :

> We cannot see any exalted place for the negro in agriculture. His methods are of the poorest and his efforts the least intelligent to be found throughout the South. It is not possible to build up waste places either through negro ownership of lands or through a tenant system which permits negroes to cultivate farms without supervision or direction of a mind better suited to the work. . . . That the negro makes a good laborer, is acknowledged by all Southern people, when his labor is under direction of competent persons. But it is seldom that sufficient executive ability is found in a negro to permit him to manage and cultivate even a small farm. When his land is paid for, his labor becomes impaired in its value to the community in which he lives, as he will subsist on next to nothing and only work when necessity compels.

The point insisted upon by those who believe with the above writer, is the need of an effective supervision. "In the cultivation, management and harvesting of the great staples of the south, cotton, sugar, rice and tobacco," writes Mr. Killebrew, former commissioner of agriculture of Tennessee, "the colored laborers are eminently successful when directed by intelligent supervision." Mr. Massey, whose favorable view of the negro as a laborer has been referred to, speaks of him as "the most docile and tractable of all laborers and under proper supervision the most contented and profitable." A correspondent of the New York *Evening Post*, June 10, 1895, quotes the superintendent of an Alabama mine as follows : "There is everything in knowing how to handle negroes. . . . I have a gang of negroes who are as good men as I should want to have under me, but put a man in charge of them who doesn't understand them and they would not be worth the powder to blow them up." And on the same point Mr. Bruce remarks: "An uninterrupted superintendence is necessary to their activity. A gang of men that will labor with the most cheerful and unremitting industry under the eye of a firm and watchful overseer, without requiring a word from him to urge them on, will, if he withdraws, begin at once to lag . . or if they continue to work, the effort will be irregular and languishing."[1]

This supervision is practiced to the fullest extent on the steamboats of the Mississippi river, where the utmost amount of labor is secured from 'roust-abouts' by methods falling just short of the actual use of the lash. But there is no rebellion, no fault found. The work is done cheerfully and effectively. But without constant supervision rapid and thorough work, such as is needed in the handling of freight, would be impossible with negro hands.

The absence of this supervision, it would seem, seriously impairs the value of the negro as a tenant farmer or small proprietor. From personal observation I incline to agree with the writer who sees little benefit accruing to the community from negro ownership of land. As a rule their "farms" are such in name only, and the cultivation of the soil and the condition of the grounds, are of the lowest order. The value of the negro as an agricultural laborer becomes impaired. The small produce of his farm, together with the earnings of his wife and children in the peanut or strawberry season, enable him to live in comparative comfort, adding little or nothing to the aggregate wealth of the community. He lives, in a word, the life of the West India peasant of whom Froude says: "The earth does not

[1] "The Plantation Negro as a Freeman," p. 179.

18

contain any other peasantry so well off, so well cared for, so happy, so sleek and contented."[1]   But in the West Indies the work is gradually passing into the hand of the imported coolies, and in our southern states it is only a question of years when the labor now passing from the hands of the negro will fall to the willing worker from Europe, or the class of southern whites described 30 years ago by Mr. Cairnes as being below the slaves in economic efficiency.[2]

The Negro as an Industrial Factor.

Previous to emancipation, the race had little opportunity to become closely associated with industrial pursuits.   There were colored mechanics, slave and free, on all the plantations, and in the towns a considerable amount of other than agricultural labor was performed by them on their own account or for the whites; but it was labor in the non-competitive sense, labor which had little or no relation to the struggle for life and the development of the qualities which would make the negroes more fit for the struggle which was to come.   But it would be a very great error to suppose that they had not a great many opportunities for the development of any latent industrial capacities, had they been disposed to exert themselves as did the white mechanics and common laborers.   The following interesting and almost unknown summary of occupations followed by the slave and free colored populations of Charleston, nearly fifty years ago, will show conclusively that the negro of antebellum days had as many, if not more, opportunities to become acquainted with the mechanical arts and trades than at the present day.

[1] "The English in the West Indies," page 78.
[2] "The Slave Power," (London, 1863), page 358, *et seq.*

REPRESENTATION OF THE SLAVE AND FREE COLORED POPULATIONS
OF CHARLESTON, AMONG DIFFERENT OCCUPATIONS.

(Census of Charleston, South Carolina, 1848.)

	Males. Slaves.	Free.		Males. Slaves.	Free.
Bricklayers	68	10	Saddlers	2	1
Carpenters	110	27	Wheelwrights	..	1
Painters	9	4	Livery stable	..	1
Plasterers	16	.	Boatmen	7	.
Wharf builders	10	.	Sailors	43	1
Barbers	4	14	Ship carpenters . . .	51	6
Bootmakers	4	3	Millwrights	..	5
Dry goods	..	1	Blacksmiths	40	4
Shoemakers	2	14	Brass foundry workers	1	1
Tailors	39	42	Coopers	61	2
Bakers	36	1	Mechanics	45	2
Butchers.	6	4	Apprentices	43	14
Confectioners	4	2	House servants	1,888	9
Cooks	3	16	Laborers	838	19
Fishermen	15	14	Porters	35	5
Hotel keepers	..	1	Stevedores	2	1
Gardeners	3	.	Janitors	..	1
Huxters	..	4	Millers	..	1
Cigar-makers . . .	5	1	Storekeepers	..	5
Tavern keepers . . .	..	1	Wood factors	..	3
Market dealers	..	1	Superannuated and		
Cabinet-makers . . .	8	.	disabled	38	1
Tinners	3	1			
Upholsterers	1	1	Total	3,534	264
Sextons	1	4	Total slave male popu-		
Book-binders	3	.	lation between 10		
Printers	5	.	and 70 years of age .		3,685
Coachmen	15	4	Total free male popu-		
Coach-makers	3	.	lation between 10		
Draymen	67	11	and 70 years of age .		349

	Females.			Females.	
Mantua makers . . .	4	128	Servants	3,384	28
Laundresses	..	45	Apprentices	8	7
Seamstresses	20	68	Laborers	378	2
Washerwomen	33	.	Superannuated and		
Cooks	11	.	disabled	54	4
Tailors		6			
Fruiters and huxters	12	1	Total	3,913	326
Market sellers	6	4	Total slave female pop-		
Hotel keepers	..	1	ulation between 10		
Pastry cooks	1	16	and 70 years of age		4,463
House keepers	..	4	Total free female col-		
Monthly nurses . . .	2	.	ored poplation bet.		
Nurses	..	10	10 and 70 yrs. of age		685

It is clearly shown in this table that the negro did
not lack opportunity to develop his latent abilities in the
field of mechanical industry; and also that he must have

been possessed of a considerable degree of ability to have been thus extensively employed in all the leading industrial pursuits of one important southern city.

A similar condition existed in other southern cities. In New Orleans we are informed by Mr. Ingle, the negroes were employed as car-men, carpenters, laborers, masons, planters, tailors, merchants and shoemakers. In Virginia, Mr. Bruce informs us, they were extensively employed as mechanics on the plantations, principally as smithies, wheelwrights, masons, and carpenters. It will be of value to compare the past with the present; which unfortunately is extremely difficult, in view of the paucity of data on the subject of the occupations followed by the colored population at the present time. The ninth and tenth censuses contain nothing on the subject, and up to this writing no information of the kind has been made public from the returns of the eleventh census.

The most important private investigations, to my knowledge, were made by the Chattanooga *Tradesman* in 1889 and 1891, covering the following points: Number of colored men employed, number of skilled and common laborers, wages paid, degree of efficiency in comparison with white labor, permanency of employment in representative industries, gain in efficiency, benefits of education to the younger generation, and the effect of education upon the negro's efficiency as a laborer.[1]

Replies to inquiries covering the above questions were received from 196 employers of negro labor, residing in the South and employing 7,395 colored laborers, 978 of whom were reported as skilled. The highest wages re-

[1] See *The Tradesman*, (Chattanooga, Tenn.) Aug. 15, 1891.

ported as paid for skilled labor was $3 per day, the low-est $1.10; the average being $1.75. The highest wages paid unskilled laborers was $1.50 per day, the lowest 60 cents, and the average $1.10. As regards comparative efficiency of common and skilled labor as compared with white labor in the same work, 27 employers, with 1,379 colored workers in their service, see no difference; 35 employers with 1,441 colored workers, prefer white labor, and 49 employers, with 3,214 colored laborers, prefer them to white men in the same capacity.

In reply to the question, "Is the negro increasing in efficiency?" 67 men employing 2,413 colored laborers, say with emphasis that the efficiency of their workmen is increasing; 43 men employing 2,279 colored laborers, say their men have not improved; 15 employers, speak-ing for 1,369 laborers, were in doubt as whether or not there had been any improvement. In reply to the ques-tion, "Does it add to his efficiency to educate him?" 30 employers, speaking for 2,860 laborers, answer that the education received by the younger negroes has been of benefit to them and that it adds to their efficiency; 13 employers, speaking for 392 men, expressed no definite opinion, while 96 employers, with 3,820 colored laborers in their service, express the opinion that such education as the younger members of the colored race have received has not been of benefit to them, and that, generally speaking, it detracts from a negro's efficiency to educate him.

The brief summary given above, shows only imperfectly the results of the investigation. The significant fact is, that so many should favor the negro as an industrial worker in view of the fault that is found with him as an agricultural laborer. An equally significant fact is that only 21 per cent. of the employers should consider education an aid to the negro's efficiency as a laborer, while 69 per cent. declare themselves convinced of its failure to increase his efficiency. It has been shown in the preceding part of this work that education has failed to improve materially the moral condition of the race; we have here the testimony of those who come in daily contact with negro laborers to the effect that education has failed to benefit the race in an economic sense. Surely such emphatic opinions must have some substantial foundation. If education, as it is at present carried on, proved to be of material value to the negro, the men who make use of this class of labor would welcome any means which would increase his efficiency as an industrial worker, since such increased efficiency would benefit alike employer and employee.

I may give in full some of the views of those who find that education has not improved the efficiency of the negro. A manufacturer of furniture writes from North Carolina: "Our observation is that those who are educated endeavor to do without work, and the effect is demoralizing to those who do labor. A limited education might not harm those who are settled, but upon the young we believe the effect is to detract from their usefulness as laborers." An employer of colored labor in mining and milling ore in South Carolina, writes as follows: "Education of the young ruins them. No educated negro will condescend to anything beneath teaching school and preaching. The educated negro will not do manual labor if he can get bread and butter in any other manner." The writers here quoted, and the great majority of the 69 per cent. who agree that education has not benefitted the race from an economic standpoint, unconsciously emphasize the position of M. Leroy-Beaulieu, that the aim of schools ought to be rather directed to the inculcation into the minds of the pupils, if not of contentment with their lot, at least of more modest ideas, and of resignation to manual labor.

But on the whole the results of this investigation of *The Tradesman* are favorable to the negro as an industrial worker. It will be observed that the great majority are unskilled; only a small number having so far succeeded in filling the more responsible positions. In the rapid development of southern industries during the period 1880–92, large numbers of negroes were employed in the coal, iron and phosphate industry, and an even larger number found work in the construction of public works and railways. Work on the latter has practically come to an end, but in the former he holds to-day an important position as a common laborer whose place could only be filled by immigration.

As regards remuneration, it has been shown that the average wages are $1.10 for common and $1.50 for skilled labor. According to the investigation of *The Tradesman* the wages of colored men are on an average about 80 per cent. of those paid to white men for the same class of work; but this difference should be charged not to discrimination on account of color, but to difference in efficiency. The real cause of the difference in wages is stated by the superintendent of an Alabama coal mine as follows: " The Englishman and the German come to us with some ambition to get ahead. The negro has no such aspiration. If he does one extra good day's work he feels so elated over it that he is good for nothing the next day, and probably stays at home. On such occasions he is always sick or resting."[1] This is the view of one who has ' as good a gang of negroes as he should want to have,' and one who

_____
[1] New York *Evening Post*, June 24, 1895.

thinks that the negro, properly handled, is of exceptional value as a laborer in the mine.

It would be contrary to our common experience if we failed to meet with considerable opposition on the part of white laborers in the same capacity. During the great miners' strike of 1894 many conflicts took place between the striking miners and negroes who had been brought from a distance to take the place of the strikers. Outbreaks of hostilities have been reported at various times from all parts of the country between whites and negroes, usually on account of labor difficulties. Near Dunbar, Pennsylvania, a riot took place between Hungarians and negroes, the result of a quarrel of many months' standing. At Spring Valley, Ill., Italians and negroes came to clash with deplorable results. At Black Rock, Ark., violence was threatened, and White Cap methods resorted to, to drive negro laborers out of the town on account of preference given them in the saw-mills. At Brookside, Ala., white and colored miners came to clash and four colored men were killed.

But the most serious outbreak of last year took place during the cotton handlers' strike at New Orleans. It was a question of colored men being employed at the same work with white men. After a period of riot, murder, and incendiarism, the colored men gained their point and the white cotton screw men agreed to work for any employer, whether he employed union hands or not, and to work with negroes. The union agreed to admit twenty gangs of negroes to membership and bound itself not to interfere with the working of the negroes. The defeat of white organized labor in this instance was a most valuable victory for the negro, since the employment as cotton screwmen and other levee work is remunerative and fairly constant. In East Boston,

Mass., colored stevedores and freight handlers a few years ago took the place of strikers on the Cunard ships and ever since the work has remained in their hands.

It would seem therefore that the difficulties arising out of labor disputes will be overcome gradually, and that the present discrimination in wages will disappear as soon as the negro acquires an equal degree of efficiency and thrift, and also the habit of constant application to his work. His efforts to adapt himself to the modern conditions of southern life, especially in the mining and transportation industries, would seem so far to have been to his economic advantage, seriously as it may have interfered with his physical and moral well being.

In the development of one great industry he has not taken part. In the cotton mills of the South no negroes are employed in any of the skilled work. The question of employment of negro labor in the mills has been very frequently discussed, but the opinion prevails generally that while he would possibly be as good a mill hand as a white person, it would be impossible to work a mill with both classes of labor. To use colored labor exclusively has been suggested, but it is asserted by many experienced mill superintendents that this would be impossible. Training schools have been suggested but such would be costly and the risk of failure would be great.

A valuable investigation into the subject was made by the *Manufacturers' Record* of Baltimore, in 1893, with the result stated as follows : " At the outset the student of this question is inclined to condemn the colored help as incapable of training for cotton mill purposes, but it will be seen from the views expressed by several managers of long experience that colored labor can be trained for almost any work in a cotton mill. The substance of the views of the majority is that in its present condition the colored laborer of the South is totally unfit for cotton-mill work, but under favorable conditions and with suitable training this labor can be utilized to good advantage."[1]

Some of the expressions of experienced mill superintendents may be worth giving here in full. Mr. H. H. Hickman, president of the Graniteville Manufacturing Co., of Augusta, Ga., writes as follows:

> I do not believe that cotton factories will be run successfully by negroes in this generation. Very few of them will ever become skilled laborers in a cotton mill. I employ a few to do common work, but none are put to a machine except to feed the pickers ; this requires no skill. White labor will not work with the negro at the machine. You cannot mix them in a cotton mill ; if employed they must run the mill alone. If we concede the fact of capability, unreliability would be a sufficient cause for not employing them.

Mr. William Entwistle, superintendent of the Pee Dee Manufacturing Co., Rockingham, N. C., writes as follows:

> We have never had a single application from any colored person for such employment, and under no circumstances would we employ them in any department where white girls are employed. Apart from this we do not think that they are adapted to the close confinement or capable of conforming to the system and discipline incident to factory labor. We employ colored men in the yard and in the dye house. As only a few are so employed we can select from the many those best suited for the work. Under such circumstances and in such cases they make very good help. A small proportion of them make fair masons, bricklayers, etc. More of them might, but for their inherent indispostion to work more than is necessary to procure a bare subsistence. . . . Over twenty years of experience and close observation in the South convinces the writer that industrious rural life is in all respects best suited to the welfare and happiness of the negro colored race and the prosperity of the country.

These opinions of experienced men are shared by the great majority of those who are in charge of cotton mills. The enormous development of this industry in the South

---

[1] *Manufacturers' Record*, (Baltimore, Md.) Sept. 22, 1893.

in recent years has naturally suggested the use of the negro as a factory worker. But so far it would seem that, leaving out a very few localities, there is an abundance of white labor, fully competent and reliable.

The number of persons employed in the cotton mills of the southern states increased from 21,150 in 1880 to 41,642 in 1890. The total wages paid increased from $2,750,000 in 1880, to $7,117,000 in 1890. In South Carolina alone the number of spindles has increased from 82,334 in 1880, to 838,036 in 1895. This enormous development will explain the frequent allusions to the possibility of colored labor in the cotton mills of the South. Not that the negro has shown any inclination towards work of this kind, but because the promoters of such industries in isolated parts of the southern states have felt doubtful regarding the supply of white labor. The question may be solved, however, by the erection of a cotton mill at Aniston, Ala., to be owned and operated entirely by colored persons. It is intended to employ about one hundred persons at the start. But even if successful the possible consequences of such a forced condition of negro labor give reason for grave consideration. From all that has been shown in regard to his physical deterioration when in contact with the forces of competitive life in the large cities and subject to the conditions of city life, it would seem absolutely certain that the employment of negroes in the cotton mills would materially shorten his duration of life.

So far I have taken into consideration only the negro in the South. If we now consider the industrial capacities and tendencies of the negro in the North, we must again draw our conclusions from very limited statistical facts.

In the North the negro rarely cultivates the ground.

Few farmers employ negroes and the inclination of the
latter is too strongly in the direction of city life to make
useful workers on the farm. It has been shown in the first
part of this work that in the North the great majority of
negroes live in the cities, where they are crowded into the
most undesirable sections. It would only be in the nature
of things that we should find them occupied in vocations which are in harmony with this condition of life ;
that we should find a tendency to seek employment
along the lines that would permit of the largest degree
of liberty, idleness, and most of all, mobility. The tendency of the negro to shift from one occupation to another,
from one employer to another, is nowhere better illustrated than in the summary of the principal occupations for six fairly representative northern cities.

From the partial returns of the state census of New
York for 1892 it is possible to obtain a fair idea of how
the various occupations are distributed among the colored
population of some of the principal cities. It is much
to be regretted that the information is not available for
New York city and Brooklyn, as no returns have been
made public for these cities. In the following table I
have consolidated the returns of the occupations of
1,314 colored males living in six cities of the state.
Syracuse, Albany, Buffalo, Auburn, Utica and Bingham-
ton contain, according to the census of 1890, 1,628 colored
males over 21 years of age ; hence the number enumerated
by occupations according to the census of 1892 may be accepted as representing with a fair degree of accuracy the
working population of the colored race in those six cities.

REPRESENTATION OF COLORED MALES AMONG DIFFERENT OCCUPATIONS IN SIX CITIES.[1]

(New York State Census, 1892.)

Agents	2	Laundry workers	1
Bakers	4	Liverymen	3
Bartenders	3	Masons	12
Butchers	1	Managers	1
Bootblacks	1	Merchants	3
Barbers	66	Mattress-makers	2
Blacksmiths	5	Messengers	4
Bell boys and men	21	Musicians	18
Butlers	3	Mechanics	1
Cooks and caterers	88	Machinists	1
Carpenters	12	Moulders	5
Clergymen	4	Printers	2
Cigars and Tobacco	2	Painters	4
Clerks	22	Peddlers	2
Coachmen	37	Polishers	1
Conductors	1	Paper-hangers	5
Coopers	3	Policemen	1
Doctors	1	Postmen (carriers)	1
Dog fanciers	1	Porters	41
Druggists	1	Shoe-makers	2
Engineers (stationary)	2	Stewards	9
Farmers, (gardeners)	10	Tailors	1
Glass-workers	1	Tanners	1
Hotel keepers	1	Teachers	1
Hostlers	34	Teamsters	72
Iron-workers	1	Tinsmiths	1
Janitors	28	Upholsterers	2
Kalsominers	8	Valets	3
Laborers	358	Waiters	337
Lawyers	1	Wood-workers	2
Lamp-lighters	1	Not given	52
Total			1,314

[1] Eleventh annual report of the New York state commissioner of labor, 1894.

Leaving "laborers" out of the consideration, we find that waiters are in the majority. Next come cooks and caterers, followed by teamsters, coachmen and hostlers. If we combine the last three we have 149 connected with the care of horses. The skilled trades and professions are represented by very few. The majority are employed at occupations which require no permanent settlement.

A waiter, a barber, a cook or a hostler can find work almost anywhere. The occupations selected are exactly those that we should expect to find on the basis of the facts previously presented. While useful in their way, these occupations, followed largely to the exclusion of others, must affect the home life and general usefulness of the negro as a factor in society. The large variety of occupations followed proves that he is not lacking so much in ability as in inclination, for the trades in which he is only slightly represented, such as tailoring, masonry and carpentry.

The argument that labor unions are opposed to his entering these trades has no force. It only proves the absence of will power in the individual to become master of his own fortune. Nor does this objection hold good in regard to such trades as shoe-making and tailoring, since the negro could easily find work enough among his own people to make these occupations remunerative. In Boston one of the leading tailors of the city is a colored man. Good colored shoe-makers are not at all rare in the South, nor are carpenters, blacksmiths and saw-mill hands. In smithcraft, we are informed by Mr. Bruce, the Virginia negro had a wide and favorable field, but from this occupation "the average young negro shrinks with the greatest aversion as it is the most exacting and confining of all mechanical pursuits."[1] In the various manufacturing industries, such as the turning out of cotton goods, hosiery, men's clothing, shirts, collars and cuffs, boots and shoes, few if any negroes are employed. In the city of Newark, New Jersey, there are some 4,000 negroes, but not one of them is employed in the thread works of the Clarks, employing some 5,000 hands. I have investigated this matter in various large es-

[1] "The Plantation Negro as a Freeman", p. 233.

tablishments in New York and New England, but I have
never found an instance where numbers of negroes were
employed as operatives in factories.

It is true, of course, that his position is exceptional
and one which in itself must produce many obstacles
difficult to be overcome by individuals. But, generally
speaking, there does not seem to be any tendency on the
part of the negro in the large cities of the North in the
direction of indoor occupations and factory work, but
rather the tendency is in the direction of the occupations
which allow him the greatest amount of liberty and require the least application of continuous labor, and
which almost always will afford him a means of making a
living in an humble way.

A comparison might be made between the occupations
followed by the Indians on the New York reservations ;
but the conditions, of course, are not exactly similar.
In a general way, taking the negro as we find him, and
the Indian on the state reservation, the comparison will
result in favor of the latter along the line of greater
economic usefulness and advancement in individual
prosperity. Out of 1,738 Indians employed in various
occupations, 590 were farmers, 712 laborers, 32 carpenters, 10 mechanics, 185 basket makers, 5 lumbermen,
etc. The Indians on this reservation cultivated during
1889–90, 20,763 acres of land, raised $97,887 worth of
agricultural produce, owned $128,120 worth of live stock,
and $63,159 worth of agricultural implements. The
total value of all the lands owned by them (the population being about 5,200) was $1,810,700 in 1890, the
value of personal property $1,309,493. Is there a com-
munity of negroes anywhere in the South that can show
for 5,000 people an aggregate of wealth and an amount
of productive labor surpassing this? Had it been pos-

sible without curtailing other matter, I should have been glad to deal with the two races at various places in this work, but this would have carried me beyond my original purpose. The comparison, whether it be made in the field of criminality, morality, industry or thrift, would result invariably in favor of the Indian of the New York reservation, for whom but little has been done, of whom but little has been said, and for whom few have even a word of kindness or regard.

As regards the difficulties which hinder individual colored men in obtaining employment in other vocations than those referred to, and which hinder women in the field of domestic labor, they are probably even greater in the North than in the South. Not long ago, in a sermon preached in the Trinity Methodist Episcopal church of Poughkeepsie, N. Y., a public plea was made for the employment of young colored people in the stores or offices of the city. In Leavenworth, Kan., a petition was circulated among the merchants requesting them to give employment to colored young men and women. About a hundred colored families agreed to patronize only those merchants who would grant their petition. So far as I can learn, in neither of the two instances was the plea successful. In not one of the large department stores of New York city, Newark or Boston, are young colored women employed as clerks or for any other purpose. On none of the surface railway lines of New York or New Jersey have I ever met with a colored man as an employee.

In the professions the difficulties are even greater. For a colored person to secure a position as a teacher in one of the public schools of the large cities in the North is almost impossible. Only very recently a case occurred in Jersey City where a mulatto woman, a graduate of the city high school, who had passed a satisfactory examination, was most bitterly opposed when appointed to a temporary position as a teacher in a public school. About the same time a case occurred in New York where a young mulatto woman of good parentage and fully competent was refused an appointment on account of her color. Even an appeal to the courts failed to aid her.

In law as well as in medicine, instances of such difficulties are not infrequent. A few years ago a colored physician brought suit against the Post-Graduate Hospital of New York city because, according to his statement, admission was refused him on account of his color. In another case a young negro lawyer was refused admission to a law students' association of New York city.

Of course such difficulties must prove a slight check on the aspirations of the race, yet only to a very small extent. The number of young colored people who have been educated at public schools or in private institutions, and who believe that they possess the ability to cope with whatever difficulties may come in their way, is very large and constantly growing. The experience of others is in this respect no check, and thousands come every year to the cities, ill-prepared for the struggle for life. The same result is met with in every direction; a scant living is eked out by those who could have lived in comfort on the farms of their fathers. By force of circumstances, by weakness of will and by evil associations, the majority are forced into localities where vice and crime are the rule and virtue and honesty the exception. In dark out-of-the-way places, in dingy alleys, or among brothels as is the case in Chicago, it is no wonder that criminals and prostitutes are common. Men and women

19

who might have lived useful and happy lives on the farm
or in the small rural towns of the South, are thus reduced
by thousands to the anti-social condition which the colored race sustains in the large cities.   Men and women
who might have been useful factors in the material development of the nation, advancing the race as well as their
own individual fortunes, become public burdens falling
heavily on those who have to bear them.   With a
marked tendency towards those occupations which
afford the least guarantee of permanency of income and
development of local attachments, the race is drifting
towards a condition which before many years will be
worse than slavery.   While here and there some able
men of the colored race have sounded the word of
warning and have preached the gospel of hard work
and self-help, the great majority of those who have
undertaken to direct the fortunes of the negro race have,
through a false education, diverted the tendencies of
the race in a direction which must lead to disaster.

Such men as Professor Hugh M. Browne of Washington, have fully grasped the danger.   As coming from a
colored man, the following observations are deserving
of wide circulation :

White men have risen to wealth and fame through the very classes
of labor which we foolishly despise as menial, and they are bringing
science and art into these to-day and elevating them beyond our
reach. . . . In my boyhood days, the household servants of the
wealthy in this section of the country were colored, but now one finds
the trained white servants, versed in ' household science' and 'domestic art.' Then the ribbons of the private equipage were held by
colored hackmen, but now they are handled by the trained white
man, versed in veterinary science and the social etiquette of his position. The walls and ceilings of their mansions received in the spring
their pure white dress from the white-wash brush of the colored man,
but now they are decorated, frescoed, etc., by the skilled white artisan.[1]

[1] Washington *Evening Star*, Dec., 1893.

And in another able paper in *The Tradesman* of Feb. 15, 1894, he writes :

> Happy will be the day for us if we shall become the preferred labor in all classes of unskilled labor. . . . I have always believed that as fast as we receive as common laborers the plaudit " well done " just so fast will we receive invitations from employers of skilled labor to come up higher. . . . The spirit of fair play is too firmly rooted in the white race to permit them to check the worthy and competent efforts of another race to rise, or to withold from that race the legitimate rewards of these efforts.

Unfortunately, for the negro, the course of the race is influenced by those who have filled his mind with false ideals, who commencing with 'forty acres and a mule,' have ended with the prospect of an education in colleges or industrial schools, not one of which can take the place, not one of which ever has taken the place, of the hard but more useful school of everyday life and work. By the substitution of artificial conditions, by misdirected education and an extravagance of charity, the race has within thirty years been reduced to almost the level to which the English poor sank through the workings of the old poor law in the thirties.

Accumulation and Taxation.

Statements as to the aggregate accumulation of property by the colored population since the war are frequent. Estimates vary from $100,000,000 to $300,000,000 of taxable values. In an address delivered by Bishop Pennick of the Protestant Episcopal church, the amount is given as $200,000,000. In another address by a colored minister on "The Progress of the Colored Race," delivered in Baltimore a few years since, the amount was estimated at $225,000,000.

In view of the fact that these statements are so very frequently made, and usually coupled with the assurance "that during thirty years no other race ever made such progress in wealth, culture and all the other achievements of civilized life," it may be of value to give a few facts as they have been compiled from official data, showing the amount of taxable property owned by colored persons, the amount of taxes paid by them and the public expenses incurred in behalf of the race.

In the first place, there is absolutely no basis for a statement of the aggregate wealth of the colored people of this country, since no data are in existence from which even a safe estimate could be calculated. In only three of the southern states is the information as regards property owned by negroes collected and published, and only for these three states, Virginia, Georgia and North Carolina, is the information obtainable. But even for these states, only the taxable property is listed, and no estimate can be arrived at, with any degree of accuracy, as to the amount of untaxed property owned by the colored population of these states.

Before I deal with the data which have been made public by the state auditors of the three states mentioned, I wish to notice briefly one indication of economic progress among the colored population, to which, probably on account of its unfortunate termination, reference is rarely made in the literature of the day on the progress of the race.

In March, 1865, Congress incorporated the "Freedman's Savings and Trust Company," and in June, 1874, the bank was closed. After an existence of less than ten years the bank failed, with an excess of liabilities over assets of one and a quarter million dollars. The bank was organized for the purpose of meeting the economic and commercial wants of the freed people, for the safe keeping of the pay and bounty money of the colored soldier, and other charitable purposes. Among its fifty incorporators were such men as Peter Cooper, William Cullen Bryant, A. A. Low and many other philanthropic and patriotic citizens. From its modest beginnings the institution grew into an institution of respectable proportions and large influence, extending all over the South by means of branch offices, reaching during the period of its active operations more than seventy thousand depositors, and handling more than fifty-five million dollars of deposits.

The bank failed on account of the inefficiency and dishonesty of the management. An amendment to the charter had been obtained from Congress in 1870, which embodied a radical and, as subsequent experience proved, hurtful change in the character of the securities in which the trustees were empowered to invest the deposits of the institution. The change opened the way for speculative loans, offered opportunities for easy infidelity to official trust, and invited a class of borrowers hurtful and dangerous to any fiscal institution.

It was brought out in the official investigation by a special committe of the Senate,[1] that the funds of the bank had been used for private purposes, that loans had been made which on their face bore the evidence of being insecure and made in the interest of the borrower instead of the lender. When the crash came at least one and a quarter million dollars were lost to the ignorant and innocent depositors, many of whom had their all deposited in the bank, the security of which they thought was guaranteed by the government.[2] How far the bank's

---

[1] Report of the select committee of the Senate, Forty-sixth Congress, 2nd session, 1880.

[2] Through the kindness of the Comptroller of the Currency in charge of the liquidation of the affairs of the failed bank, I am able to give the following additional facts. At the time of the company's

influence extended, how largely the colored people availed
themselves of the opportunity for investing small savings
and had faith in the security it offered for their hoarded
sums, is seen in the following table, showing the aggregate amount deposited each year as well as the annual
gain.

BUSINESS OF THE FREEDMEN'S SAVINGS BANK, 1866–1872.[1]

Years.	Total Amount of Deposits.	Deposit Each Year.	Balance Due Depositors.	Gain Each Year.
1866 . . .	$ 305,167	$ 305,167	$ 199,283	$ 199,283
1867 . . .	1,624,853	1,319,686	366,338	167,054
1868 . . .	3,582,378	1,957,525	638,299	271,960
1869 . . .	7,257,798	3,675,420	1,073,465	435,166
1870 . . .	12,605,782	5,347,983	1,657,006	583,541
1871 . . .	19,952,947	7,347,165	2,455,836	798,829
1872 . . .	31,260,499	11,281,313	3,684,739	1,227,927
1873 . . .			4,200,000	
1874[2] . . .	55,000,000		3,013,670	

[1] Senate Report, No. 440, 46th Congress, 2nd session, p. 41, Appendix.
[2] Bank failed in 1874.

The table is complete to the year 1872. The balance
due depositors in 1873 was $4,200,000, representing the
accumulated savings of less than eight years. The total
amount that had been deposited to the end of 1872 was
over $31,000,000 ; by the end of 1874, when the failure
came, over $55,000,000 had been on deposit in the bank
at one time or another. While, therefore, the remnant was
not so very large, the sphere of influence of the bank as
an educator in thrift must have been very great.

The faith of the depositors in the bank was implicit,
and the reports issued by the bank gave not the slightest
hint of possible danger. In 1872 when the bank was
practically insolvent, the seventh annual report closed

failure in 1874, it consisted of 33 branches with 61,131 depositors, and
the balance due these depositors at the time was $3,013,699 . . . .
The total payments to March, 1896, were $1,722,548, leaving a bal-
ance unpaid of $1,291,121. The present cash balance in the hands of
the government receivers amounts to $30,476.

with the following remarks: " There are no stock-holders in this company, and all of the profits, over and above expenses, go at each interest day to the credit of the depositors' interest. . . . The past history of the bank is a matter of just pride to all. . . . trustees and depositors alike. . . and its future is full of promise. Before the next annual meeting we shall be able to re-port five million dollars due depositors." Less than two years after this was written the bank failed and with its failure went the confidence of a large body of colored people in institutions for savings.

Not that the amount lost was so very great : to the average depositor the loss was probably small ; but it was the wrecked hopes, the loss of faith in thrift and accumulation as a means towards improvement of their humble condition, that injured the race to such an ex-tent that its effects will be felt through several genera-tions.

For the crimes thus committed against a helpless people, no one seems ever to have been punished. An investigation was made into the conduct of the officials, but the president and the actuary of the bank had in the meantime died, and the other persons sharing the responsibility, so far as they came before the Senate committee to be questioned, pleaded forgetfulness or ignorance of the violated law, or good intentions and philanthropic motives, and, all other excuses failing, placed the responsibility for all questionable acts upon their dead associates.[1]

Previous to emancipation, the slaves and freed people of color owned but a small amount of property. The ownership of land to any extent by slaves was out of

[1] Report of the select committee of the United States Senate, 1880) p. vi.
(

the question and no institutions for savings existed to encourage thrift in this direction. Many, however, accumlated a sum sufficiently large to purchase their own freedom ; and since the value of a slave was considerable during the last twenty or thirty years of slavery, their capacity for self-denial for a future end was of considerable economic importance. Of course the underlying motive in this habit of thrift was the desire for bodily freedom, in contrast with the underlying motive of modern thrift, economic freedom.

We have no information for years previous to 1879 in regard to the accumulation of property by the colored population of any southern state. But since 1879 the information is available for Georgia, although the data refer only to taxable values and not to property in general. In none of the last three census enumerations, dealing with wealth, debt and taxation, has an effort been made to obtain information on this most important point. Hence the statistics for Georgia, as a representative southern state, extending over a period of nearly twenty years, are of more than ordinary interest and value. For the purpose of comparison the amount of property owned by white persons is also given in the table below, which covers the period 1879–1895.

ASSESSED VALUATION OF PROPERTY OWNED BY WHITE AND COL-
ORED PERSONS IN GEORGIA, 1879-1895.[1]

	Whites.	Colored.
1879	$219,911,021	$ 5,182,398
1880	233,169,833	5,764,293
1881 · ·	247,773,679	6,478,951
1882	261,930,100	6,589,876
1883	277,300,555	7,582,395
1884	286,863,845	8,021,525
1885	290,993,408	8,153,390
1886	297,852,280	8,655,298
1887	316,605,329	8,939,479
1888	318,232,060	9,631,271
1889	335,523,507	10,415,330
1890	365,044,781	12,322,003
1891	388,389,733	14,196,735
1892	406,189,434	14,869,575
1893	410,644,753	14,960,075
1894	388,428,748	14,387,730
1895	370,739,521	12,941,230

[1] Reports of the Comptroller General of Georgia.

It will be observed that in 1879 the aggregate amount
of taxable property owned by colored persons was
slightly in excess of five million dollars. We may
properly consider this amount as representing the accumulations during the period 1865–79, or during a
period of about fifteen years. In 1894 the aggregate
amount was in excess of 14 million dollars, or about ten
million dollars above the amount for 1879. Hence if
the period 1865–79 is represented as the first period of
freedom, and the last fifteen years the second period,
we have an indication that the rate of increase in wealth
during the last period was twice that of the first. Of
course in this calculation no account is taken of the increase in population.

To represent more clearly the rate of increase in
wealth and at the same time the contrast with the
wealth of the white population, I give in the table below

the per capita wealth for the two census years 1880 and 1890.

ASSESSED VALUATION OF PROPERTY AND PER CAPITA VALUATION
IN 1880 AND 1890.

	White Population.		
	Population.	Value of Property.	Per Capita.
1880	816,906	$233,170,000	$285.40
1890	973,462	365,044,781	374.90
	Colored Population.		
1880	725,133	5,764,293	7.95
1890	863,716	12,322,003	14.26

According to this table the per capita value of assessed wealth has increased from $285.40 to $374.90 for the white population, and from $7.95 to $14.26 for the colored, during the ten years, 1880–90. For every dollar owned by the colored people, the whites own and pay taxes on about $27; and of the aggregate wealth owned by both races, the colored in 1879 owned 2.3 per cent., and in 1892, 3.5 per cent. The percentage of colored in total population was 47.02 in 1880, and 47.01 in 1890. The disparity between the ratios of wealth and population is seen to be still very great, and it is also shown that even an addition of $10,000,000 in wealth during the period 1879–92 has affected but slightly the percentage of wealth owned by negroes. To this must be added the fact that during the period 1891–94 only slight additions have been made to the aggregate value of property owned by the colored population. The disparity between the wealth of the whites and that of the colored is still very great. While progress has been made, and some property has been accumulated, the colored race holds but a very small share of the aggregate public wealth in Georgia; and we shall find the same condition prevailing in the two other states for which the facts are available.

For the state of Virginia the data as to property owned by colored persons has been made public since 1891 in such detail that a more complete view of the economic condition of the race is possible for this state than for any other. In the table below I have brought together the returns of the state auditor for five years, showing for both races the aggregate amounts of taxable values on both real and personal property.

ASSESSED VALUATION OF PROPERTY IN VIRGINIA, 1891-1895.[1]

| | Owned by White Persons. | | |
	Real Estate.	Personal Property.	Total.
1891	$286,192.615	$93,5:6,029	$379,708,644
1892	291,292,281	92,525,131	383,817,412
1893	296,371,055	90,373,044	386,744,099
1894	300,038,625	83,349,044	383,387,669
1895[2]	291,308,592	79,955,026	361,263,618
	Owned by Colored Persons.		
1891	8,995,514	3,094,451	12,089,965
1892	9,425,085	3,342,950	12,768,035
1893	9,829,583	3,465,370	13,294,953
1894	10,162,889	3,241,144	13,404,033
1895[2]	10,759,548	3,174,450	13,933,998

[1] Reports of the auditor for public accounts, 1891-1895.
[2] Re-assessment.

The table shows that the whites in 1895 owned 361.2 million dollars worth of real and personal property listed for purposes of taxation, while the aggregate wealth of the negroes is given at 13.9 millions. Of the total wealth of both races the negroes, therefore, in 1891 owned 3.1 per cent., or 0.4 per cent. less than the proportion for Georgia. The per capita wealth in 1891, according to the foregoing figures, was approximately $374.20 for the whites, and $18.90 for the colored population. While the whites of Virginia and Georgia have about the same amount of taxable values per capita, the colored population of Virginia shows $4.60 per capita more than the colored population of Georgia.

The distribution of the accumulated wealth of the two races in Virginia, according to various kinds of real property, is given in the table below, which shows the amounts assessed against lands, houses on lands, lots and houses on lots, together with the number of acres of land owned and the proportion of each class of property to the aggregate amount of real property. A comparison is also made for the two years, 1891 and 1895 ; but the period is rather too short to afford a clue as to the tendency of the colored population in the accumulation of real property.

COMPARATIVE VALUATION OF REAL PROPERTY OWNED BY WHITE AND COLORED PERSONS IN VIRGINIA, 1891 AND 1895.

	Owned by White Persons.			
	1891.	Percent-age of Total.	1895.	Percent-age of Total.
No. acres of land	25,285,981		. 25,154,781	
Value of land	$123,497,236	43 28	$113,129,317	38.83
Value of bldgs. on land,	39,362,942	13.75	40,408,200	13.87
Value of town lots . . .	52,590,894	18.38	63,074,643	21.65
Value of bldgs. on lots,	70,356,543	24 59	74,696,432	25.65
Total value	286,192,615	100 00	291,308,592	100.00
	Owned by Colored Persons.			
No. acres of land	698,074		833,147	
Value of land	2,938,064	32.66	3,450,247	32.06
Value of bldgs. on land,	1,393,766	15 49	1,909,154	17.74
Value of town lots . .	1,954,394	21.73	2,142,196	19.92
Value of houses on lots .	2,709,290	30.12	3,257,951	30.28
Total value	8,995,514	100.00	10,759,548	100.00

It is shown in this table that in 1891 the whites owned 25,285,981 acres of land, decreasing their holdings to 25,154,781 acres in 1895. The colored population owned 698,074 acres in 1891 and increased their holdings to 833,147 acres in 1895. In 1891 the whites owned 97.3 per cent. of the aggregate acreage as against 96.8 per cent. in 1895.

The increase in the ownership of land held by

negroes in this state has previously been referred to. It
is here shown that during the depressed condition of agriculture the colored population has been gaining by
what the whites have lost. That is, the increase in the
holdings of the colored population has been due not so
much to an increase in the aggregate acreage by a
utilization of former waste lands, as to purchase
for cash or on time, of the land formerly under culture
by the white. Of the aggregate taxable values of real
estate, the whites owned 57 per cent. in agricultural
values (lands and houses) in 1891, and only 52.7 per
cent. in 1895, showing a decrease of 4.3 per cent.
or an increase by that much of the values of city real
estate. The colored people's taxable accumulations consisted of 48.2 per cent. in agricultural values in 1891, and
49.8 per cent. in 1895, showing an increase of rural over
urban valuation of nearly two per cent. Hence during
the past five years the tendency among the colored
population has been in the direction of acquiring agricultural property rather than lots and houses in town,
whereas among the whites the tendency has been the
other way. It remains to be seen whether this condition will be persisted in under more favorable conditions
as regards the returns from labor upon the land in this
state. In view of the considerable migration of negroes
from the country to the cities, it is remarkable that
those who remained in the country should have been
able to acquire and to keep as much property as the returns show they actually hold.

In North Carolina the assessment of 1891 gave the
value of real and personal property owned by each race
in that state. According to the reports of the state
auditor, the whites owned $234,109,000 worth of taxa-
ble property, while the negroes owned a little in excess

of $8,000,000. Or, of the aggregate taxable wealth, the negroes owned about 3.3 per cent. The per capita wealth of the whites was $223.10 and of the negroes $14.10. The returns for this state as well as those for Georgia and Virginia have been consolidated in the table below for the purpose of easy comparison. The general agreement of the figures supports the claim that the official data are approximately correct in their representation of the taxable wealth of the negro in these three states.

COMPARATIVE VALUATION OF TAXABLE PROPERTY OWNED BY
WHITE AND COLORED PERSONS IN NORTH CAROLINA, 1891.

	Whites.	Colored.	Percentage of Total Property Owned by Colored Persons.	Per Capita Value of Property Owned. Whites.	Col'd.
N. Carolina, 1891	$234,109,568	$ 8,018.446	3.3	$223.1	$14.1
Virginia, 1890 .	379,708,644	12,089,965	3.1	374 2	18.9
Georgia, 1890 .	365,044,781	12,322,003	3.5	374.9	14.3
Three states	978,862,993	32,430,414	3.2	322.3	15.7

In the three states the whites own 978 million dollars worth of taxable property as compared with 32 million dollars worth owned by the negroes. The per capita wealth is $322 for the whites and about $16 for the negroes. Of the aggregate the colored population owns 3.2 per cent.

It is shown in this summary that there are only slight differences between the three states as regards the proportion of wealth owned by the colored population. The per capita is largest in Virginia and lowest in North Carolina. The largest per capita wealth of the whites is in Georgia, and the lowest in North Carolina. The total white population of the three states is 3,037,333, the colored 2,071,755. Hence with 40.5 per cent of the population the negroes own only $3.20 out of every hundred dollars of taxable wealth in these three states. The claim of an aggregate valuation of one hundred million dollars is probably based on this average, since a per capita of $15.70 applied to the aggregate colored population of the southern states would give about 110 million dollars. But it is extremely doubtful whether this average would hold good for all the southern states. For such states as Mississippi, Louisiana and South Carolina, the average per capita wealth is probably much less than for Georgia and Virginia.

But valuable as these figures are in indicating how far there may be a tendency to a higher economic stage, the data are insufficient, and fall far short of presenting a true picture of the economic progress of the race. The aggregate amount of taxable values is only one measure of economic progress. The amount of taxes actually paid, not merely on the property assessed, but also from other sources is even more significant. And in addition to this we should know, for a full and comprehensive view of the negro as an economic factor in the development of the South, the proportion that he bears of the public burdens.

It is only for the state of Virginia that these important questions can be answered with any degree of exactness. For North Carolina my information is limited to the amount of taxes paid for school purposes only. In Virginia taxes are paid on real estate and personal property, on incomes over $600 per annum, and a capitation tax on males over 21 years of age. The aggregate amounts received from these sources are given in the table below, which covers the five years 1891-95.

AMOUNT OF TAX ON REAL ESTATE, PERSONAL PROPERTY AND
INCOMES ASSESSED IN VIRGINIA, 1891.

	Assessed Taxes.	
	White Population.	Colored Population.
1891	$1,796,576	$163,175
1892	1,816,134	171,144
1893	1,824,153	172,391
1894	1,807,698	172,124
1895	1,808,234	174,808

The above table shows the assessed taxes only. It will
be observed that while the whites in 1895 were assessed for
$1,808,234 of taxes, the colored population were assessed
for only $174,808. It is not possible to give the exact
amount of taxes actually paid, but I have been favored
with an explanatory letter from Mr. Morton Marye, the
auditor of public accounts of Virginia, which enables
me to present the following facts bearing on this point.

Of the total taxes, those assessed on real and personal
property as well as on incomes are practically all collected, but of the capitation taxes a large proportion is
not collected. In 1895, the whites failed to pay $55,233
of the capitation tax, or 23.6 per cent. of the total capitations assessed against them, while the negroes failed
to pay $57,925 or 48.3 per cent. If we compare the
unpaid taxes with the aggregate of taxes assessed for
all purposes we have the following result.

APPROXIMATE AMOUNT OF TAXES PAID BY EACH RACE IN VIR-
GINIA, 1895.

	Total Assessed Taxes.	Unpaid Capita-tion Taxes.	Taxes Paid.	Percentage of Taxes Paid.
Whites . .	$1,808,234	$55,233	$1,753,001	96 4
Colored . .	174,818	57,925	116,893	66.8

Of the aggregate amount of taxes paid, only 6.2 per
cent. was paid by the negroes, although they form 38
per cent. of the total population. On the basis of the

census of 1890 the per capita taxes paid by the whites amounted to $1.75, as against a per capita tax of only 18 cents paid by the colored population of the state. The economic consequences of this anomaly can hardly be overestimated.

It has been stated that the unpaid taxes fall largely on the assessed capitations, and it may be of value to know the proportion of capitations to the whole amount of assessed taxes. The following table will show for the year 1895, the proportion of each class of assessed taxes to the aggregate amount assessed. The table affords other valuable information, especially with respect to taxes on incomes, which it will be observed amounted to only $16 for the colored population in 1895.[1]

DISTRIBUTION OF THE ASSESSED TAXES IN VIRGINIA, 1895.

Kind of taxes.	White Population.	Percentage of Total.	Colored Population.	Percentage of Total.
Real estate.	$1,210,688	66.95	$ 41,823	23.92
Capitation	234,268	12.95	120,152	68.73
Personal Property. .	320,269	17.72	12,827	7.34
Income.	43,009	2.38	16	1
Total.	$1,808,234	100.00	$174,818	100.00

It is shown in the above table that of the total taxes for the white population, 12.95 per cent. are assessed on capitations, and for the colored 68.73 per cent. That is to say, the kind of tax most easily evaded comprises almost two-thirds of the total assessed taxes of the colored population, and as a result we find that the amount of public revenue is materially reduced by the non-payment of the capitation tax. For the whites only about one-fifth of the total is assessed

[1] Besides the taxes enumerated in this table, the state assessed taxes upon railroads, insurance companies, banks, and license taxes, to the aggregate amount of $1,136,603, all of which is collected, and of which the colored people practically pay nothing.

20

on capitations, and the non-payment of the amount given affects the aggregate returns to a much smaller degree. Thus the proportion of the public burden borne by the colored race comes down in final analysis to a per capita tax of only 18 cents.

It will be noticed that of the income taxes, the whites paid $43,009; while the colored population paid only $16, this amount coming from Richmond, and Charlotteville, and Chesterfield county. The tax on incomes is one dollar for every hundred in excess of six hundred dollars; hence in only two cities and one county were there found negroes who paid tax on incomes in 1895 exceeding $600. Of course there are hundreds, perhaps thousands, whose incomes exceed this amount, and the fact that the tax is not paid shows that the class of the colored population of which we hear so much in the newspapers and sermons, the class who it is claimed have made such exceptional individual progress, accumulating wealth anywhere from five to one hundred and fifty thousand dollars, are wanting in that sense of public morality which demands that a man shall pay the taxes which his income, property or political privileges impose upon him.

Income taxes have always been disliked and no doubt there are thousands of the whites who do not pay them. But it must be taken into consideration that the whites pay a larger proportion of taxes on real and personal property, and further that of the capitation tax only 23 whites per 100 fail to pay, as against 48 negroes. The amount of the income tax has declined in recent years, and the decline for the colored race has reduced the amount to practically nothing. Only about a year ago a correspondent of the New York *Sun* in an article on the negro section of Richmond, gave a list of 12 colored persons whose aggregate wealth, it was stated exceeded a quarter of a million dollars. There was one woman who was said to own $150,000 worth of property, and five cases were given where men owned more than $10,000 worth; yet only $1.75 was paid in taxes on the incomes of the entire colored population of this city. This evasion of the payment of taxes is very general among negroes throughout the South, excepting for real property, on which the negro is usually prompt to pay.

In North Carolina the data available do not afford a clear insight into facts. The table below will show for the state the amount of taxes for school purposes levied during five years, but the reports do not show the amount actually paid.

TAXES FOR SCHOOL PURPOSES ASSESSED IN NORTH CAROLINA IN 1891-1895.

	General Property Tax.	White Population. Poll Taxes.	Total.
1891	$283,953	$299,994	$583,947
1892	364,012	237,461	601,473
1893	354,221	240,912	595,133
1894	378,248	243,992	622,240
1895	363,158	250,458	613,616
		Colored Population.	
1891	8,735	90,420	99,155
1892	12,373	93,589	105,962
1893	12,274	92,870	105,145
1894	13,071	92,139	105,210
1895	12,861	94,436	107,297

The total amount of school taxes levied in 1895 was $765,510, 80.17 per cent. of which was assessed to the whites, and 14.01 per cent. to the colored, the remaining 5.82 per cent. being derived from other sources. In the same state the school population in 1890 was 64.9 per cent. white and 35.1 per cent. colored. Hence with 35.1 per cent. of the school population, the colored people were charged with only 14.1 per cent. of the taxes. It would be interesting to know what proportion of these taxes were actually paid. Since the larger proportion of the taxes levied against the negroes were poll taxes, it is doubtful if more than half of them were collected.

The economic consequences of this disproportion of taxes to population, and the great differences between benefits received and services rendered, are nowhere better illustrated than in the case of Virginia.

In his work on "The Old South," Mr. Thomas Nelson Page has called attention to the fact that during twenty years (1870–90) the total cost of negro education alone was equal to nearly six million dollars, while for the whites during the same period 17.5 millions were expended for this purpose. These expenditures Mr. Page compares with the taxes assessed in 1891, and shows that while 25 per cent. of the public funds for school purposes were devoted to negro education, the negroes were charged with only 8.3 per cent. taxes. Mr. Page, moreover, gave the assessed taxes and not the actual amount of taxes paid, which for the colored would approximate, on the basis of the figures for 1895, only 6.2 per cent.

Mr. Morton Marye, the auditor of Virginia, a few years ago was asked by a representative of the American Association of Educators of the Colored Youth, "What is the negro doing towards his own education?", and replied with the following statistics:

By the tables which have been prepared from the official records it appears that the colored people of the state pay into the treasury the sum of $103,565, and that the state pays out in their behalf:

For criminal expenses	$204,018
For education.	324,864
For care of lunatics.	80,000
Total expenditure	608,383

These figures show that so far from contributing their own support the colored people cost the state in criminal expenses $100,453 more than the entire sum they pay into the treasury. These figures also show that not only do the colored people fail to pay one cent towards the regular expenses of the state government (other than that of criminal trials) such as salaries of the governor, judges of the court of appeals, of circuit, corporation and county courts and of other state officers, cost of the general assembly, public printing, interest on the public debt, etc., but they cost the state for criminal expenses, education and care of their lunatics, $504,817 more than they pay into her treasury.

It is difficult to arrive at definite conclusions on the basis of the foregoing information. In one sense the statistics show a certain degree of economic progress : some lands have been acquired, some personal property has been accumulated, and some taxes are paid ; but after all the general condition of the race from an economic standpoint is far from what it ought to be to make the negro a positive and determining factor in the economic life of the nation.

That he should try to evade the payment of his taxes is what might be expected. In this respect the white race has always set an example of which there is nothing to be proud. It was the conclusion of Professor Ely, that "a study of taxation is calculated to give one a rather pessimistic view of American laws, American institutions, and American character." And the fact that the negro should prove himself an unscrupulous tax-dodger is only another proof of his tendency to acquire the vices rather than the virtues of the white man's civilization.

The tendency would seem to be in the direction of the purchase of land and property in the agricultural sections ; although a considerable portion of the assessed wealth owned by negroes is in city property. Whether their ownership of land will prove a benefit to the state is very doubtful. From such data as have been at my command, it would appear that the negro on the land is,

contented with making a living and no more. This conclusion is supported by personal observations in various
portions of the South. Hence it follows that, while the
settlement of the negro on land which is his own may
insure a happier and less burdensome existence, it is
very doubtful whether such a condition would not, in
the end, prove more of a hindrance than a help to the
economic progress of the South.

In the large cities the vast majority of negroes lead a
precarious existence, accumulating little property and
making but scant provision for old age, disease, and death.
The evil influence of the failure of the Freedmen's Bank
will be felt for generations to come in an indirect way.
Some attempts have been made to induce the negro
to save, but in most cases they reach only a small
class of individuals. Northern societies for the amelioration of the condition of the colored population have made
some efforts to induce the negroes of the large cities to
save small amounts by means of cards and stamps, but
such instances as have come to my notice seem to
prove that very little has been accomplished. I have no
data, however, in regard to the amounts saved, and the
sums thus laid aside may be larger than would appear.

And in the accumulation of the property which the
negroes actually own, there is one fact which must not
be ignored, that is, the effect of the ' unearned increment',
which, proportionately speaking, has probably benefitted
the race more that the whites. The enormous development of the southern states during the past ten years,
the growth of new cities and the extension of old, the
development of suburban tracts and the growth of the
railway systems have, in very many instances
made rich people out of colored persons who accidentally owned a piece of land which under new condi-

tions became desirable because of its location. In many instances to my own knowledge, especially in the vicinity of Chattanooga, large sums were paid to negroes for land on account of its proximity to valuable land in a particular section in which negroes were not wanted. Of course the same shifting of fortunes occurs everywhere, but it particularly modifies the amount that the negro can show in the way of taxable property as the result of his own labor.

As a general conclusion it may be said that the negro has yet to learn the first elements of Anglo-Saxon thrift. He has yet to be taught, or left alone to learn the lesson of the consequences of the old English poor law. What Mr. Mackay says of the workings of the factory laws and other philanthropic efforts in behalf of the English poor, holds equally for the negro of the South :

As they have not been obliged to learn the first steps, so they have difficulty in proceeding further and are constantly looking to the state to aid them under conditions in which the state is powerless. The working class gained, no doubt, some of the advantages which the factory acts were intended to give, but these acts have made a break in the continuity of individual efforts. They have deprived men of a most invaluable educational process, and this loss perhaps more than balances the gain. Workmen have gained their present position by the short cut of state interference, and they hardly know how to utilize the advantages which they have acquired. The natural course of economic evolution is slower but surer in the end.[1]

But the consequences of this disregard of a fundamental law of economic and social life, namely, that the individual shall develop his faculties and abilities, not in accordance with the preconceived ideas and notions of others, but as a result of his own individual struggle for success in life, have even more seriously affected the progress and development of the white race, if for no other reason, because there was more to be lost.

[1] Mackay, "The English Poor," p. 263.

The method employed by Mr. Marye in showing that
the negro is a heavy burden to the state of Virginia, may
understate, but it does not exaggerate the burden of a
large negro population. If it were possible to obtain
correct information in regard to the annual cost of the
negro population and its annual contribution to the
public fund, I feel sure that the indirect gain to the
public through the productive ability of the negro would
be shown to be far less than is supposed. Shirking its
duty towards the state to such an extent that even those
most able to pay evade the payment of a paltry income
tax, much missionary work will still have to be done
before the negro race will understand the rudimentary
ethics of social life.

With an inordinate rate of mortality, with an excessive degree of immorality, with a greater tendency to
crime and pauperism than the whites, the negro race has
also, as shown by the facts just given, a far lower degree
of economic activity and inclination towards accumulation of capital and other material wealth. It seems from
all the facts relating to their economic condition, that the
great majority leave the earth as poor as they entered it,
and are fully satisfied with a degree of comfort too low to
prove of economic advantage to the state. It is not too
much to say that if the present tendency towards a lower
degree of economic efficiency is persisted in, the day is not
far distant when the negro laborer of the South will be
gradually supplanted by the immigrant laborer from
Europe, just as the coolie in the West Indies has supplanted the native laborer.

Land at the present rates is very easily obtained by
negroes in the Southern states, and once obtained it is
very easily held. The genial climate and the pro-
ductiveness of the soil will supply with little labor the

wants of a negro and his family, leaving but a small amount of work to be done to supply those necessaries of life which have to be bought for cash. This is practically the condition of the negro in the West Indies;[1] and this is the tendency disclosed by the available facts in the southern states. The drifting towards a proprietorship of small holdings may insure to the negro the comforts of life, but such a proprietorship will add little to the progress and prosperity of the state. And as a result of this probable condition, the state will in return be slow to provide for its citizens those advantages of modern civilized life, without which the majority of the people are no longer willing to get along. Such public improvements as good roads, canals, hospitals, asylums, institutions for higher and technical education, adequate provision for paupers and other dependents, will be largely impossible in states where the whole burden of public support is carried by a comparatively small proportion of the population.

[1] The remarks of Mr. Froude in regard to the negro in the West Indies are equally applicable to the negro throughout the larger part of the South. "If happiness is to be all and end all of life, and those who have most of it have most completely attained the object of their being, the 'nigger' who now basks among the ruins of the West Indian plantations is the supremest specimen of present humanity." ("The English in the West Indies," p. 50.)

CHAPTER VII.

CONCLUSION.

Of all the vulgar modes of escaping from the consideration of the effect of social and moral influences on the human mind, the most vulgar is that of attributing the diversities of conduct and character to inherent natural differences.[1]—*Mill.*

In treatises on pathology we find much as to the influence of age, sex and temperament on disease, and concise descriptions of affections peculiar to certain countries, but almost nothing as to the influence of race.[2]—*Topinard.*

The central fact deducible from the results of this investigation into the traits and tendencies of the colored population of this country, is plainly and emphatically the powerful influence of *race* in the struggle for life. In marked contrast with the frequent assertions, such as that of Mill, that race is not important and that environment or the conditions of life are the most important factors in the final result of the struggle for life, individual as well as social, we have here abundant evidence that we find in race and heredity the determining factors in the upward or downward course of mankind.

In the field of statistical research, sentiment, prejudice, or the influence of pre-conceived ideas have no place. The data which have been here brought together in a convenient form speak for themselves. From the standpoint of the impartial investigator, no difference of interpretation of their meaning seems possible. The decrease in the rate of increase in the colored population has been traced first to the excessive mortality, which in turn has been traced to an inferior vital capacity. The mixture of the African with the white

[1] "Principles of Political Economy."
[2] "Anthropology," p. 413.

race has been shown to have seriously affected the longevity of the former and left as a heritage to future generations the poison of scrofula, tuberculosis and most of all of, syphilis. This racial inferiority, has in turn brought about a moral deterioration such as is rarely met with in civilized countries at the present time. Already subject to an inordinate rate of mortality, especially from all of the most destructive diseases, the sexual immorality prevailing between colored females and white males of a lower type, as well as between colored males and colored females, has also brought about a diminished power of vital resistance among the young, as is to be expected from the recognized fact that the death rate for illegitimate children is about twice that of children born in wedlock. As a general result there is diminished social and economic efficiency, which in the course of years must prove not only a most destructive factor in the progress of the colored race, but also in the progress, social as well as economic, of the white race brought under its influence.

Racial inferiority was the keynote of the pro-slavery argument. On the other hand, racial differences were explained away by those who saw in freedom the sure prospect of speedy amelioration of the lot of the southern slave; yet thirty years of freedom in this country and nearly sixty in the West Indies have failed to accomplish the original purpose of the abolition of slavery, that is, the elevation of the colored race to the moral, mental and economic level of the white race.

Nothing is more clearly shown from this investigation than that the southern black man at the time of emancipation was healthy in body and cheerful in mind. He neither suffered inordinately from disease nor from impaired bodily vigor. His industrial capaci-

ties as a laborer were not of a low order, nor was the
condition of servitude such as to produce in him morbid conditions favorable to mental disease, suicide, or
intemperance. What are the conditions thirty years
after? The pages of this work give but one answer,
an answer which is a most severe condemnation of modern attempts of superior races to lift inferior races to
their own elevated position, an answer so full of meaning that it would seem criminal indifference on the part
of a civilized people to ignore it.   In the plain language
of the facts brought together the colored race is shown
to be on the downward grade, tending toward a condition in which matters will be worse than they are now,
when diseases will be more destructive, vital resistance
still lower, when the number of births will fall below
the deaths, and gradual extinction of the race take place.
Neither religion nor education nor a higher degree of
economic well-being have been able to raise the race
from a low and anti-social condition, a condition really
fostered by the very influences which it was asserted
would soon raise the race to a place even more elevated
than that of the whites.

It is not in the conditions of life, but in race and
heredity that we find the explanation of the fact to be
observed in all parts of the globe, in all times and
among all peoples, namely, the superiority of one race
over another, and of the Aryan race over all.   To what
must we attribute this superiority?   To what inherent
traits must we attribute the marvelous conquest of nature by the Aryan race?   I cannot do better than quote
from the work of Mr. Morris, who defines in an admirable manner the essential differences between the four
most important races:

If the negro is indolent both physically and mentally, the Mongolian energetic physically but undeveloped mentally, and the Melanochroi active physically and to some extent mentally, in the Aryan we find a highly vigorous and developed mental activity. Though by no means lacking in physical energy the mind is the ruling agent in this race, muscular work is reduced to the lowest level consistent with the demands of the body and the intellect, and every effort is made to limit the quantity of work represented in a fixed quantity of product. Waste labor is a crime to the Aryan mind. Use is the guiding principle in all efforts. It is to this ruling agency of the intellect over the energies of a muscular and active organism that we owe the superior quality, the restricted dimensions, and the vast quantity of Aryan labor products. In his work pure thought is far more represented than pure labor.[1]

If we consider the negro race . . . . it is to find a lack of energy both physical and mental. Nowhere in the region inhabited by this race do we perceive indications of high powers of either work or thought. No monuments of architecture appear, no philosophies, or literatures have arisen. And in their present condition they stand mentally at a very low level, while physically they confine themselves to the labor absolutely necessary for existence. They neither work nor think above the lowest level of life needs ; and even in America under all the instigations of Aryan activity, the Negro race scarcely displays any voluntary energy either of thought or work.[2] It goes only as far as the sharp whip of necessity drives, and looks upon indolence and sunshine as the terrestial paradise.

The white race has great physical vigor, capacity and endurance. It has an intensity of will and desire which is controlled by intellectuality. Great things are undertaken, readily but not blindly. It manifests a strong utilitarianism, united with a powerful imagination which elevates, enobles and idealizes its practical ideas. The negro can only imitate, the Chinese only utilize, the work of the white ; but the latter is abundantly able to produce new works. He has a keen sense of order as the yellow man, not from love of repose, however, but from the desire to protect and preserve his acquisitions. He has a love of liberty far more intense than exists in the black or yellow races, and clings to life more earnestly. His high sense of honor is a faculty unknown to other races, and springs from an exalted senti-

[1] Morris, " The Aryan Race : its Origin and Achievements," p. 277-8.

[2] " Even so highly developed a type of mind as that of the negro— submitted, too, as it has been in millions of individual cases to a close contact with minds of the most progressive type, and enjoying as it has in many thousands of individual cases all the advantages of a liberal education—has never so far as I can ascertain executed one single stroke of original work in any single department of intellectual activity."—Romanes " Mental Evolution of Man," (New York, 1889,) p. 13.

314

ment of which they show no indications. His sensations are less intense than in either black or yellow, but his mentality is far more developed and energetic.

Thus the Aryan stands as the type of intellectual man, the central outcome of the races in which the special conditions of dark and light, North and South, emotional and practical have mingled and combined into the highest and noblest states of mind and body.[1]

In other words, the Aryan race is possessed of all the essential characteristics that make for success in the struggle for the higher life, in contrast with other races which lack in either one or the other of the determining qualities. A statement so far-reaching must needs have a considerable body of facts in its support, and the whole history of human effort is witness to the fact that no other race since the Aryan appeared on the scene, has, in the end, been able to resist the onward march of its progressive civilization. Here, in the contrast between the white and colored races we have the most complete historical proof of race superiority, a superiority extending into all the intricate and complex phenomena of life. Wherever the white man has gone, he has become master of the conditions of life. The whole history of Anglo-Saxon conquest and colonization is one endless proof of race superiority and race supremacy. In countries where the very forces of nature were at first against him, he has, after years of struggle, gained his end and mastered the conditions of life surrounding him.

It has been shown in this work how the mortality of the white troops in the West Indies has gradually decreased during the past seventy years. It may not be out of place to give a few additional facts.

In the abbreviated table below I give some of the most important statistics bearing on the question of the ability of the white race to live in the tropics. Here we have for four large sections and for a very long

[1] Morris, "The Aryan Race: its Origin and Achievements," p. 28.

period the experience of the British and Dutch armies
in the East and West Indies. Without exception the
fall in the death rate has been very great. It is immaterial for our present purpose to know to what causes
this diminishing mortality may be due; we here have
merely to consider the fact that those countries are no
longer "the white man's grave."

MORTALITY OF THE BRITISH TROOPS IN BENGAL.

1825–29	77.7 per 1,000
1881–90	14.5

MORTALITY OF THE BRITISH TROOPS IN MADRAS.

1801–1809	68.0 per 1,000
1881–1890	13.0

MORTALITY OF THE BRITISH TROOPS IN THE WEST INDIES.

1819–1836	78.5 per 1,000
1886–1892	9.7

MORTALITY OF THE DUTCH TROOPS IN THE EAST INDIES.

1819–1828	170.0 per 1,000
1879–1888	30.6
–1892	16.0

Were not the conditions of life extremely unfavorable to the white race in those countries in the early part
of the century? Is not the climate the same, the heat
still as oppressive, the jungle still as malarious, the life
in itself still as totally different from the life at home?
Are not these statistics proof that the white race must
have been able to master the unfavorable conditions of
life in order to have made possible such enormous re-
ductions in the death rates? Even if it is admitted that
in certain sections it is not as yet possible for the white
race to increase and multiply, is it not proof of a superior vitality to have been able to make at least a stationary condition possible at the present time? And will it
be doubted that where so much has been accomplished

the race will be able to improve its condition still further, to adapt itself still more completely to the prevailing conditions, and thanks to superior race traits and consequent moral, intellectual and economic superiority, in the end to become absolute master of the conditions of life, even in what were formerly considered the most fatal regions of the earth?

Let us consider one experiment of this kind. The colonization of Algeria by France was most bitterly opposed fifty years ago. In numberless instances the claim was made that never under any circumstances could the French population become so acclimated that it would increase and multiply. Major Tulloch (who wrote extensively on the mortality of the white race in the tropics during the first fifty years of the present century,) in a paper on "The Mortality among Her Majesty's Troops in the Colonies", speaks of the colonization of Algiers as follows:

To ascertain the races of men best fitted to inhabit and develop the resources of different colonies is a most important inquiry, and one which has hitherto attracted too little attention, both in this and other countries. Had the government of France, for instance, adverted to the absolute impossibility of any population increasing or keeping up its numbers under an annual mortality of seven per cent., (being that to which the settlers are exposed at Algiers), it would never have entered on the wild speculation of cultivating the soil of Africa by Europeans, nor have wasted a hundred million sterling with no other result than the loss of 100,000 men, who have fallen victims to the climate of that country. In such questions military returns, properly organized and properly digested, afford one of the most useful guides to direct the policy of the colonial legislator; they point out the limits intended by nature for particular races and within which alone they can thrive and increase.[1]

What are the facts of subsequent experience? Was ultimate failure the result of this struggle of the white race against such unfavorable 'conditions of life?'

---

[1] *Journal of the Royal Statistical Society*, Vol. X, (1847), page 259.

Algeria became a colony of France in 1837, when the last provinces were conquered. Nearly seven years had passed since the first attempt was made to conquer the territory, and during this time 6,592 persons of French descent had settled in the new colony. The total European population in this year was 16,770, exclusive of the military force. Nearly twenty years later, or nine years after Mr. Tulloch wrote his essay against colonization, the population of French descent had increased, largely of course by immigration, to 92,750. Twenty years later, that is, by the year 1876, the French population numbered 156,365; while at the last census, 1891, the number had increased to 271,101.

During the same period other races, most of all the Spanish, had settled in Algeria and were increasing at a rapid rate. From 5,189 Spanish settlers in 1837, the population of Spanish descent increased to 151,859 by the year 1891. The Jews, who numbered 6,065 in 1837, increased to 21,048 by the year 1856, and to 47,-564 by 1891. Only the Germans, who numbered 782 in 1837, and 5,440 in 1856, have shown a tendency to decrease in population, numbering only 3,189 at the census of 1891.[1]

Thus, it is clearly shown that those races which Mr. Tulloch concluded could not possibly survive the early unfavorable conditions of life, half a century later had increased, partly by immigration but in no small part by natural increase, to a total European population of nearly half a million. And only forty years later Mr. Playfair, the British consul, could say : " Who shall estimate the gain to humanity by the transformation of a nest of pirates and robbers into the beautiful colony which Algeria now is ?" The enormous mortality of

[1] "Statistique Générale de l'Algerie," Alger, 1894.

21

the early years has long since decreased, and to-day the births exceed the deaths, year after year, with a favorable tendency upwards.

I have calculated the ratios of births to deaths, for the period 1881–93, which shows that for all Europeans in Algeria the ratio is one death to every 1.15 births, those of French descent have a ratio of one to 1.17, while the Jews have a ratio of one to every 1.65 births, the most favorable of all. The native population of Algeria has frequently shown an excess of deaths over births, but the statistics for this part of the population must of necessity be wanting in completeness. Surgeon F. L. Du Bois, writing in 1880 to the Navy Department,[1] expressed it as his opinion that the native Mussulman population would rapidly disappear, but so far this has not taken place. For while at times the births have fallen below the deaths, at other times the reverse has occurred. If the race is destined to disappear it will be a very gradual process of extinction, increasing perhaps in rapidity in course of time.

Such extinction has been almost invariably the rule where white races have permanently settled among what the Germans call the " Naturvoelker." It would carry me beyond my purpose were I to deal to any extent with this point; but on account of the close relation between the extinction of native races in various parts of the world and the settlement of those sections by the white races, it may not be out of place if I give here the following table showing the decrease in the native Indian population of this country, and of the natives of the Sandwich Islands and New Zealand.

[1] Annual report, Secretary of the Navy, 1880, p. 439.

ACTUAL AND RELATIVE DECREASE IN THE NATIVE INDIAN POPULA-
TION OF THE UNITED STATES, THE HAWAIIANS
AND THE MAORIES.

North American Indians. 68 Years.		Hawaiians.[1] 67 Years.		Maories. 48 Years.	
Year.	Population.	Year.	Population.	Year.	Population.
1822	471,417	1823 . . .	142,000	1843 . . .	114,890
1850	388,229	1853 . . .	71,019	1858 . .	56,049
1870	313,712	1872 . . .	49,044	1881 . . .	44,099
1890	248,253	1890 . . .	34,436	1891 . . .	41,993
Total decrease,	223,164		107,564		72,897
% of decrease,	47.4		75.8		63.4
Av. annual %,	0.69		1.12		1.32

[1] ANNUAL DEATH RATE IN HONOLULU (SANDWICH ISLANDS), 1893–94.

Per 1,000 of Population.

	1894.	1893.
Native	33.6	29.5
Asiatic	24.3	20.8
European	16.8	17.7

I have confined myself in this table to periods of observation for which the statistical data are fairly reliable
and which would tend rather to understate than over-
state the native population at the earlier periods. It
will be observed that the annual rate of decrease has
been highest for the Maories, slightly lower for the
Hawaiians, and about half the rate of the former for the
native Indian population. These figures are interesting
from a number of standpoints, but we must confine our-
selves to one or two. It goes without saying that the
conditions of life have been the most unfavorable for
the Indians in comparison with the Maories and Hawaiians. Of the Maories it need only be said that they lived
in a land where the dominant white today enjoys the most
favorable rate of mortality of any race on earth excepting
the Norwegians. Of the Hawaiians it need only be said
that the very name of the group of islands, the " Paradise of the Pacific," indicates that the conditions of life
must have been fairly favorable for success in the
mere struggle for physical existence. Of the three races

the American Indians have without question been exposed to the greatest hardships and the most unfavorable conditions of life, if only on account of the enormous increase in the white population.   Yet the rate of decrease has been only one-half that of the others, and the reason for this becomes plain if we go a little deeper into the life history of the three races.

Of the Maories, Mr. Archibald Hamilton wrote in 1869 as follows :

It is frequently asserted that, under any circumstances the natives must disappear before the advance of European civilization ; that they are a doomed race.   For the sake of humanity, I trust that some means may be found of terminating the present state of chronic hostilities, so that there may still be a fair opportunity for preserving by far the finest and most intellectual race with whom Anglo-Saxon colonists have yet come in contact.   There is ample room for both : no wide extent of country is required for hunting ground : and a glance at the map will show how small a portion of the island has been yet appropriated.[1]

Another writer observes :

The Maories, such as they were found by Tasman and Cook, no longer exist ; they were a people of great force of character and superior intellectual powers, and it is proper that their memory should be perpetuated ; for their descendants are no longer the typical representatives of the ancestral stock ; they are the degenerate offspring of a superior people, who within a longer or shorter period will become entirely extinct.[2]

In regard to the conditions of life, Mr. F. D. Fenton in his able report on the Maories, printed in 1859, wrote as follows :

A similar abundance of fertile soil, extreme facility in obtaining the necessities of existence, and a climate of even greater salubrity (than the United States) place the aboriginal inhabitants of this island in circumstances of similar advantage for developing to the utmost the powers for rapid increase possessed by the human race generally.[3]

Thus, with conditions of life exceptionally favorable, conditions which enabled the white population to reduce

[1] *Journal of the Royal Statistical Society*, September, 1869, p. 303.
[2] Featherman, "Oceano-Melanesians," p. 166.
[3] *Journal of the Royal Statistical Society*, December, 1860, p. 514.

its annual mortality to less than 10 per 1,000, and as a result increase its average longevity far in excess of that enjoyed by the whites of this country, the native race, though exceptional in character, failed to meet the final test of the survival of the fittest; and before another half century the most of its members will have passed away. It was racial inferiority, therefore, and not the conditions of life that brought about gradual extinction of this race.

Of the Hawaiians we have so many accounts that it is extremely difficult to select descriptive statements that would not contradict others of equal value from the standpoint of personal observation. Mr. Featherman speaks of them at the time the missionaries came to the islands, as "the uncorrupted children of nature." Mr. Bishop in a paper read before the Social Science Association of Honolulu, spoke of the women of the race as natural prostitutes, incapable of conceptions of sexual morality.[1] Mr. Charles Gulick in "A Footnote to Hawaiian History" speaks of the race at the time of the missionary settlements as "of incomparable physique, open-hearted, generous, and hospitable to a fault.[2] While Mr. Bishop speaks of the Hawaiian female as "aggressive in solicitation," Mr. Gulick asserts, on the strength of forty years residence in the islands, that he has "discovered no such custom or weakness." That the women were weak and willing to submit to irregular sexual relations with the whites is not to be doubted. It would be contrary to all other experience with native

[1] "Why are the Hawaiians dying out?" By S. E. Bishop, Honolulu, Nov., 1888. (Reprinted in Appendix 2, "Foreign Relations of the United States," 1894, p. 769, *et seq.*)

[2] "A Footnote to Hawaiian History," by Chas. T. Gulick. (Reprinted in Appendix 2, "Foreign Relations of the United States," 1894, p. 745, *et seq.*)

races if it were otherwise. This, however, would prove
nothing further than that the whites who came to the
island were not slow to take advantage of the child-like
ignorance of the women or the foolish vanity of the men
who in the words of Mr. Featherman, "were proud of
the attentions shown and the intimate relations cultivated by their better halves when visitors or distinguished strangers claimed their hospitality." [1]

Yet in the "Paradise of the Pacific," under the influence of missionary efforts for more than seventy years,
subjected to all the religious and educational influences
prevailing among the white race, and practically under
complete influence of preachers and teachers, the race is
dying out at a rate which will make its complete extinction only a question of a few years. And why is it thus
becoming extinct? Mr. Bishop attempts to answer this
question :

> As the leading and most efficient element of weakness in the Ha-
> waiian race, tending to physical decay, we predicate : *Unchastity*. A
> general impairment of constitutional vigor in the people by venereal
> disease caused them to fall early victims to other maladies, both native
> and foreign. All diseases ran riot in their shattered constitutions.
> They became especially incapacitated to resist pulmonary maladies.
> The greatly increased prevalence of colds and consumption is doubt-
> less due to this syphilitic diathesis rather than to change of habit as to
> clothing, although the latter may have had some unfavorable effect. [2]

It is not, therefore, to any unfavorable conditions of
life but to a race trait, an inordinate amount of sexual
immorality, that Mr. Bishop attributes the downward
tendency of the race, "a race," he adds, "well worth sav-
ing. With all their sad frailities, they are a noble race
of men physically and morally. They are manly,
courageous, enterprising, cordial, generous, unselfish.

[1] "Oceano-Melamesians," p. 241.

[2] "Foreign Relations of the United States," Appendix 2, 1894, p.
771.

They are highly receptive of good. . . . In an unusual degree they possess the capacity for fine ardent enthusiasm and noble ends. Should the Hawaiian people leave no posterity, a very sweet, generous, interesting race will have been lost to the world." Lost to the world, Mr. Bishop could have added, in spite of more than seventy years of missionary and educational efforts, and in spite of the possession of all the virtues, it would seem, except one,—the absence of which in civilized life is as fatal as in the life of the native who inhabits the "Paradise of the Pacific." With every possible chance that improved conditions of life could offer, with all the churches and schools that were needed, with willing hands ready to help, to support, to save,—this race, "sweet, generous and interesting," has in the short space of three score and ten years been reduced to less than one-fourth its original numbers.

The North American Indian, has been at times a very troublesome factor in the growth of the American nation. Years of strife has reduced his original habitation to a few limited reservations, most of which are constantly being encroached upon by the aggressive white population. Few races have made such a brave struggle for their own preservation; few races can boast of so high a degree of aboriginal civilization. If the race had produced nothing better than the "League of the Iroquois," it would have left its mark in indelible imprints on the history of the human race. The race made a brave and persistent struggle, but all to no avail.

Those who have had opportunity to study the original paintings in the Catlin gallery of Indian portraits,[1] must have been struck by one predominating trait in the

---

[1] Smithsonian Institute, Washington, D. C.

Indian countenance, a trait met with in nearly every instance, from chiefs ever so humble, to the mightiest whose fame still lingers. An iron will can be traced upon the countenance of nearly every Indian of note. That trait, a race trait, is still met with, and the faces of Sitting Bull, the Sioux chief; Piah, the Ute chief; Tomasket, the Nez Perce chief; Keokuk, the Sac and Fox chief; White Bird, the Crow Indian,[1] still show the inflexible, unbending nature of the Indian of long ago. This race could never be permanently enslaved, it could never be brought to accept the customs and ways of the white race. More subtle methods and power were necessary to civilize it away. Neither the poison of adulterated whisky, nor the frightful consequences of sexual immorality, spread around the forts and settlements of the whites, were sufficient. The most subtle agency of all, governmental pauperism, the highest development of the theory of easy conditions of life, did what neither drink nor the poisons of venereal disease could do, and today the large majority of the tribes are following the Maories and Hawaiians towards the goal of final extinction. There are exceptions and it is in the exceptions that we find the most emphatic lessons—lessons which if heeded by those remaining will alone effectually check the downward course of the race.

The facts on which the following table is based have been in part obtained from two valuable papers on gynecic notes among the Indians, contributed by Dr. A. B. Holden, former agency physician, to the *Journal of Obstetrics*,[2] and in part from the reports of the Commissioner of Indian affairs. I have selected the two years 1882 and 1895 for comparative purposes, since the

[1] Census report on Indians, Washington, 1890.
[2] *American Journal of Obstetrics*, June and July, 1892.

former year covers about the period at which the notes were compiled in regard to the prevailing state of morality and association with the whites. The table shows the population of each tribe in 1882 and 1895, and contains a statement of the prevailing degree of chastity and prevalence of venereal diseases.

TRIBES HAVING LITTLE OR NO INTERCOURSE WITH THE WHITES.

Name of Tribe.	Population.		Remarks.
	1882.	1895.	
Flatheads, Montana . .	1,381	1,695	Adultery rare; no venereal diseases.
Cheyenne Riv., Mont.	3,188	2,539	Chaste; venereal diseases rare.
Sioux of Devil's Lake, Montana	933	1,021	Chaste, and venereal diseases rare.
Klamath, Oregon . . .	707	982	Chaste; venereal diseases rare.
Total	6,209	6,237	Increase in population, 28.

TRIBES HAVING COMMON INTERCOURSE WITH THE WHITES.

Name of Tribe.	Population.		Remarks.
	1882.	1895.	
Gross Ventre, Mont.	950	624	Unchaste; venereal diseases excessively prevalent.
Assiniboine Sioux, "	850	763	Unchaste; venereal diseases excessively prevalent.
Crows, Mont.	3,500	2,133	Without chastity; venereal diseases excessively prevalent.
Assiniboine of Fort Peck, Mont	1,300	716	Morals; low venereal diseases prevalent.
Yanktomains, Mont. .	3,800	1,276	Morals low; V. diseases prevalent.
Neah Bay, Wash. . .	1,019	754	Unchaste; all are tainted with syphilis.
Round Valley, Cal . .	645	623	Chastity unknown; 75 per cent. affected with syphilis.
Total	12,064	6,889	Decrease in population, 5,175.

In the words of Dr. Holden, " Venereal diseases prevail in any tribe in exactly that degree in which men and women of that tribe have ceased to be chaste and faithful in wedlock. " And further : " Tribes who have been isolated, or who have held aloof from the whites, retained their tribal relations, and declared for non-intercourse, are chaste and free from taint. The tribes who have opened their arms to receive the white man, or who have been seduced by him, have been debauched and inoculated." This plain and emphatic condemnation of intercourse between unlike races, or attempts at their amalgamation in violation of the "law of similarity," is supported by the table before us, which shows that while the tribes that have little or no illicit intercourse with the white race are holding their own or making slight gains in population, those that have "opened their arms to receive the white man" have decreased to nearly one-half their number during the short period of 13 years. Hence the decrease in the Indian population is due largely to the rapid decrease among certain tribes while others are holding their own or gaining slowly year by year.

These instances of the results of intimate contact of the lower races with those of a much higher degree of culture and morality, will suffice to show the preponderating influence of race in the struggle for life. Given the same conditions of life for two races, the one of Aryan descent will prove the superior, solely on account of its ancient inheritance of virtue and transmitted qualities which are determining factors in the struggle for race supremacy. The lower races, even under the same conditions of life must necessarily fail because the vast number of incapables which a hard struggle for life has eliminated from the ranks of the white races, are still forming the large body of the lower races. Easy conditions of life and a liberal charity are among the most destructive influences affecting the lower races; since by such methods the weak and incapable are permitted to increase and multiply, while the struggle of the more able is increased in severity.

The two essential virtues of modern progress, self reliance and chastity, have not been the result of easy conditions of life. Self reliance in the Anglo-Saxon race is the result of the struggle of ages rather than of book education or missionary efforts. No missionary or educator or philanthropist extended aid or comfort to the English peasant class during its darkest days, to the earliest settlers on the coast of New England, or the pioneer in the forests of the far West. History is replete with instances of men of mark emerging from the most unfortunate conditions of life; but it is extremely rare to find a case where easy conditions of life or liberal charity have assisted man in his upward struggle. Self reliance in man and chastity in woman are qualities that must be developed, and thus far they have not been developed by the aid of charity or liberal philanthropy.

A study of the race traits and tendencies of the negro in America makes plain the failure of modern education and other means in encouraging or permitting the development of these most important factors, without which no race has ever yet been able to gain a permanent civilization. Easy conditions of life, a liberal construction of the doctrine of the forgiveness of sins and an unwarranted extension of the principle of state or private interference in the conduct of individual life, have never yet raised a race or individual from a lower to a higher plane. On the contrary, the world's failures are largely those of races and individuals in whose existence the struggle for a higher life had practically come to an end. "For carrying on the chief objects of our life on earth, very little of what is now called civilization is really wanted;"[1] and, unfortunately, it is just the useless adjuncts to civilization that the lower races in their contact with the higher races first acquire.

The downward tendencies of the colored race, therefore, can only be arrested by radical and far-reaching changes in their moral nature. Instead of clamoring for aid and assistance from the white race the negro himself should sternly refuse every offer of direct interference in his own evolution. The more difficult his upward struggle, the more enduring will be the qualities developed. Most of all there must be a more general recognition of the institution of monogamic marriage and unqualified reprobation of those who violate the law of sexual morality. Intercourse with the white race must absolutely cease and race purity must be insisted upon in marriage as well as outside of it. Together with a higher morality will come a greater degree of economic efficiency, and the predominating trait of the white race, the virtue of thrift, will follow as a natural consequence of the mastery by the colored race of its own conditions of life. The compensation of such an independent struggle will be a race of people who will gain a place among civilized mankind and will increase and multiply instead of dying out with loathsome diseases.

The day is not far distant when, in the words of Mr. Kidd, "The last thing our civilization is likely to permanently tolerate is the wasting of the resources of the richest regions of the earth through the lack of the elementary qualities of social efficiency in the races possessing them." When the ever increasing white population has reached a stage where new conquests are

[1] Max Mueller, "The Savage."

necessary, it will not hesitate to make war upon those races who prove themselves useless factors in the progress of mankind. A race may be interesting, gentle and hospitable; but if it is not a useful race in the common acceptation of that term, it is only a question of time when a downward course must take place. All the facts brought together in this work prove that the colored population is gradually parting with the virtues and the moderate degree of economic efficiency developed under the regimé of slavery. All the facts prove that a low standard of sexual morality is the main and underlying cause of the low and anti-social condition of the race at the present time. All the facts prove that education, philanthropy and religion have failed to develop a higher appreciation of the stern and uncompromising virtues of the Aryan race. The conclusion is warranted that it is merely a question of time when the actual downward course, that is, a decrease in the population, will take place. In the meantime, however, the presence of the colored population is a serious hindrance to the economic progress of the white race.

Instead of making the race more independent, modern educational and philanthropic efforts have succeeded in making it even more dependent on the white race at the present time than it was previous to emancipation. It remains to be seen how far a knowledge of the facts about its own diminishing vitality, low state of morality and economic efficiency will stimulate the race in adopting a higher standard. Unless a change takes place, a change that will strike at the fundamental errors that underlie the conduct of the higher races towards the lower, gradual extinction is only a question of time.